A CELEBRATION OF POETS

MIDWEST
GRADES 7-9
SPRING 2014

A CELEBRATION OF POETS
MIDWEST
GRADES 7-9
SPRING 2014

AN ANTHOLOGY COMPILED BY CREATIVE COMMUNICATION, INC.

Published by:

creativeCOMMUNICATION
A CELEBRATION OF TODAY'S WRITERS

PO BOX 303 • SMITHFIELD, UTAH 84335
TEL. 435-713-4411 • WWW.POETICPOWER.COM

Authors are responsible for the originality of the writing submitted.

Thank you to our student artists whose work is featured on the cover:
Marcus Leonard - Grade 10, Vanessa Schnurer - Grade 12, Samantha Laffrey - Grade 8, Olivia Long - Grade 9, Cami Rose Olson - Grade 12, Sarah Hammond - Grade 11, Lilly Wikner - Grade 7, Sophia Cai - Grade 8, Yaeji Lee - Grade 12, and Karen Yang - Grade 9.
To have your art considered for our next book cover, go to www.celebratingart.com.

ISBN: 978-1-60050-634-5

FOREWORD

Dear Reader:

Recently my first grader made this statement.

"Dad, I think words are very important."

Language is what separates humankind from the animal kingdom. Language and words are what have allowed us to move forward and progress as a species.

As students move through the various grades in school, their command of language develops. One of the rewarding aspects of publishing student writing is seeing the changes from the early grades to the later grades. The words move and shift, create images, relate ideas. These ideas change and impact lives. We have all heard the phrase "the pen is mightier than the sword." Throughout history it is words that have changed the world. From the constitution of governments, to a simple "I am sorry," words are what convey and share ideas.

The words in this book range from a simple description of the world that surrounds the author, to a meaningful sharing of thoughts and ideas. Every great idea started with a single thought and then a single word. The myriad of pens that created these words come from student writers who show the power of words. From these pens may emerge future authors, teachers and statesmen. I hope, as you read these words, you feel their power, and agree with my response to my son.

"You are right son. Words are important."

Sincerely,

Thomas Worthen, Ph.D.
Editor
Creative Communication

WRITING CONTESTS!

Enter our next POETRY contest!
Enter our next ESSAY contest!

Why should I enter?
Win prizes and get published! Each year thousands of dollars in prizes are awarded throughout North America. The top writers in each division receive a monetary award and a free book that includes their published poem or essay. Entries of merit are also selected to be published in our anthology.

Who may enter?
There are four divisions in the poetry contest. The poetry divisions are grades K-3, 4-6, 7-9, and 10-12. There are three divisions in the essay contest. The essay divisions are grades 4-6, 7-9, and 10-12.

What is needed to enter the contest?
To enter the poetry contest send in one original poem, 21 lines or less. To enter the essay contest send in one original non-fiction essay, 100-250 words, on any topic. Please submit each poem and essay with a title, and the following information clearly printed: the writer's name, current grade, home address (optional), school name, school address, teacher's name and teacher's email address (optional). Contact information will only be used to provide information about the contest. For complete contest information go to www.poeticpower.com.

How do I enter?
Enter a poem online at:
www.poeticpower.com
or
Mail your poem to:
Poetry Contest
PO Box 303
Smithfield, UT 84335

Enter an essay online at:
www.poeticpower.com
or
Mail your essay to:
Essay Contest
PO Box 303
Smithfield, UT 84335

When is the deadline?
Poetry contest deadlines are December 5th, April 16th, and August 19th. Essay contest deadlines are October 15th, February 17th, and July 15th. Students can enter one poem and one essay for each spring, summer, and fall contest deadline.

Are there benefits for my teacher?
Yes. Teachers with five or more students published receive a free anthology that includes their students' writing. Teachers may also earn points in our Classroom Rewards program to use towards supplies in their classroom.

For more information please go to our website at **www.poeticpower.com**, email us at editor@poeticpower.com or call 435-713-4411.

TABLE OF CONTENTS

STATES INCLUDED IN THIS EDITION:

ILLINOIS
IOWA
KANSAS
NEBRASKA
NORTH DAKOTA
SOUTH DAKOTA

Spring 2014 Poetic Achievement Honor Schools

*Teachers who had fifteen or more poets accepted to be published

The following schools are recognized as receiving a "Poetic Achievement Award." This award is given to schools who have a large number of entries of which over fifty percent are accepted for publication. With hundreds of schools entering our contest, only a small percent of these schools are honored with this award. The purpose of this award is to recognize schools with excellent Language Arts programs. This award qualifies these schools to receive a complimentary copy of this anthology.

Belle Valley School
Belleville, IL
Rhonda Hatridge*
Ms. Junghan*

Boone Central High School
Albion, NE
Cheri Blocher
Cassie Olson*

Cambridge Jr/Sr High School
Cambridge, NE
Rami Albers*
Katie Helms*
Carol Ommert

Canton-Galva Middle School
Galva, KS
Tina McMannis*

Central Jr High School
West Frankfort, IL
Megan Deason*

Chadron Middle School
Chadron, NE
Barbara Waugh*

Chapman High School
Chapman, KS
Collette Erickson
Patty Stout

David City High School
David City, NE
Valarie Barnhart*

Divine Infant Jesus School
Westchester, IL
Megan Angellotti
Joanne Macpherson

Edgebrook Elementary School
Chicago, IL
Leslie Carroll
Caroline Delia
Gloria Fields*

Florence Nightingale Elementary School
Chicago, IL
Brandon Barr*

Gilbert Middle School
Gilbert, IA
Virginia Beecher
LisaJane Gildehaus*

Glenwood Middle School
Glenwood, IA
Susan Reed*

Hannah Beardsley Middle School
Crystal Lake, IL
Lynette Fennell*
Jodie Treptow
Mrs. Van Dorpe

Holy Cross Catholic Elementary School
Omaha, NE
Mr. Fisher
Carolyn Taylor*

Hoven High School
Hoven, SD
Colette Maier*

Immaculate Conception School
Morris, IL
Loreen R. Vlk*

Jane A Neil Elementary School
Chicago, IL
Ms. Booker
Mr. Dimos
Richard King*
Mr. McMorris
Mr. Pham

Jefferson Middle School
Dubuque, IA
Carol Schmitt*
Katherine Thimmesch

Jordan Catholic Middle School
Rock Island, IL
Mrs. Marlier*

Kimball School
Kimball, SD
Patti Lee Konechne*

Learn To Write Now
Naperville, IL
Aruna Davis*

Logan View Public School
Hooper, NE
Sheryl Uehling
Tammy VonEssen

McPherson Elementary School
Chicago, IL
Pamela Barreda*

Mercy High School
Omaha, NE
Kate Adams
Mrs. Brousek
Mary Coyle*
Mandi Marcuccio

Morton Magnet Middle School
Omaha, NE
Sharon Oakman*

Mother Teresa Catholic Academy
Crete, IL
Michele Nowak*

Nathan Hale Middle School
Crestwood, IL
Jen Battistoni*

Northlawn Jr High School
Streator, IL
Nancy K. Hepner*

Oblong Elementary School
Oblong, IL
Laura Collier*

Olpe Jr/Sr High School
Olpe, KS
Leanne Garcia
Marilyn Stueve*

Peck Elementary School
Chicago, IL
  Kathe Myers*
  Ms. Ramirez

Peoria Christian School Monroe Campus
East Peoria, IL
  Valerie Painter*

Perry Middle School
Perry, IA
  Abbey Gerzema*

Providence St Mel School
Chicago, IL
  Sharrell Anderson
  Sheila E. Foster
  Ms. Staskel

Rochester Jr High School
Rochester, IL
  Suzanne Pettyjohn*

Rossville Alvin Grade School
Rossville, IL
  Brianna Jorgji*

Sandwich Middle School
Sandwich, IL
  Jamie L. Duvick*

Southeastern Jr/Sr High School
Augusta, IL
  Cindy Twidwell*

St Francis De Sales School
Lake Zurich, IL
  Kathy Butler*

St Francis Middle/High School
St Francis, KS
  Lisa Holzwarth*

St Gilbert School
Grayslake, IL
  Diane Dolan*

St Mary School
DeKalb, IL
  Marissa Dobie*
  Mrs. R. Pedryc*

St Philip Neri School
Omaha, NE
  Christine Mohr*

St Philip the Apostle School
Addison, IL
  Gina Sannasardo*

St Robert Bellarmine School
Chicago, IL
  Susan Peters
  Meg Ryan*

Summit Hill Jr High School
Frankfort, IL
  Mrs. Beck
  Laura Goebel*
  Patrick Sullivan*
  Beth Zinsky*

Thomas Middle School
Arlington Heights, IL
  Deborah Burner
  Jodi Cyr
  Susan Ward*

Tonganoxie Middle School
Tonganoxie, KS
  Kim L. Woodall*

Whittier Middle School
Sioux Falls, SD
  Lindsey Kuipers
  Emily Leitheiser*
  Andrea Olson
  Rebecca Olson*
  Angie Schlenker*

William Fremd High School
    Palatine, IL

        Gary Anderson
        Marilyn Berdick*
        Jaclyn DeRose Han*
        Judy Klingner
        Laura Marsh
        Eric Schaefer
        Trish Weathers-Weidig

Language Arts
Grant Recipients
2013-2014

For over 20 years, we've offered language arts grants and are proud that we have provided over $100,000 to schools across the United States and Canada. After receiving a "Poetic Achievement Award" schools were encouraged to apply for a Creative Communication Language Arts Grant. The following is a list of schools who received a two hundred and fifty dollar grant for the 2013-2014 school year.

A F Maloney Elementary School, Blackstone, MA
Allegan High School, Allegan, MI
Benet Academy, Lisle, IL
Birchwood School, Cleveland, OH
Blessed Sacrament Catholic School, Seminole, FL
Boyce Middle School, Upper St Clair, PA
Brookville Intermediate School, Brookville, OH
Durant High School, Durant, IA
Elbridge Gale Elementary School, Wellington, FL
Holy Cross High School, Delran, NJ
Li's Academy, Arcadia, CA
Our Lady Star of the Sea School, Grosse Pointe Woods, MI
Outley Elementary School, Houston, TX
Parkway Christian School, Sterling Heights, MI
Pleasant View Middle School, Grove City, OH
Ramsay School, Ramsay, MT
Rochelle Middle School, Rochelle, IL
St Stanislaus School, Meriden, CT
Stevensville Middle School, Stevensville, MD
Thomasville Primary School, Thomasville, NC
Troy Intermediate School, Troy, PA
Vacaville Christian Schools, Vacaville, CA
Valley Academy Charter School, Hurricane, UT
Wattsburg Area Middle School, Erie, PA

Please note, effective Fall 2013, our grants program has now been replaced by Classroom Rewards. This new program allows any teacher to be eligible to earn points towards much needed classroom supplies. There is no limit on eligibility and there are no purchases required for a teacher to earn rewards. Any teacher with students accepted and published in our contests or who refers another teacher to our contest will receive points.

Top Ten Winners

List of Top Ten Winners for Spring 2014; listed alphabetically

Alexandra Angrim	Grade 8	Olive Tree School	CO
Shridhar Athinarayanan	Grade 7	White Station Middle School	TN
Gracie Cook	Grade 7	Walter E Harris Public School	ON
Jacqueline He	Grade 8	Joaquin Miller Middle School	CA
Amity R. Irving	Grade 7	Mark Twain Middle School	OR
Jackson Knizhnik	Grade 7	Science and Arts Academy	IL
Will Lane	Grade 8	The Bement School	MA
Milind Mishra	Grade 9	Stanton College Preparatory School	FL
Jaclyn Rothman	Grade 8	Harvard Westlake School	CA
Elena Smith	Grade 7	North West Central School	SK

All Top Ten Winners may also be seen at www.poeticpower.com

Vesuvius Awakening

The roar of a dragon,
Waking
from the slumber of a thousand years. Stretching his wings,
Slowly at first, then rhythmically,
Pounding against his cold cell walls.

Furious panting has turned the sky ash gray;
Rocky ground rumbles as he takes wary steps toward freedom.

Deep in a marketplace
donned with crimson banners,
Men clad in dusty woolen robes
Lean out from rickety wooden stalls, knocking jars of peppercorn
To the ground; gaping at the swirling sky above.

The dragon, paid no mind as his infamous plan unravels;
Bursts forth from his jagged prison; tumbling through the sky.

Soot-smeared wings, no longer fettered,
Beat desperately through smoggy air.
Scales dancing to the ground,
Impaling themselves into the minute landscape below.

Jaclyn Rothman, Grade 8

India

The sun streams a sweltering, luminous flood,
Pouring into the parched ground.

I saunter along the arid path:
A dangerous road brimming with rickshaws and cattle.

The mellow scent of fragrant clove drifts in the dusty air;
Every whiff I take forms a louder sneeze than the last.

Sounds blend impeccably:
Heart-stopping horns mix with howling merchants
Creating an enticing anthem.

Children with slender arms and burnt flesh
Tear their clothes while playing cricket.
I hear the sound:
The sound from the ball slamming into the bat
In a single, sonorous strike.

Desolate faces scour and beseech for food.
Beggars, they call them.
Their bodies so thin,
So fragile.

I continue down the path, leaving footprints in the dusty earth.
They are my marks of discovery.
My discovery of India.

Shridhar Athinarayanan, Grade 7

In a Poem

In a poem, I am a yellow fish
Diving deeper and deeper
Through tangles of text
Searching for a bottom that I may never find.

In a poem, I am a stray dog
Romping and playing
Through streets of stanzas
Sniffing among trash and treasure for my nose alone.

In a poem, I am a white bird
Flying lower and lower
over vineyards of verbs
Dipping my wings through clouds of rhymes.

In a poem, I am an icy comet
Moving faster and faster
Past miles of metaphors
Cosmic forces all around me but only silence in my ears.

But in this poem, I am a kid in a candy store
Touching the wrappers of words
Smelling the sweetness of similes
Seeking another sugary sonnet
The coins in my pocket ready to jingle free.

Will Lane, Grade 8

Hear the Reverberations of Long Ago

the memories are stenciled onto her soul
in gold and aquamarine ink
the thoughts are tucked away into little matchboxes
(painted in pretty pastel tints)
and adorned with acorn buttons and ribbons and bows
amid the soft lilt of tangerine sunlight
her head is an attic of treasures
(faded, clean, drawers brimming with secrets)
we sit and talk in there, over the soft violin music
for centuries, years, days
about everything and nothing all at once
(our hands clutching steaming porcelain cups of hot lavender tea)
while we let the stately grandfather clock
drone the slow seconds away
(tick. tock. tick. tock.)
once she asked me if I remembered
(the stark moon was a symmetric white outside)
I hesitated, tried to forget the past
sipped my tea of guilt and shook my head
(the sting of my conscience brought forth
the sharp aroma of cold mint)

Jacqueline He, Grade 8

The Raindrops

I step outside and hear the call
of countless raindrops as they fall
and hit the pavement with a splat
as many more repeat the act.

No one's out to greet the sun;
I'm the sole pedestrian.
instead they all are safe inside
and from the water droplets hide.

I look upon the road and see
a vehicle that passes me.
the driver just ignores the drops
and keeps on going, never stops.

The driver's life is one straight line,
monotonous in rain or shine.
on days like this I realize
that life passes before our eyes,
and some of us don't ever stop and take a look at life's raindrops.

Jackson Knizhnik, Grade 7

Perfect

What does it mean to be perfect?
To always be the best?
Maybe it means to try your hardest
And never second guess.

To always be happy!
To never have a doubt!
To listen to what your heart says!
To simply let it all out!

Don't let anyone bring you down;
Keep your head held high;
Let your soul be free;
And don't ever let your spirit die.

Yes indeed, perhaps being perfect
Is different than I thought;
It is simpler and easier
And cannot be bought.

Nobody's perfect
Is what people say
But I think everyone's perfect
In their own unique way.

Gracie Cook, Grade 7

Sipping in the Dark

Steam, silent, like a mouse, wafts from a mug.
Tea.
As toasty as a kitten in my hands.
I clutch my 'little cat.'
Dependent on its heat.
Sipping in frigid, muted light.
Always sipping, never drinking.
A repeated ritual: An echo.
Shadows lurk around me,
In the early morning light,
Yet the tea creates fiery warmth within.
Half-awake.
The aroma of fresh peppermint blends in with the darkness,
Making the perfect shade of ebony.
A blank mind, void of all thoughts.
Restless rain glides down window panes.
Empty mug on a counter.
Another gradual entry to a
New day.

Amity R. Irving, Grade 7

Evening Falls

Evening falls
A raven calls
And all around, the light grows dim
A breeze sighs
A dove cries
From the edge of an oak tree limb

Yawning loud
The sun goes down
It sinks into the earth
But it will
Come back again
To grant morning its birth

And while it's gone, it sends along
Its glowing cousin Moon
To sail across the twinkling sky
And set the nighttime tune

It baffles me
Perplexes me
That people love machines
When all around them, land and sky
Act out amazing scenes

Alexandra Angrim, Grade 8

Winter's Puzzle

I never figured out winter's puzzle
I tried to solve it but the
fireplace burned out and the
hot chocolate tipped over and ruined it
My mother insisted that I
keep trying
over the noise of the frying fish
A wind sneaks its way into my home.

I take a break and gaze at
the earth-like walls cake with
dust, disuse, disarray
and yet
browned into a hearth that houses
the homily habits
of winter.

The wind finally catches up to my thoughts
and tickles my ear as it whispers
its wonders
and beckons me to look out the window
and stare at its
secrets and answers

Milind Mishra, Grade 9

Greatness Is Within Her

She walks down the long hallway
The thud of her skates echoes and fills the silence running through the rink
She steps onto the smooth, glistening ice
She slowly dumps the bucket of pucks
Bang bang bang
The sound of her blades as she cuts through the ice is too familiar
Crick crick crick
She takes the puck and races down the ice
Her ponytail flies through the air as fast as she does
The whistle of the wind plays through her ears
Whoosh whoosh whoosh
She lets the puck go off of her stick
It hits the post and the sound rumbles through the entire arena
Ting ting ting
She knows that she is better than most boys
They will never believe it though…
She is used to being judged because a ponytail hangs down her back
Yet she will never take no for an answer
Because greatness lives within her.

Elena Smith, Grade 7

Grades 7-8-9
High Merit Poems

Lasting Peace

Waves, they thrash.
Thunder, they crash.
Lightning, the flash.
But calm in the end,
the ocean lay flat,
no storms at all, nothing of that.
The sun starts to drop,
into the ocean with a plop.
The wind is a cool breeze,
flowing with ease.
The moon rises high,
so high up in the sky.
The stars they shine so bright,
being the only light to the night.
Stephanie Stark, Grade 8

Birds

Flying high above the world
Living in trees
Getting worms from the ground
Hollows or nests are best

Living in trees
Babies learning to fly
Hollows or nests are best
Condors soar above the rest

Babies learn to fly
Getting worms from the ground
Condors soar above the rest
Flying high above the world
David Alepra, Grade 8

I'm Not Very Good at This

I've never been good at poems,
and I can't think of words to use.
I'm not very good at many things,
and I'm not very good at this.

I sit here and I think of words to use,
but the distractions are too much,
I don't know what to write about,
and I'm not very good at this.

I still try and contemplate words to use,
but nothing really fits.
I'm frustrated at myself,
because I'm not very good at this.
Genesis Estrella, Grade 8

Hidden

My appearance is as bright as the sun
Inside I feel down
My heart is as broken as the liberty bell
But my smile I try to sell
Cassidy Anderson, Grade 7

Winter

Winter is cold like solid ice.
Jackets, gloves and hats are needed to prevent frostbite.
The glistening white snow adds cheer to the season,
as vibrant Christmas lights do for the very same reason.
The smell of hot cocoa dominates my surroundings
blending with the faint smell of the cool breezy air.

There are many activities in the season of winter.
With sledding, skiing, tubing, snow boarding and more,
winter is definitely no mere bore!
Snow boarding is the best
as it puts you to the test with its deceiving yet plentiful tricks,
that make you plummet towards the hard ice and "BAM!"
You experienced a hard hit!

Although winter projects lots of magnificent scenery and awesome activities like
snow boarding there are still more important things about the season.
The joyful season is truly about spending time with those who you love.
It is not a crime to be with the ones you care about and to pray to family above.
If you take the time to do this simple task you will have a permanent place in that
person's heart.
Forever happy that you followed these instructions from the very start!
Zach Favia, Grade 7

Originality Makes a Difference

What does originality mean to me?
It's when people stop pretending and be who they are
So why don't people just be what they're meant to be?
Unfortunately for some of us, No matter what we do, we're constantly ridiculed
I once had a dream of a wonderful world
There was so much color and creativity everywhere
I was confused, what separated this world from the one we live in?
However, I didn't take me long to find out what was different
Everyone was just being themselves
We are all different, but we're all human as well
We make mistakes, we all mess up
It all depends on how you fix your mess ups
And what you make of them

We are teased, made fun of, and mocked for being us
STOP making fun of me and others, what did we do to you?!
I get it constantly, home, school, and the bus.
I try being strong but sometimes it's just too hard
People make others feel miserable, and die, just too feel on top
Sometimes it's hard to keep moving forward
I am different, I am original
And try as you might, you can't make me fall.
Sydney Trombley, Grade 8

Jigsaw Puzzle

Life is like a jigsaw puzzle
without the picture
on the front of the box.
Also you're not even sure if you have all of the right pieces.
You find one match, and more, and more. until there are no more pieces to put on.
Zack Jurgens, Grade 7

The Love for Cattle

Raising and showing cattle is my passion,
It takes a lot of hard work and dedication;
Your calf becomes your best friend,
The love you share never seems to end.

The first time you see a baby calf,
They always seem to make you laugh;
When you watch them run and play,
It's hard to just turn and walk away.

As you try to make their hair grow,
A chance to be a champion, you never know;
All the hard work spent to win,
They always seems to make you grin.

In the ring for the final drive,
You feel as if you're so alive;
As you look your calf in the eye,
You try so hard not to cry.

Dalton Wagner, Grade 9

Loss…

I lost you somewhere along the way
I remember how you always knew what to say,
When I was down you were there always.
And that's why I called you my best friend forever and always.

Yes, we had our fights
It's usually over by the end of the night
We were just that tight,
Be this way again we just might.

Don't get me wrong I'm just fine
But I need you to keep me in line
I'm starting to think that apologizing to you is a waste of time,
You think I'm lying any ways and that's fine.

I think I'm done
We had so much fun
The last 3 years have been a blast
I really hoped it would last.

Emma Humpal, Grade 8

Willow

That which was once sleeping
But now with bright shades of yellow and green, it awakens.
Still drooping through the seasons
As the wind softly rattles its branches.
It's like the tree is whispering its secrets,
Yet they are just out of reach to hear.
How much fun it was hiding and climbing within its branches.
In ten years it grew so much.
From a shoot off of another tree
To a mighty tree itself.
As long as it stands it will always be my weeping willow tree.

Nicholas Josten, Grade 8

Unknown Man

He is a normal man.
He has a house.
Clothes, food, water and a family.
No one knows his past.
Except for one.
She was a wise woman.
She told me about him, I couldn't believe what I had heard.
He was beaten.
By his own mother.
She made him kneel on raw grits for hours and hours and hours.
She made him scream until his lungs ached.
She made him pick cotton until all ten fingers were blistered.
She made him do the goriest of things so she wouldn't have to.
She was a slave.
But she was a slave driver to her own son.
This boy was now a man.
He leads a normal life.
He has a house.
Clothes, food, water and a family.
But he does not lead a normal life in the footprints of his memories.
He is the unknown man.

Emma Hoover-Grinde, Grade 7

My Special Treat

You find your way into my dreams,
You're always raiding my thoughts,
Just a chance to taste your sweet symphony
Gets my mouth to water,
But no, they say moderation is good,
Once in a while, that's acceptable,
But your shiny glow, frosty sparkles,
Many flavors to pile on top,
Oh no, you've burrowed yourself into my mind again,
Temptation, you cloud my thoughts,
Maybe once a week, no that's too often,
When can I go on a binge?
Who would've thought resisting would be so hard,
Trying? Yes, I'm trying hard,
But it's been a while, my taste buds miss your company,
For today I may slip, just today,
Just one savory bowl, only two toppings,
But I can wait longer, just be strong,
Sweets or salad, pudding or yogurt,
I feel like I'm in a child's battle,
Today, just today, I'll treat myself, so bring me the ice cream!

Casey Hayes, Grade 7

As One Together

Together we share everything.
As one we speak for our country.
We are together on a never ending journey.
We share one light, one future, and one ground.
As one, we answer the call of history
and carry the precious light into our future.
Together we are one country on a journey.

Cristian Raya, Grade 7

04/28/1988

Come with me to April 28, 1988
See
the panicking of all the passengers
the plane as it carefully falls apart
Hear
the screaming and crying of all the people
listen close as the plane screams too
Touch
the radio as your thinking everybody is in your hands
the ground as you carefully land
Smell
the burning parts and jet fuel smell the air in high altitude
Taste
the scariness as they scream taste the victory as you landed safely

Jaden Carmel, Grade 7

In Just 500 Years

What flavor do you want for your house?
Chocolate, strawberry, or peppermint mouse?
And how do you want your robot to smell?
Like lemons or water fresh from the well?
What color will your eyes be today?
Purple, red, or maybe gray?
(Hey, want to teleport to Mars?
Just feed your robot two chocolate bars!)
Look, we found a disease's cure!
Wow, it's bound to work for sure!
Now, it's been such a long day.
Simply press your sleep button and you'll drift away.
But be prepared for fun tomorrow —
We'll rid the world of even more sorrow!

Jenna Fischels, Grade 8

Sometimes…

Most days I'm flamboyant orange
teeming with excitement, love and laughter
making jokes about anything and everything
living my life to its fullest.
Sometimes I'm flat black
tired, hopeless, and depressed
not very talkative, wanting to lay down and sleep
hoping to be alone.
There is always a dark side.

Kyle Eaheart, Grade 7

Bury the Dagger

Why is it wrong to express feelings?
But it's okay for us to casually participate in violence?
I'm embarrassed to be part of this race
Where we still discriminate for the differences
I'm bleeding out for humanity
I cry for the future generations
Teach the kids to become affectionate
Bury whatever the dagger might be
And let peace fly

Baylee Miller, Grade 8

The Weather

Some people say that the weather affects our emotion.
Such as how we are happy when it's sunny out,
and sad when it's raining.
But not for me.
As I look out my wet window,
I want to run.
Want to dance.
See, the rain feels like the world is finally giving off some of its love.
Finally sweating some of its happiness,
into the sad world we live in.
When it's sunny,
I feel sad.
I feel like the sun overpowers everything in her way.
Like she's showing off her magnificent rays,
so the rest of the world will be jealous of her beauty.
So I will leap in the rain,
and draw the blinds to the sun.
For I'm not like normal people.

Sophia Magruder, Grade 8

In the Boxing Gym

I remember the first time I went to a boxing gym.
I was nervous yet eager to try it out.
The gym smelled like sweat and hard work.
Some guys were sparring in the ring.
They moved too fast for my eyes to see.
They left me in awe with their skills.
I still remember the "thud thud" sound they made.

As I looked to the left I saw another guy training.
He had the look of determination in his eyes.
Sweat fell from his face.
He was giving it 110%.
But he still had more energy.
I would like to be like that man.
One day…

I still remember the "thud thud" sound he made.

Jose Lavin, Grade 8

A War

War is an awful and
Disruptive disaster,
Many people lose their families
And their lives,
You are called and soon are holding a gun
And fighting because two countries just can't get along
Every night you lay in the wet hole you dig
Hoping this nightmare would come to an end.
Thinking every day how stupid you had to be
Just to join the army
To look cool in front of your friend,
That is if you ever see them again.
Every night you write letters
Hoping a few words will make it better

Antoni Lipski, Grade 7

Resting in Peace
A wise man once said:
"Dream as if you'll live forever
live as if you'll die tomorrow"
— Oscar Wilde

I liked to live by that.
everyone should.
I'd like to be remembered as an adventurous,
fun loving creative soul,
That I made a difference in peoples lives
left this earth knowing I won't be forgotten.
I know I'll be leaving someone behind on this earth to carry
on my legacy.
I don't know yet, but hopefully it's a good one.

Kim Marass, Grade 8

New York City
Big city, shining lights, millions of people
Broadway, Funny Girl, Wicked
Times Square, 42nd Street, Statue of liberty
Fun, exciting, loud
Gucci, Chanel, Tiffany & Co.
Fashion, performing arts, journalism
Breakfast at Tiffany's, Ghostbusters, Maid in Manhattan
Glitz, glam, jewelry
Busy sidewalks, taxi cabs, crowded streets
Iconic skyline, tall buildings, Empire State Building
Manhattan, Queens, Long Island
Dancing, singing, painting
Vogue, Seventeen, Glamour
The city that never sleeps

Kayla Hayes, Grade 8

Winter Must Go
A cold blistering day, a blanket of snow
The trees, crystallized with ice
Patches of green grass, surrounded by snow
Chilling winds burning your nose, some sun would be nice
The frost is a wonder, how could it be
The flowers are gone, the petals fallen
Toasty fireplaces, mugs of hot tea
Waiting inside, the world is frozen
No longer leaves of orange, but leaves of gray
Trees bare naked, nothing to cover their arms
Still November, endless months till May
Resorting to hot oatmeal, instead of Lucky Charms
The vast cover of blistering white snow
Will not be missed and now must go.

Ysabel Lee, Grade 9

I'm Here
When you are sad or when you are in a crying mood,
I'll be right beside you, and comfort you will find.
If you need an ocean or a loving helpful person,
I'll be right here for you, I truly understand.

Makayla Short, Grade 8

Fandoms
I opened a book and in I stepped,
into a world of promises kept.
My world of hopelessness disappeared,
becoming a reality that seems so real.

Doctors, heroes, and a 74th Game.
Tributes of a district set aflame.
I met a girl who speaks the unspoken,
and a guy whose spirit has been broken.

I close the book and back I came,
my room and life all the same.
Back to the mundane black and white colors.
After all, some infinities are bigger than others.

Ashley Peters, Grade 7

Why
I do not understand
Why people think that talking out of turn is okay
Why the world is in such bad shape
Why America feels that they have to intervene in every affair
Like a curious child interrupting someone's conversation
But most of all I do not understand
Why people intentionally break the law
Risking their life's freedom for a moment's worth of fun
Knowing that their consequences are going to be severe
What I understand is why people decide to be alone
Being alone gives one time to think things through
When there is no one around to interfere
And nature is the only thing that surrounds them
The only noise that they hear is the wind passing by

Alexander Wysocki, Grade 9

Basketball Life
Basketball is a game for great technique.
I'm looking around to find an opening;
I shoot for a basket and hope it will sink
just like an anchor dropping.
The crowd went ballistic when I was focusing.
The defense was playing like they were on an ice skating rink
while I acted like the court king.

The sweat dripped down
like a water from its faucet.
Looking at the clock countdown,
wondering if I should toss it.
Basketball is so fun
because of the feeling that you just won!

Zane Miller, Grade 8

Basketball
Running down the court with the wind in my hair
Feeling like Michael Jordan flying in the air.
Putting the orange ball through the hoop
Winning the game by a whoop.

Tori Schoof, Grade 8

Good Enough?

Today she was walking
Out by the sea
When she noticed
A lady crying on a dock

As she walked on up
She heard "I am not good enough anymore."
She told the lady a bit strict
"Everyone has a reason, so do you."

For the lady looked at her
She started to smile
"Thank you for saying that, I now know,
I have a reason that is not here at all."

The lady walked away
And later that day
She saw the same lady
This time helping others
In the same way.

Jadyn Leiseth, Grade 8

Continuing On

When I look up,
Everyone is staring right back at me.
Trying not to get nervous,
I continue on with speaking.

My stomach starts to talk like a rumbling monster,
then my voice starts shaking;
I take a deep breathe and
I continue on with speaking.

My arms are the window
when the train goes soaring by;
Trying to stand still,
I make eye contact and
I continue on with speaking.

My face is a
red ripe juicy tomato;
Soon enough, though, I am relieved because
I am finally done speaking.

Sarah Hinners, Grade 8

A Good Book

I don't see the world around me
Instead I see another place
One full of mystical creatures and new people
A place that is hard to find if you're not looking
A place that is like no other
A place that is hidden between pages
The pages of a good book waiting to be read
And until I finish the book a new world will be open to me
Away from reality

Audrey Paisley, Grade 7

Grandma

Oh dear grandma…
I would like to hear your voice again.
I would like to see you again.
I would like to hug you again.
I would like to kiss you again.
I would like you to be there for me again.
I would like you to support me again.
I would like to taste your food again.
I would like to talk to you again.

I would like you to believe in me again.
I would like you to care for me like no one else did again.
I would like to go shopping with you again.
I would like to laugh with you again.
I would like to go to your house just to be with you again.
I would like to have fun with you again.
I would like to have you again.
I would like you to tuck me in at night again.
I would like to be with you and have you forever.
I would like to say I love you.

Karen Ramirez, Grade 8

Be Different

Have you ever been left out
or felt like you don't belong
and then tried to convince yourself
that there's nothing wrong?
Then we have more in common
than I thought
In fact I'm still an outcast
and I wouldn't be proud of myself
if I said that I'm not
Being different
is what it really means to be cool
To be an individual means to be yourself
and everyone is different
So face it
there are no REAL outcasts
there are only those that choose to flaunt their individuality
but get left out
because others don't understand
that everyone should strive to be an individual
To be DIFFERENT

Kelsey Anne Harper, Grade 9

Fall

Looking at the red, yellow, and orange leaves
Watching them fall thousands of feet
watching the horse as if it can gallop forever
as peaceful as the deep blue sea
looking at the grass cover thousands of ground
as the white fence cuts the land into parts
the water quietly makes it's way around
so peacefully quiet watching nature
wishing that this day can last forever

Rahwa Beyene, Grade 7

In Your Shoes

You say I don't understand.
You ask "How would you know?"
But I've stood where you stand,
And I really do know.

I've seen things that would kill any other man,
And done things that would shame another.
But I've felt more pain than anyone could plan,
And yet I would never tell anyone, not even my brother.

I've lived in fear and in guilt,
But those insecurities were shadowed by stolen arrogance.
My common good nature, which was desperately built,
Was all gusto, with pretended confidence.

So look at your shoes.
Where have they trod?
Have they led you down a brighter avenue,
Or some ruined clod?

So listen and I'll tell you a secret, for you, and you, and you.
Those shoes you're wearing? They were mine once too.

Seth DeVries, Grade 9

Eternity of No Choices

E verybody acts like they know. Never to let their knowledge show.
T hey think they're the judges of your heart,
E ven if their judging only pulls your life apart.
R eally all you want is to make your own choice.
N o one should be able to have their own voice?
I t's torture to know your wishes are behind a chalk line,
T hat is guarded by evil monsters and a land mine.
Y ou close your eyes, run and hope you won't explode

O nly because you know your bottled feelings will soon implode.
F unny that the people who made the same mistakes

N ever take your side when it's your case
O ver and over you watch as your life is thrown away

C aused by choices you have to make every day
H ow does a person live through this hell?
O nly the happiest of couples can tell.
I t is worth the heartbreak and the years.
C hoices can cause pain and tears.
E ventually though, you will find the one
S o just trust your heart until its job is done.

Cindy Mauck, Grade 8

Fall Forest

Flowing water over rocks.
Feeling of love, and mystery.
Leaves releasing from their branches.
Fall overcoming Summer seasons.
Nature doing no harm to anything but your emotions.

Emma Scott, Grade 7

Aurora

In the dew-filled field of dawn,
Within the inner atmosphere of darkness,
From the flat, rigid horizon spawns
The great ball of light intensity.

Pink squeezes into the orange of day
As it becomes her golden locks.
The red roses become moist and fray,
While heat dries them

The rooster is the messenger, bringing her notice to all,
Whilst the dear savages her tears for its thirst.
Insects manage to calm down their buzzing and crawl
As she, the inching barrier of shine crawls upward.

Squinting children are awakened by her gleam and voice,
And then summoned by her smell;
The glorious smell of a mist's choice
Mixed in with the natural orchid's scent

Dear Aurora, only lasts for half-an-hour or so,
Until the sun sets, hence appearing her foe.

Lucy Limanowski, Grade 9

The Answer to Doors

Doors mean leaving
Or do they?
Some are heavy
Causing work to get in
Others are new
Like they are only there for you
Sometimes just handles
Other times under lock and key
"GET OUT!" some say
Begging you in
Brothers and sisters
Moms and dads
Their doors may be the same as yours
You may find yourself stuck out
But that can always lead to more adventures
Some doors are not right for you
Their rooms smelling sour
Others greet you with the sweet smell of incense
And some nice warm air
Doors may mean leaving
But they can also mean beginning

Samantha Goodmanson, Grade 8

Evolving

Walking through the depths of our souls
Sinful shadows bring us to all-time lows.
But with Our Father lighting the way
On the correct path, our feet shall stay.
Friendship guides our growing minds
And with God's help, we will succeed in ways of all kinds.

Sara LaMantia, Grade 8

A Reflection of the Past

As I walk through the camp
Realizing what happened here
I look around wondering
How many died so dear
Imagining all these skinny, almost weightless beings
Sitting in the corner afraid to move
I look around more, tripping in a hole,
It must have been someone trying to escape
This terrible place gave me goose bumps
Thinking how much these men had to be filled with hate
As I walk by a small, run-down building
There is quite a raunchy stench
As I walk I drag my feet on the ground,
I kicked something, and it was the sound of a ding
It was chains that of which
The prisoners' were bound
During this war the Nazis lost
That is now known as the Holocaust

Jeremiah Hoffmann, Grade 8

The Road…

As I walk down this gravel dirt road.
I look around a flower is blooming,
A tree is growing its beautiful green leaves,
Plants are sprouting all around,
Birds are singing.
After a harsh winter everything is back to normal;

Then I shiver,
I am brought back to reality.
Look all around,
I am not joined by flowers and bright colors,
No, I am joined by a cold white blanket of snow.

I take myself to that place,
To that warm spring evening,
But the cold always brings me back,
I will never be in that spring evening.
I will forever be stuck in the cold…

Jada Ranslem, Grade 8

Listen

People sometimes don't make good decisions,
And they have to pay the price.
It is not very nice but you can't control,
What people do.
It is not your fault!
You can't blame yourself.
You tried to help.
Some people just won't stop.
They don't know how to get away,
But just stay strong.
All you can do is be there for them,
And always remind them,
That you love them.

Katelynn Arrington, Grade 8

Music

Music cleanses every living soul.
It can sing a meaningful song
That expresses one's deepest feelings.
The music makes us feel like we belong.
Even if times are rough, love will always shine through the dark.

Music makes people feel excited.
It can sing a loud boisterous song
That makes people want to get up and dance.
Fun music makes us all sing along
Together, to stand against boring and dullness in the world.

Music makes people feel alive.
It opens our oblivious eyes
That were closed in our fake sense of reality.
The music makes people realize
How beautiful a combination of twenty-six letters can be.

Music is sound that is not heard through ears.
We listen to music through the soul.
People can listen to whatever they want to,
Such as genres like pop, rap, or rock and roll.
Just let the music belong to you, the one and only you.

Mia Peterson, Grade 7

Shattered Promises

Remember the day you pulled up your sleeves?
The day that marked our friendship.
The sorrowful look in your watery eyes,
The doubt in your innocent voice.

Remember you promised not to forge a smile?
But I still see you smiling your plastic grin.
Laughing at the jokes of those plastic people,
But they slam the door on your face when you're in need.

Remember you promised you'll be ok?
But you still leave the scarlet marks on your arm.
You hide the marks with fabrication,
But they all know the truth.

Remember you promised that you'll be happy?
But you still cry your mournful cry.
You inhale their beautiful lies and their painful truth.
They hurt your delicate skin and your delicate soul.

Remember you promised me?!
Of course you remember.
But why do I see your shattered promises resting at my feet?

Marlen Gongora, Grade 8

Ocean

I watch as it moves along in a timid manner,
nonchalant to the world when it leads a silent life,
alone and careless to the worries of the rest of us.

Eric Brown Jr., Grade 7

Spring Weather

It is warm outside
The sun shining bright at last
Beautiful cloud shapes

Rainbows and sunsets
Puddles in all of the streets
The sun shining back
Lisa Demas, Grade 7

My Mother

My mom has always been there for me
she has been there through
thick and thin
my mom has always been there for me
she takes care of me when I'm sick
feeds me when I'm hungry
my mom has always been there for me
Monique Carlock, Grade 7

Invisible Art

Rising land scraping skies
Covered in thick invasive trees
With invisible art in the world
Created by us
But we are oblivious to it
Weaving around the invading trees
That destroy our beautiful art
Rachel Klein, Grade 7

Emotions

Love
Warm, significant
Loving, caring, fulfilling
Heart, rose, wound, injury
Fighting, arguing, yelling
Harmful, terrible
Hatred
Alivia Lantz, Grade 7

Opposites

Feline
Fluffy, cuddly
Purring, meowing, lounging
Scratching post, catnip, cop car, bones
Patrolling, lurking, spotting
Vicious, sneaky
Canine
Kaytlyn Moore, Grade 7

Free

I am running fast
Leaving the world behind me
Forgetting the past
Fleeing the negativity
Finally, I can be free
Lauren Martin, Grade 8

Summer

Summer is here
and the children are excited.

Flashes of sandy beaches pop in their heads
while they lay in their beds.

After a cold blustery winter
they are ready for a sprinkler.

Swimsuits are bought and flip flops as well
and maybe a super soaker or a water spraying bell.

The sun beams down on the hot pavement
making illusions of water down the road giving the sign that summer is here.

Little girls set up lemonade stands
hoping for some business.

As each car passes
they get full glasses.

The hotter it gets outside
the more customers come.

The money that is raised
goes toward a water gun.

Hopefully they will get enough money
to make the start to their summer great.
Lexi Helland, Grade 8

Basketball

A sport where you need stamina,
you need the ability, the energy to do it.
If you play it every day, all the time
you can end up being one of those athletes on television.
The only key to the game is to have perseverance.
As you see athletes running back and forth,
the intensity in the game grows.

You hear the ball dribbling, you hear it swoosh off the net
the fans start yelling and you feel as if you lost your hearing
Watching the players, they make you want to be in their shoes.
You can consider this sport just a sport but to others it's a way of life.
Sometimes you feel like if the ball players were just as us,
but when you think about it they go through a lot of sweat.
Basketball is an inspiring sport, that gets you thrilled to do and to watch.

At a game, you smell the food and the players sweat,
the crowd goes crazy, you see the players speed get faster
The clock starts to tick.
The last shots are going in, people's hearts are beating
you start to get excited.
Coaches and players start to get upset. Swish! The last shot is made.
That's what makes this sport so inspiring and fun.
Cristian Alvarez, Grade 7

My Love Took Flight*

The birds tell me
That my love is gone
That she has taken flight with the rest of them

The birds whisper to me
That I should not cry
That even though she is gone
Life still goes on.

The birds show me their wings
Their radiant flight
and they tell me that even though it's dark
The moon still shines bright

The birds tell me
That my love is gone
That she remains watching
and she wants my smile to shine on

Roxana Arroyo, Grade 8
Dedicated to an unforgettable woman.

Ride On

As I ride on,
I have a really big fear,
If I do one thing wrong, something might happen —
Something bad, big, or broken.

If the ride is smooth,
I will be just fine.
If the track is rough,
I might hit something and fly off like a bird.

When I hit the ground
I'm not going to hear a sound;
I could be hurt,
Or I might break something.

Despite the risk
I do it anyway.
When you love something,
You risk it all.

Gage Poling, Grade 8

Her

Her name inspired the angels!
Her beauty was that of an angel!
Her love seemed as strong as the Lord's!
Her love seemed to take up all of the heavens!
Her love was my refuge!
Her love gave me something to live for!

My love for her was vaster than the Dakota prairies!
My love for her was stronger than a bull ready to charge!
My love for her gave her refuge!
My love for her gave her something to live for!

Luke Pond, Grade 8

Ultimate Training

I remember training, for the start of the year,
there was a lot of sweat coming out of my body
and the coach wanted everything to be perfect.
They treat us with a hard attitude.
We have to do everything the best we can
because our parents are paying the money
so everyone gets along,
and everyone likes the training.

I remember the first day I was scared
that everything I did went wrong.
I got yelled at but these
yells reminded me why I was here
and it helped me concentrate on
why I was there.
When I was injured all
I wanted to do was train with him.
All the memories seem clear
and I understand why he trained us like that.

Trinadad Ruiz, Grade 8

What Lies Ahead

The thoughts in my head are spinning,
Soon there will be a new beginning.
New people, new faces,
New buildings, new places.
Leaving behind the old familiar ways,
Feeling anxious about the upcoming days.

Will I fit in? Will they be nice to me?
All I've known for so long is my SGS family.
The time is now where things begin to change,
"Goodbye" and "Farewell" are the words we all exchange.

Each day I find my eyes smiling with delight,
Ready for a great challenge ahead to fight.
The nerves kick in as this new time approaches,
Getting advice from my long-time coaches.

We will eventually go our own way,
Hoping we will meet again someday.

Ava Speer, Grade 8

Cold

It is white, and I am losing sight
I am sad, but at the same time I am mad
I see snow every day, I just want it to go away
I want to see the sun, then have lots of fun
In the winter I am alone, so I just stay home
I listen to music day and night, do I think that's right
I try to forget everything, but I remember it's nothing
There's nowhere to go, so I just go with the flow
It is December, and I don't want to remember
I am now in the sun, everyone is having fun
I want to stay, here in Mexico till May

Ailyn Torres, Grade 8

The Swing
When I was a little girl
I would run down to my swing
Hop right on then twist and twirl
Pretending I was flying

"Push me, Daddy, push me!"
I would yell over to him, captivated
Wanting him to set me free
From stale to animated

Holding on with all my might
My dad would start to push
Back and forth high as a kite
Until the world all looked like mush

I felt just like a bird
Then sadly flew back down
"Again, again!" I cried until he heard
And he always smiled big and round

I oft think back to those days
When all it took was asking
Then I remember it's still that way
And my daddy will always be listening
Maggie Wiele, Grade 9

Sadness...
Your eyes,
The windows to your soul,
Feelings,
Your peace of mind,

The way you move,
Something's wrong,
Trust me,
I know you,

I am right in front of you,
Yet I don't know what to do,
You're crying,
And lying,

About how you feel,
I want you to heal,
But I can't repeal,
The pain you feel,

So today,
I have to say,
By the end of the day,
I know you'll be okay.
Matrik Hartman, Grade 8

Noon Wash
The sun is rising;
All is waking up;
The salty smell of the sea;
There is an orange glow.

The sun is high in the light blue sky;
A slight breeze is blowing;
The green sea sprays salt water;
The pure white wash is blowing.

The sun is setting;
It is radiant;
All is winding down;
Soon, everything will be still.

The sun is gone;
The moon is high;
It's a silver sequin;
In the pitch black sky.
Isabella Martello, Grade 7

The Four Seasons
The apple blossoms are in bloom
And can be seen by the light of the moon;
The trees are all beginning to green,
It makes the most beautiful scene.

It is lovely to hear the breeze
Whistling through the green trees;
Let the cattle in the fields graze,
All you need to do is sit and gaze.

The leaves are now being brightly dressed
And now have clothes which look the best;
The geese are all flying away;
While in the fields are piles of hay.

The wind is surely one cold bite;
Then something nice and fluffy white,
Thick and fast through the air,
Snowballs are flying everywhere.
Felicity Wohletz, Grade 8

Peace
To find peace
Within your soul
Is not an easy thing to accomplish

You have to find people
That you love
And goals you want to reach

You are filled with such
Happiness,
That you can't help but
Smile,
Every second of every day

You have to forgive all the people
That have hurt you
In the past
And look towards the future

You trust in God
And follow his wishes,
To gain a permanent spot
In Heaven
THIS is PEACE
Haley Mosley, Grade 7

Gymnastic Meets
Chalk on my hands
Bruises on my feet
All I can think about
Is winning the meet.

My adrenaline is pumping
As I go to the floor
My music begins
With an ear-piercing roar.

A great starting position
Will add extra to my score
And with a beautiful flip-flop
I land feet on the floor.

Next a back tuck
With beautiful form
Then a front layout
The crowd cheers up a storm.

And when the results come in
It's a perfect ten
I have so much fun
That's why I do it again and again.
Clare Collard, Grade 7

Nebraska
Full of snowy winters
Deathly hot summers
Corn fields full of crops
The biggest zoo in America
Founders of Arbor Day
Creators of Kool-Aid and the Reuben
Fun football games in the fall
Husker spirit fills the air
A perfect place for family
Sitting in the center of the U.S.
Nebraska is a great place to live
Carissa Schaben, Grade 8

One Lost Mind

Colors of freedom reflect off the large windows,
faintly illuminating the already bright space.
As salt water rains to the ground,
searching for bobbing curls that never show.

Their eyes never stop wandering,
ears never stop listening,
until the facts are faced.
Some will have weights locked in their chest,
others will have a hope lift them.

From top to bottom lies a box filled with treasures,
upon an untouched bed.
As the storm rolls in,
with piercing and pounds,
unable to forget what happened when the sun went down.

They carried the stone strapped on their hearts.
Unable to give them one last token of love,
their farewells are unspoken.
The wound unfixable.

Some hear faint laughs echoing in the distance,
almost as if the heavens are whispering.
Unable to let go, it was cut. All because of one lost mind.

Karina Hotchkiss, Grade 7

Rockets Volleyball

When the refs blow their whistles,
So that the game can start while I hit the first serve,
As it goes over the net,
The team cheers; it's an ace!

After we receive a ball,
Although it was a bad pass up,
Wherever it soars, as long as it's high,
Our setter can reach it and give a good set.

Since she pushes a nice set while we wait on the tip line,
Where the ball is in our sight
As if our hitters are hammers,
They whack the ball down: KILL! "RELOAD!"

But that isn't enough,
Because we can show them the rest of our skills,
While their passers wait for a hit, before they have time to spring,
Our front row tips the ball delicately to the ground!

No matter what team,
Whether they're tall or short, strong or weak,
Supposing everyone is trying their best,
When it's the end of the game,
WE WILL WIN!

Maddie Schurman, Grade 8

My Sister Hannah

T rying to do her best in school
E ager to learn new things every day
E verytime wears a huge smile on her face
N ever gives up on herself, no matter what
A plus student every single time
G ives a huge effort to get those A+'s
E xcited to learn about poisonous frogs
R eally enjoys doing the impossible in school

Shelby Wolff, Grade 7

An Amazing Place

My favorite place to be is Fargo, North Dakota
I will be going there this summer in June
I visit my family and go to the lake while I'm there
I see the clear lake water and the Fargodome
I hear the football fans cheering the NDSU Bison
I choose to spend time shopping and watching Bison football
I will go back there next summer with my sister
I love being in North Dakota spending time with my family

Zoe Sundstrom, Grade 8

Who Am I?

Silently I question who I really am.
Some say I'm too small; some say I'm like a bird.
Some say I'm not good enough, but I don't really care.
Everyone has opinions, lots of variety.
Some say I'm like a sapling; I'm not yet full grown.
I know I still have much to learn, and must keep pushing on.
I know I must keep working hard, for I know what's at stake.
One day when I don't give my all, I know that is all it takes.

Haylee Weiss, Grade 7

In the Grandstands

F un for the whole family
O utstanding players to watch
O pponents are whimpering with fear
T elling the opposing team to get out of here
B est thing to watch on Friday nights
A stonished to see how hard the players hit
L oud cheering is what I hear
L oving how amazing our Indians are

Kaleb Hays, Grade 7

My Favorite Sport

B all in the air about to be caught
A bird flies over the field
S omeone yells, batter up, my favorite words
E veryone looks at the pitcher
B all cracks off the bat when it's hit
A ll the people in the stands watch the ball soar
L ooking around, trying to find the ball
L aughing starts when the outfielders hit one another

Connor Keller, Grade 7

There Is Still Hope

On a cold autumn night
As I look to the red field
The moon shined bright
And made me yield
I saw a young boy
Along with the rest of the dead
One who should be filled with joy
From my eye a tear began to shed
This young boy all alone
I searched and searched to learn something of him
But his name was still unknown
Now everything bright and beautiful was now dim
I thought could there still be hope from deep within
Yes there is always hope
I fight now for not just my country
But now I also fight for him!
From here on out I don't fight to push the enemy back
From now on I fight to win!
And I fight for him.

Hunter Zielinski, Grade 8

Horror in the Dark

Looking in a dark room,
Nervous, scared, afraid to roam.
Because of you, I am scared to death
chilled to the bone.

The many legs you have
are all thin as thread;
You're always prepared to attack.
When I see you, I feel dead.

The thought of an encounter with you
is constantly on my mind.
I always prepare myself for what I should do
If your body is what I might find.

Your presence to me is always a fright,
But I know I'm going to have to face my fear.
Even when I hear crawling during the night,
I know that facing my fear is right.

Morgan Egeland, Grade 8

The Tide of Life*

"Like as the waves make towards the pebbl'd shore
So do our minutes hasten to their end."
Each tide comes in, another day is gone,
How many waves are left 'til there are none?
Some are forceful, full of rage and destruction,
Others gentle, bringing calm and peace,
Day in, day out 'til we reach the last
Breath of the ocean to come to pass —
The end for which we have so long aimed,
The tide draws back, eternity is gained.

Julia Varnado, Grade 9
*Inspired by William Shakespeare.

Fearing Enduring

Hearing the applause from the crowd below
As I walk up I keep my head low
Looking down I see my hands shaking
When I look up I see smiles in the making.

I try to read but my mind is busy
Suddenly I start to get nervously dizzy
As I speak my tongue suddenly slips!
And when I try to walk down I start to trip.

I hear a snicker, then two, then four
My face turns red as I get up from the floor
People are laughing like bees all around
I just want to cry listening to the sound.

Everyone points with amusement in their eyes
People all around, girls and guys
Pointing and shouting while I'm sheepishly pouting
Walking away, it's myself that I'm doubting.

Savannah Eaton, Grade 8

My Beach

The tiny grains gliding through your feet,
Packed tight to make a fantasy,
Millions together all for this beach,

The hot sun warming the skin of people,
Being tan is a dream of many,
Bathing suits show the lines between winter and summer;
These lines remind us how cold it once was,

The sun dances on the water,
Jump in and soothe heating skin,
Surfing day and night,
Watch the sun sink below the water,

The beach is a home,
The beach is a dream,
The beach is a playground,
The beach is a sanctuary,
The beach is my vacation

Olivia Ruby, Grade 8

White Butterflies

The hot summer day
Brings a warm feeling in my heart
I know we are going to the Sunny Meadow
The long car ride there fills me with anxiousness
We arrive and start running around
I grab a baseball cap and wait
The hot settle wind brought the beautiful white butterflies
I jump and run
Trying to catch the beautiful butterflies
The sun sets
And I await the next day we come visit

Fatima Serna, Grade 8

She Lived

She laughed, she loved, she traveled and learned.
She served, she was blessed, she was loved and she lived her life.
She never grew out of her passion for traveling.
She circled the world, traveled the globe…and around again.
Paris, Greece and Alaska to see the Northern lights,
Unlike anything she had ever seen.
She loved being a missionary,
Parasailing, and swimming with dolphins.
It was a blast,
Even the many years at school,
And learning new languages, (trés français!)
There were hard times,
Happy times,
Down times
And silly times,
But she lived with no regrets,
And loved it all.

Rose Neff, Grade 8

Snowstorm Warning

S lipping and sliding all around,
N o sunlight to be seen,
O ld memories of the past snowstorms,
W hite snow falling heavily,
S chool is out because of the storm,
T oo much snow to compute,
O ther people like the snow,
R unning around in the snow,
M others calling children indoors,

W anting to drink the warm hot cocoa,
A rranging a movie around the warm fire,
a **R** ranging a snowball fight,
N avigate the direction the storm is going,
ask **I** ng parents if they could teach you to ski,
N egotiate with the parents about a trip,
G o skiing with friends.

Julian Mikesell, Grade 8

A School of Superb Satisfaction

I love St. Mary School.

We students are the best;
We welcome any guest.

Our teachers are so great;
They won't let students be late.

We learn so much Catholic knowledge,
So we'll get accepted to college.

With service we spread so much love,
And teach people to pray to the Father above.

I love St. Mary School.

Carlie Merola, Grade 7

Shoes

Shoes, shoes, shoes
Nike, Adidas, and Jordans
Are the ones I use.
Shoes are the best invention
there could be.
Jordans are the best out of all.
I wish I could have as many Jordans
That fit in a UHaul.
Then with so many shoes,
I can go to the park and ball.
I don't know what I would do without shoes.
Shoes, shoes, shoes,
Nike, Adidas, and Jordans are the ones I use,
And they are the best brands of shoes
I would choose.
Sometimes shoes just make me feel happy
Because they are just beautiful

Luis Salazar, Grade 7

You Must Go On

Even if many bad things happen,
and the world seems horrible,
you must go on

Even if life seem pointless,
and think you're worthless,
you must go on

Even if you can't afford everything you want,
you must go on

Because before you know it,
it would be the end of your life

And cherish all of the wonderful things in life,
that's why,
you must go on.

Angela Estrada, Grade 8

The Light Shines Down*

The light shines down
on the bright
spontaneous city
down to the calming
aqua water

The light shines down
Making the whole city joyful
Making the whole city calm

The sunshine
Makes the proud birds chirp
Making the building show
Their reflections

Lia Tzoubris, Grade 8
*Inspired by "Lower Manhattan from the River" by John Marin

Spring

After the snow melted,
I thought the ground would be soaked,
the sky would look vapid,
plants would wilt,
and the cracks on the street would materialize themselves.

After the snow melted,
I thought I'd be gloomy,
I'd forget the sun's existence,
and that rain would revisit me everyday.

After the snow melted,
I would've never expected the sun to shine,
the grass to turn green,
flowers to sprout,
or have heat torture me at night.

After the snow melted,
I would've never have thought spring would come.

Yadira Corral, Grade 8

Am I Really Alone?

We're together always, every day
Days upon days, hours upon hours.
We say we will never leave each other's side
It was as if we were glued together, forever.

I've been so happy
Or maybe I'm just on your drug
I'm drowning in your love
And I love the feeling

But lately I've been having dreams, nightmares
you leave, and never return
as I wake, I'm screaming
I'm now falling from cloud nine

I hope it's just a nightmare…
but it's not; we slowly start to drift apart
I am still in denial; I don't believe it,
but it's the truth: you're really gone…you're really gone…

Ashley Tolle, Grade 8

Avery, My Inspiration

You are my inspiration, my role model, my guide.
You give me confidence to try my best.
You have an immaculate smile and a bubbly personality.
You're always happy and full of energy.
You're hard working, dedicated and clearly committed.
You're super sweet and you encourage others to keep going.
You always see the good side in people.
You're extremely talented, and I look up to you.
You're there for others when they need you.
You include everyone and make them feel welcome.
You're brave and truly an inspiration!

Kate Preston, Grade 9

The Path of Time

The path of time has an endless journey
One that started before anyone has ever known.
Not one journey will ever be the same,
But they can have similarities.

We share the path with everyone,
Like loved ones, friends, and strangers.
Your journey flies by when you're having fun,
And slows down when you're not.

The hills you go up represent difficult times,
Because they're harder to deal with.
But the downhill journey is tons of fun;
It's no doubt the best part!

Just remember for every hill you go up,
You will eventually get to travel down.
Not all journeys start or end the same.
Yours has just begun.

Lillian Gossett, Grade 8

Showing Cattle

working all summer in the heat
pulling, tugging, and sweating
finally the time has come
the frenzy of the people
trailers everywhere
water sloshing, feed spilling, dirt everywhere
cattle mooing
drenched cattle
blowdryers drying
combs flying
aerosol cans spraying
switching from rope to leather
lastly, polishing the hooves
the adrenaline rush of entering the ring
the voice of the judge roaring
leading in circles
ribbons handed out
washing again
put it all away till next year

Kenidee Urling, Grade 9

Friends

Friends stick together 'til the end,
They are like a straight line that will not bend.

They trust each other forever,
No matter if you're apart you are together.

They can be your hero and save your day,
They will never leave your side, they are here to stay.

They help you up when you fall,
Your true friends are the best of all.

Jasmine Lamon, Grade 7

If I Were a Butterfly

If I were a butterfly
I could fly
I could spread my wings
And take whatever life brings

If I were a butterfly
I would be free
I could fly across a desert
Or even across the sea

If I were a butterfly
I could go with the flow
And I wouldn't care
Wherever that I may go

But I am not a butterfly
At least I can dream
The only thing I will ever be
Is just plain old me
Cassie Rich, Grade 8

April

April is the spring season,
Flowers are blooming.
People are walking.
People love spring.

A fresh smell of grass growing,
People mow the new grass.
The swimming pool opens.
Kids go to the parks until dark.

In April, it rains and rains.
A rainbow and flowers pop up!
Bugs crawl out of their holes.
And people make goals

Green grass, flowers, and trees grow.
Kids playing outside their house
People paint their house.
April is the spring season.
Haleema Rehman, Grade 8

Fall Is The Best

Fall, the best season.
It gives me great happiness
With colorful leaves.

With its great weather,
We can play fun basketball
With only sweatshirts.

Our friends are waiting
To meet with us after school
To play in the fall.
John Tijerina, Grade 7

Overcoming

All eyes are on me
Watching like a hawk watches prey
Trapped *in* a vice of expectation
My muscles tense, I'm breathing heavy
Head starts to spin

Breathing, *focus* on the breathing
Tethered to it, it allows me to *hold on*
My heart pounding in my ears
There's no stopping now

Momentum builds and it becomes easier
If I choke up now, it's all over
Nearing the end, I know *I can do it*
But the eyes are still watching
This time with a different emotion

Finished, relief crashes over me in a wave
The roar of applause rings in my ears
The fear and anxiety slinking away
To find someone else
Someone else who can overcome
Sam DeMoss, Grade 8

Soccer

Soccer.
 Green grass
  Players breathing heavily.
Fancy ball.
 Fans yelling, coach screaming
  Sidelines.
Referee whistles.
 Contact sport
  Always watching — pay attention
   No advantage.
Drop, passes, through balls.
 Lines
  Smacking cleats.
Sweaty, cold, hot, wet.
 Focus on position
  Shoulders pushing across
   Pressure —
    Pushing.
No mistakes, no fear.
Take the shot!
Soccer.
Benjamin Schellenberg, Grade 7

Family Love

Your family will always love you
No matter what you do
They will stick by your side
Every day you are on this planet Earth
You always love your family
Even until the end of time
Grant Goral, Grade 7

Drumsticks

The way it swings down,
 To the plastic skin.
The vibration through,
 The wood.

The way it chirps, like a bird,
 When it hits the bronze.
Feeling the rotation, like a windmill,
 As it twirls in my hand.

The way it chips,
 From the steel rim.
Then it cracks from
 Wear and tear.

The way it swings down,
 To the plastic skin.
The vibration through,
 The wood.
Jason Krause, Grade 8

Music

Music makes me dance and move
Music makes me move to the groove
Sad songs bring some people to their knees
Other songs make them feel free

Some music makes me cry
Other music makes me happy inside
Songs give off different emotions
For music I have full devotion

Although people make me sad or mad
Music is there to make it not so bad
Different music enlightens our day
I think music is the only way

Get lost in the music, carried away
Music is in my life every day
The passion is in my heart
It's been part of my life from the start
Sara Stapleman, Grade 9

The Masked Man

There is a man that stands very tall,
He will take all the thugs out in a brawl.
He's strong, he's slick, he moves very quick,
He never has time to rest or be sick.
He dresses in black,
And is always ready to attack, but
Only when the time is right,
He also has the very best of eyesight.
No, he has no fear of rats,
Nor a fear of cats,
Just a fear of bats.
Chris Alvey, Grade 8

Milk Is Best Out of the Jug…
The milk we just bought
was tasty out of the jug,
Very refreshing, I thought,
very cold, very thick.

You wanted it for the donuts,
Soaked in white Heaven
Damped in deliciousness,
Regret it, I don't think so.

Sorry not sorry
Yummy on my tongue,
Would do it again…and again,
Milk is best served out of the jug.
Zach Reichen, Grade 7

Snowy Winter
Snow glistens in the sunlight
the flakes starts to fall all around
its beauty is blinding and white
cold light fluffs that make no sound

Each flake is beautiful and unique
so I lay down in a blanket of white
as they land on my eyelash and cheek
my arms and legs outstretched in spite

I feel the cold seep through my clothes
and breathe the frozen air through my nose
I know I must not stay too long
although the pull of it seems so strong
Ethan Robey, Grade 8

Spring Is Here
S tart of baseball season,
P lants begin to grow
R ain pours down,
I am relieved there is…
N o more snow.
G reen grass improves the landscape.

I ntelligence stops, school is almost over,
S unshine all day long!

H eat is very mild,
E arly tans will appear,
R unning in the sun,
E veryone is happy; spring is here!
Ben Chapman, Grade 8

Dream On
Everyone can dream
Dreaming is what keeps people going
Dreaming is what people need
Dream on forever
Genny Johnson, Grade 8

Snow Land
Wouldn't it be pretty to live in land of snow?
Where beauty covers the land, stars speckled up above in the silk of navy blue sky,
Crystal icicles hanging in the fresh evergreen pine trees,
And a cozy warm house in the middle of it all.
In this land, time stands still in icy crystal winter,
And love and happiness is all around and survives through the bitter wind outside,
If only regular life was as good as that, where time never moved,
And it was never sad or cruel as the world is now.
Because in Snow Land there are no terrible things, to be worried about
There is no pain or sorrow.
In Snow Land there is no one that has to be perfect to enter.
No matter what your past is or where you come from you are received with love and care.
If only this was more than just a precious dream for the world peace.
I wish there was a place like that in this cold world,
A place where my dream would come true.
Kimberly Baez, Grade 7

Heavy Snowfall
H eaping snow seems to fall on my lawn,
E ven though I lay still, my energy is drawn.
A t the heart of my yard, I stand in the thick snow,
V igorously I move, but the snow continues to grow.
Y elling and frustrated, I give up and decide to stop.

S ome people wait all year and live for winter,
N ot for me, though, it's like an annoying splinter.
O ver the years I learned to think of snow as chore,
W ith all the shoveling I have to do, it's like a never ending war.
F or my sister, though, it's the stuff of absolute happiness,
A nd when I watch her, I just see total madness.
L ike many other people, though, I'm not alone in my opinion,
L iving in my world, if I ruled the world, it would be a snow free dominion!
Matthew Tungett, Grade 8

The Lively Lake
I come here all the time, mainly in the summer
When I am here, I learn different water sports and make new friends
I see people swimming and having fun, beautiful beaches and many people
I hear motorboats roaring, waves crashing on the shore
The screams of laughter from children, and music coming from boats
I choose to have fun and live life to the fullest; I try new things and
Become excellent at the water sports I have learned
When I come home, all I can think is when I can go back
I never want to come home because the lake is where I can be me
Madison Tice, Grade 8

The Beach
I go there all the time mostly during the summer.
When there, I play catch on the sand and dive for passes in the water.
I watch the water as it flows upon the sand.
I hear the sound of birds chirping loudly among the waves.
I have a great time there no matter when I go.
I am always sad to leave, but I know I'll be back next summer.
I love the beach more than anything in the world.
It's the best place I could be.
Jake Faulkender, Grade 8

Synonyms

Happy
Bright, Cheerful, Festive, Glad.
Happiness it the opposite of mad.

Pain
Sting, Ache, Anguish, Strain.
pain hurts and will always remain.

Laugh
Cheer, Mock, Ridicule.
laughter against you make you like a fool.

Fantasy
Illusion, Mirage, Delusion, Daydream.
A fantasy is not what it seems.

Fireworks
Blast, Flame, Fire, Spark.
You can see fireworks in the dark.

Denzell Smith, Grade 7

Poisonous Rope

The reptile is slithering through the garden;
Plants move as the ants rant,
Black and red and very viscous;
I run inside as fast as a cheetah.

I hear his tail shake;
It rattles over and over,
The most frightening reptile I've ever seen,
But there's no time to waste.

It's the longest I've ever seen,
And I know it is very poisonous;
The snake was a rope lying in the sun;
This wasn't just an illusion.

It was sneaky not to make a sound,
Then he crept up on his prey,
Eyeing it very closely,
And suddenly he struck the mouse.

Nick Thielen, Grade 8

You Are…

You are the fire that lights my way,
The blue in my sky,
The sun in my summer,
The snow in my winter,
You make my heart beat fast.

You are the thrill in my life,
The notes in my song,
The steps in my journey,
The pencil to my paper,
You make my life wonderful.

Lauren Brand, Grade 7

Miss Him

Is it ok to miss him,
Even though he hasn't been in my life?
Is it all right,
That my heart aches for him to show up?
He hasn't been the best father,
No, he hasn't been a father.
But I still love him,
So is that wrong?
Is it wrong,
To want him to show up?
To act like I'm his baby girl again?
To erase the past,
And let him into my future?
Is it wrong,
To look at his picture twice a month?
Wanting to see him,
So badly.
Cause I miss my daddy,
So,
Is it wrong?

Rachelle Lumpkins, Grade 9

Us

you and I
me and you
physically one
mentally two
I am a prisoner you are my cage
but I committed no crime and I feel no rage

we are bound together
neither the best
stuck forever
yet never at rest
constantly at war
yet always at peace

you are my cage I your prisoner
lost in a jail and rare is a visitor
still we are content
as the one that is two
you and I
me and you

Heather Pump, Grade 7

A Poem Is a Puzzle

A poem is like a puzzle
Which are challenging
Making you think about it
Piece by piece
You're putting words together once you
Find the picture
You see words start to run
You take all the words and mix them up
As they leave your mind

Amber Crague, Grade 7

Whispers of Spring

There's a whisper in the breeze,
A soft breath,
Singing through the trees,
"Wake up, wake up, it's time."

There's a little bit of green,
Peeking underneath,
Changing my yard's sheen,
"Can I come up now?"

There's a sky oh so blue,
Brighter than in winter,
And clouds sailing too,
"Is it time to water the ground?"

Quietly, quietly, things are growing,
And before you know it,
Their colors are showing,
"Welcome, welcome, sunshine!"

And I watch and I smile,
Breathe in the breeze,
Hearing all the while,
"Wake up, wake up, it's spring!"

Hannah Van Sickle, Grade 7

Why Are You So Skinny?

Get some meat on you
Are you anorexic?
Are you on a diet?
You're skinny

You're like a bag of bones
Are you okay?
You are a twig
You're skinny

You need to be fattened up
Why are you so scrawny?
Is there something you aren't telling me
You're skinny

In reality,
Absolutely no eating disorders
Eat junk to try to put on weight
I'm sorry I'm skinny

Slim, Curvy
Tall, Short

Love yourself

Rachel Dever, Grade 9

Speak

Speak
Or maybe I won't
Speak
Why should I?
Speak
What if I don't?
Speak
Or what if I do?
Speak
What does that matter?
Speak
Maybe I will
Speak
Tomorrow
Speak
Fine, today
Speak
Now?
Speak
You're right, Speak
Ellie Johnson, Grade 8

I Have a Dream

True racism
True alienation.
True neglect.
True addictions.
True negativity.
I have a dream.
These are most of the things
That scare us away from success.
Almost 50 years.
Martin Luther King died long ago.
His dream will be complete.
If not today…one day.
I have a dream.
true Positivity.
true Education.
true Happiness.
true Love.
true Peace.
I ask, have we really joined hands?
I have a dream.
Monique Wilson, Grade 9

Time

We are here for a while
In time must move on
The days lay before us
Then they are gone

Our purpose on earth
Who can say?
It is a mystery forever
Take it day by day
Brandon Ray, Grade 8

Grandpa

Memories flowing through
My head like
Clouds in the sky

Thinking of my grandpa
When I last saw him
While sitting on his lap
I remember it like yesterday

Questioning him if he was okay
While he was feeding me Cheerios
He tried being strong and brave
For the sake of the family
We all knew he would be gone
One day
Whether we liked it or not
Till this day my grandpa
Will forever be in my heart
Abigail Espinoza, Grade 8

Why We Celebrate

The land of the free
The home of the brave
That's why we celebrate Veteran's Day

Some men and women
Went overseas
Lost their lives
Taken prisoner or even injured

We are so thankful
For those that served
The Army, Navy, Air Force, and Marines
So that our safety will be ensured

November 11th
A day to remember
And honor the veterans
So we can enjoy freedom every day
Victoria Denison, Grade 7

Puzzles

Poems are puzzles,
Being difficult to understand at first.
Trying to figure out
The right piece to fit.

Poems are puzzles,
Being built to tease
The imagination of the reader.
But when finished,
It seizes your eyes to observe it.
You step back to take a closer look.
You'll then see the full picture,
Full of mystery and wonder.
Justin Hernandez, Grade 7

Put It Down (Suicide Prevention)

As the blood rushes down your arm
As you puke up your very last breath
Why do you do this self-harm
Why do you want to be close to death

Put down the knife
Put down the pills
Don't end your life
Don't find the white hills

As you fall to the ground
As you say your last goodbye
We all have tears and a frown
We all ask "why?"

Put down the gun
Put down the blade
Dying isn't fun
Nor is it to see your life fade

But we can help you
We can help rid you of that frown
Just tell us what to do
How to help you put it down
Tristian McCann, Grade 8

My Own Worst Enemy

In this dark cave
I call my mind
A path is paved
And a coil unwinds

In this dreary place
Where sin and madness play
Joy and love race
Without further delay

In my own cage
I am my own worst fear
But diminish the rage
And my heart starts to clear

In that filthy jail
When I lose all hope
A light will prevail
And I grasp a rope

In this crumbling room
That crashes to the ground
There is no longer any doom
Because I have been found.
Leah Murfin, Grade 9

2014

Since 2004
The door to my education has been open
Around 2005 the door opened a little bit more
A little bit too much, maybe?
Things started to change
It was no longer about what you knew
It was — can you spell encyclopedia or corkscrew?
No longer was it about learning and going home
You stayed there all day and still didn't learn a thing.
Then you get called stupid and wonder why
They just want to memorize and mesmerize these celebrities
But people like me
We care
We know
It shows
In our grades
In our lives
But not on the news
Or TV alike
We're seen as depressed and stupid
I wonder why.

Angelica Horton, Grade 9

The Light

My dreams lay shattered, broken.
I am searching for more than I know.
I wrestle achingly though each day.
Simplicity and peace left in a flurry,
Cold, icy, and far.
My heart was left empty and heavy.
But, there is more than meets the eye.
A light is shining brightly,
Glowing, beyond the clouds, dark and ominous.
They loom mercilessly over me, threatening to smother.
Yet, I will not be consumed.
The winds may blow and all I know may crumple.
But I will hold tight, for I know what is coming.
The rain will pass.
Though the season is not over yet, I will carry on.
For now I see the light far in the distance.
It is bright with glorious beams.
Clouds, they will pass, the darkness will fade.
Night, after all, will come to an end.
Dawn is ringing.
I am almost there.

Graciela Acosta, Grade 9

The Silent

Tears from these friends without a voice
Being beaten without a choice
Their tears are pouring down
Heavier than rain from a cumulus cloud
We notice their sorrow on TV screens
But shy away from giving them their needs
Do they deserve this? Nobody knows
But when opportunities to help arise
The abuse towards these friends grows
Have they committed a felony?
Do they deserve to cry their sad melody?
Friends are supposed to be loved
But under the bus is where they are shoved
This problem requires escalation to the extreme
Before somebody of authority intervenes
Tears from these friends without a voice
Will hopefully have a choice
If everyone speaks up for the unspoken
Their silence will finally be broken
These friends should have a voice
We have the choice

Jailen Billings, Grade 9

The Forest

It's a secret world.
Hidden, so to speak.
Hidden between the lies that society keeps.
Where the dreamers can explore deeper.
Where the adventures can climb.
Where my mind still wonders
from time to time.
It's where the bark becomes faces —
Both cruel and devious.
The animals run within their infinite playground,
and live between it all.
The snow will eventually coat every living thing here.
But if you stay with me,
we'll be lost in the summer clear.
Even with the cold of winter —
Our hearts will never freeze.
We'll watch the changing season,
but we won't feel the breeze.
It's where the leaves still shimmer until they fall.
And even with that icy glaze cover —
The forest, is still the most majestic place of all.

CC Johnson, Grade 8

Spring

Pine cones litter the ground like inanimate hedgehogs
as tiny blossoms lay beside them in their rosy dresses.
Craggy bark pieces protrude from beneath the debris,
resembling moss-covered benches for the insects that investigate.
Winter still shows signs of wear on the crinkling, thin, paper-like
pieces of leaves and pine needles
but still a warm breeze gives a promise of the spring to come.

Maiya Orstad Brings, Grade 7

Summer Days

Happiness seems light blue
Like lying down in the grass watching the sky
I see white clouds rolling by in the blowing wind
I hear birds singing their beautiful song in the trees
I smell fresh air and green grass being cut nearby
I touch the soft grass and feel the cool earth
I taste icy cold lemonade which has been freshly squeezed

Taryn Zweygardt, Grade 9

World

Walking down the street,
I see a homeless man on the floor,
trying to pick himself up
I offer my help, he denies it
has he given up?
Is this what the world has come to?
People giving up on life?

Turning on the tv, I watch a commercial,
People suffering from hunger,
all over the world,
they still have hope.
Is this what the world has come to?
People dying from hunger?

Eduardo Botello, Grade 8

Summer Is Already Here

The birds singing and dancing
The sun so bright
Flowers are blooming
Grass is growing
Butterflies are flying

Fresh wind
Beautiful sky
Summer oh summer
Fireflies flying
Dogs outside
A warm summer sky
And the warm air
Summer is already here.

Stephania Lopez, Grade 7

Bugatti

Sleek and cool I look at you
Fast and sharp
Smooth as a baby's skin
The more I look, you grab my heart.

But when I see the price
My jaw drops to the floor
And I turn away,
I can see you no more.

The Bugatti's roaring engine fades away
As it leaves to seek a new driver.
A Bugatti cost beyond my dreams.
I leave and I feel lost.

Juan Fragoso, Grade 7

Society

Sometimes I feel like I don't belong.
They only let us know
What they want us to know.
Reality isn't real.

Kayla Aguilar, Grade 9

The Colors of the Ocean

Look over there! Did you see?
Let's go in a bit deeper.
Imagine you go on a scuba adventure.
The Colors of the ocean
You splash into the ocean, the water is cold, and you can taste the salt in your mouth.
Instantly, you see the colors of the reef
You keep on swimming, suddenly you see a fish.
You notice the colors and patterns on its scales.
Suddenly, you stop…You see a jellyfish, be careful.
Look at its shimmering colors.
Keep on swimming.
Notice the pretty seashells close to the floor?
Close to the shells you see a star, a starfish.
Its got a pretty color too.
You feel the warmth of the sun, glistening through the water.
It makes some of the rocks sparkle.
Oh no! Your air is running out!
As you get to the top, tiny bubbles appear.
You can feel the nice breeze on your face, as your friends help you into the boat.
You can still smell the salt of the water, and can hear your flippers as you swam.
As the sunsets, and the waves crash into the boat, you remember, the colors of the ocean.

Yarely Contreras, Grade 7

Soccer

Soccer is my passion.
Exercising and relaxing on a beautiful day
Is somewhat like Heaven to me.
As I start running I can feel the wind gently pressing among my face.
WHOOSH,
Goes the wind.
I start to feel an adrenaline rush.
Can it be the wind?
Or is it my strong love for the sport?
Maybe it is both.
I hear my cleats ripping through the grass
As I dribble the ball to the goal.
I smell the plants and trees strong odor around the field
Allowing me to taste fresh oxygen.
You see that round object filled with air around my feet?
It is more than a toy,
It is my partner throughout the wonderful sport.
Long drips of sweat pour down,
I then realize the sun's dazzling rays beaming down on me.
But I don't mind one bit,
For soccer is my passion.

Javier Saucedo, Grade 7

To Keep Going

Uncertainty seems purple
Like the eerie mists, spring brings every single year
I see the rain droplets trickling down carefully from the sky
I hear the "plop, plop, plop" the droplets make as they hit the ground
I smell the wet dirt in the warm, humid air
I touch one last time, my tense and nervous hands
I taste the salty, gritty mud being flung at my lips as I go with my uncertainty

Makayla Rogers, Grade 9

Poetry Is Like Candy

Poetry
Is like candy
Strikes you with
Words that inspire
You

Sometimes sweet but
Sometimes sour
Long or short
You understand them all

Soft or hard
Your tongue speaks
Its words

Siri Landers, Grade 7

America!

Dear fellow people
Who fought for us
You served your time
I thank you so much

For the freedom you give us
Thank you so much

For the people who defended our country
For some soldiers who almost died for us
Thank you so much

For schools, houses, able to walk on streets
Thank you so much for our freedom

Marine Robinson, Grade 7

Our Veterans

Our veterans answered a call
To support our country in fight
Their country had requirements for
The essential skills they brought

We salute every one of them
The noble and the brave
The ones still with us here today
Or the ones who rest in an honorable grave

So here's to our country's veterans
They're above all the rest
Let's give the honor that is due
To our country's very best

Katelyn Leggitt, Grade 7

Stars

Stars are lanterns
Shining the way
I follow their footsteps
I must not stray

Angela Davis, Grade 7

My Secret Oasis

My favorite place is found within my heart, but only I can find it.
I go there when I have trouble with life or need strength to get through the day.
When I'm there, I let Him know everything that has been bothering me,
Plus exciting experiences which have boosted my spirits.
The images I see are of Him and me talking in the clouds.
I hear His deep voice telling what I should do to help my family and me.
While I'm at my oasis, I listen to what He says and take every word to heart.
I go back there, to my oasis, every night and every morning.
Prayer has helped me through many things.
If I listen, the Lord will answer me with an open heart.

Reagan Beims, Grade 8

A Recipe for a Great Basketball Player

3 gallons of aggression
2 quarts of determination
1 tablespoon of luck
5 cups of endurance
5 gallons of skill
7 ounces of patience
9 cups of hard work
In a large bowl, combine your ingredients;
however, don't over-mix or else your player might become a little grouchy.
Display neatly on a freshly waxed basketball court and enjoy!

Karsyn Hay, Grade 7

Amusement Park

I can smell the food, popcorn and the cotton candy
I can hear the people screaming on the roller coaster
AAAAAAAAAAHHHHHHHHHH
It goes as fast as a cheetah
I can see people, food, rides, and drinks
I can touch the food, the cement on the road, and the metal on the rides
I can taste the popcorn and the cotton candy
The food dances in my mouth, it's so good
There are a billion people in the amusement park
I love going to the amusement park.

Isaac Moreno, Grade 7

Nebraska — My Home

The corn in the huge fields, their green stalks waving in the breeze.
The sky, a perfect blue, not a cloud to be seen.
The sandhill cranes form shadows on the ground from the sky.
Strong, tall cottonwoods cast seeds everywhere making people sneeze.
The lakes, ponds, and rivers sparkle like someone threw glitter on the surface.
The capital building towers over the streets of downtown Lincoln.
All these things and many more make up one special place,
NEBRASKA — my home.

Katrina Dienstbier, Grade 8

It's Time for Bed

Little child is waiting in his mental state.
Singing to him, soothing and distracting, enabling him to more peace.
An underbelly of anxiety needs to be gentled.
The child is finally full of pleasure.
Mothers sit close by, keeping a watchful eye, changing experiences with Works of art.

Kyra KoballRunyan, Grade 7

My Hijab

What do you see when you look at me?
Do you see someone limited or someone free?
All people do is just look and stare,
Simply because they can't see my hair,
Others think I'm controlled and uneducated,
But truly I'm not that sophisticated,
They are so thankful that they aren't me,
Because they would like to remain "free,"
They think I don't have an opinion or a voice,
They think that being hooded is not my choice,
They think that the hood makes me look caged,
They think that my religion is harsh and outraged,
All they can look at me in fear,
 And in my eye there is a tear,
My Hijab is like a beautiful jewel,
Even though people think I'm a fool,
My Hijab gives my look a POP,
I love Hijab from the bottom of my heart to the top,
My Hijab is always going to be my best friend,
I don't need people judging me about my split ends,
Because my Hijab is with me till' the end…

Lina Syed, Grade 8

A Complex Fear

The fear of disappointing is strong,
So I work at something all day long.
I do not want to let them down.
Pressure like deep water keeps me going;
I have to stay focused, fierce, and fighting!

I do not want to feel the shame,
For I am the only one to blame.
I often ask for help;
I always want to do my best,
But the stress is often heavy, like a boulder on my chest.

This fear with all its might can still win the fight,
And it often brings on stinging tears.
This fear has developed in the past two years,
And this fear feels like torture.

I'd like to not know this fear;
I wish I was just normal:
To try my best and just my best,
But this fear, it is just too strong.

Caroline Knutson, Grade 8

Blissful Beauty

Joy seems teal
Like the rolling waves of the bright, alluring ocean
I see many schools of fish floating about the water
I hear dolphins chattering amongst their friends, big and small
I smell the ocean breeze in the surrounding world of artistry
I touch the water full of life and wonder through a dreamer's eye
I taste the salt in the air above the sea creatures' home

Katie Schmid, Grade 9

Follow Me to the Pages

Follow me, and see all the amazing things I see
Follow me, to a world where you can be who you want
Follow me, to a new place where you can live
And it all begins with the turn of a page.
Follow me, and take part in countless adventures
Follow me, and struggle through grave disasters
Follow me, and survive through everything
And it all begins with the turn of a page.
Follow me, and discover teachings you will live with
Follow me, and reflect in newfound ways
Follow me, and make acquaintances that never fade
And it all begins with the turn of a page.
Follow me, and trust that you can do anything
Follow me, and do what is true
Follow me, and experience a thousand lifetimes
And it all begins with the turn of a page.
Follow me, to go some place new
Follow me, for who knows how long
Follow me, because part of you is there waiting
And it's just a page away.

Grace Frickenstein, Grade 7

Just Because I Tore My ACL in the Eighth Grade

Just because I tore my ACL in the eighth grade
Doesn't mean I won't get to play sports again
Doesn't mean I will never be an athlete again
And doesn't mean I can't be successful

Just because I tore my ACL in the eighth grade
Doesn't mean I'm afraid to take a hit
Doesn't mean I'm fragile
And doesn't mean I won't play till the end

Just because I tore my ACL in the eighth grade
Doesn't mean I won't be a college athlete
Doesn't mean I will listen to people telling me I won't
And doesn't mean I rehab for nothing

Just because I tore my ACL in the eighth grade
Why do many people doubt me?
Why can't I be like you?
How come people tell me that I won't or I can't?
Just because I tore my ACL in the eighth grade

Beau Jersild, Grade 8

My Morning

Every morning at six o'clock I wake up
I go downstairs and pour some milk in a cup
I go up to my bedroom and get dressed
I go to the mirror and my hair is a mess

I splash water on my face to wake up
My sister yells at me to hurry up
I wear too much perfume; I need to wear less
I sat on the couch; I was ready to rest

Terra Saunders, Grade 7

Basketball

Basketball is a game of determination.
It's also a game of concentration.
One must need physical and mental awareness,
And treat each and everyone with fairness.

After you have won the tip off,
You look for a shot to get off.
Like Kobe, you don't have to pass it.
Now you drive hard to the basket.

As you drive closer, it's a test.
You soon take a hit to the chest.
You must focus on the free throws
Almost like you are Derrick Rose.

Now it is the time to defend,
Just try not to have a goal tend.
Block every shot like Dwight Howard,
Make each opponent a coward.

The gave is just about over,
You do one final crossover.
Each speaker turns up the amps.
People now scream, "You are the champs!"

Tony Whitmarsh, Grade 7

Drag Racing

Get on the track
Put some oil on the street
And never look back
When drag racing

Kick it into first gear
Make sure nobody is near
And burn some rubber
When drag racing

The man asks if you're ready
Nod your head
Make sure your hand is steady
When drag racing

He flicks the switch on the lights
The green light is shown, you go
When you hit 150 the car starts to fight
When drag racing

The car passes the finish line
The smell of Nos. and gas roam through the air
I wish the winning car was mine
When drag racing

Joe Corban, Grade 8

What It Does to Me

It does amazing things,
It brings wonder,
Some wonderful people to meet.
In some ways it makes you braver.

I can't explain how emotional it is.
You may laugh you may cry.
There is nothing that can stop you.
But for some reason you can never say goodbye.

It may be a teacher,
It might be someone smart,
Or maybe not,
But to me it's how the child gets to your heart.

It makes me sad and happy,
I just love people like this.
You may not understand,
Why I am obsessed about this.

But believe me,
If you step out of your prism,
Then you'll understand,
That it's just wonderful Autism.

Kaitlyn Milligan, Grade 8

Do You Remember?

Why don't you look very familiar,
But nothing strange or peculiar
We used to be best friends
Do you remember?

I hope you remember me
We even used to go play in the deep blue sea
Summer or winter we used to go play together
Do you remember?

We were tight like brothers and sisters
You've protected me to the point where I won't get a blister
But sadly we both moved away
Do you remember?

It's been seven long years since I've seen you
I honestly missed you and I hope you missed me too
Your name I could never forget
I hope you remember

Now I'm seeing you face to face
We're both walking towards each other at the same pace
We have so much to catch up on
This day I will cherish and forever remember

Michelle So, Grade 9

Death

Death is something we all fear,
I believe we should be respectful,
Listen closely and you will hear.
Death is something we all fear,
It's strong and can draw a tear,
Soon we will be part of a death toll.
Death is something we all fear,
I believe we should be respectful.

Peyton Phillis, Grade 8

Cheerleading

Cheer is awesome
It makes me blossom
Yelling for a victory
Your team will go down in history
Win or lose you love your team
They are the best it would seem
Cheering is fun
Especially when my team has won

Skylar Reed, Grade 8

Open a Book

Feel the magic as books pull you in
Explore a world unknown
Go to places, only pages can show
Feel the magic as books pull you in
Lose yourself to the world; give it a spin
Make it a place all your own
Feel the magic as books pull you in
Explore a world unknown

Haley Selvidge, Grade 8

Acrostic

All I have to do is
Create an acrostic poem.
Rhyming is not necessary.
One word in each line will do.
Stop worrying about your grammar.
Try to teach others how to write.
It will be interesting,
Cool and fun.

Whitney Cole, Grade 7

America's Favorite Pass Time

Ball boy hands the bat to the competitor
  A finest hit I've ever seen, but the
    S hort-stop just snagged the ball
  E very fan started to cheer,
B ut then the umpire called an out
A nd all the fans began to squeal
L ow and behold the final inning
  L astly, we started winning

Draven Houtman, Grade 7

Life

A lways someone there for you
B e careful who you trust
C an you make it a good day?
D on't be what people want to see, be what you want to be
E ven though sometimes you may be down, things will get better
F inish what you start, **G** o out and have fun
H ave a positive attitude as much as you can
I n everyone's mistakes, they always learn something
J ust be careful what path you decide to take
K eep going through rough spots with a smile
L augh at the people who try to bring you down
M ake every day exciting, **N** o one decides your future but you
O pen up your mind, and don't judge people
P ick your friends very wisely
Q uit all the things that are not good for you
R unning from your problems won't fix them
S ay what is on your mind
T hings will get better in life, it may be stormy now, but it never rains forever
U nique isn't a bad thing, **V** ery fun times need to be cherished
W ho is a good influence on you? **X** crossing; pick your path
Y ou only live once, **Z** oodikers, what a good life!!

Nicole Thomas, Grade 7

Red Light

A moment of impact
The light goes from green to red
We stop, slow down and hit the brake
Maybe we run out of gas
Or the pedal broke
But in the green light you have power
In that moment your heart can fly
Because you are the bird flying south in winter
It's threaded in your bones
The green light is you!
So we hit a moment of impact,
The green just had to turn red
You get two choices,
Will you fall or take flight?
Somewhere in the red light your heart comes through, love is unpredictable
But passion is like oil on our hands
You can turn the other direction,
Fight gravity, but it just won't do
From time to time again, the light will turn red
After all the tears have dried, your problems stand in front of you,
Staring blankly into your red eyes

Liana Wallace, Grade 7

The Blues

Sadness seems blue
Like the sparkling ocean on a hot summer day
I see a little boy crying for his mother's grief
I hear a puppy's plea for its mother on a winter's night
I smell the lake on a warm summer day winding down
I touch my grandmother's quilt I helped assemble on a Friday afternoon
I tastes my aunt's cookies on a brilliant spring day

Julia Davis, Grade 9

3 Seasons

A cool breeze outside
Flowers swaying side to side
In the meadow near.

The sun shining down
The calm waves splashing the shore
The summertime roars.

Red leaves are long gone
The white snow covers green grass
Cold weather veers in.
Kelly Millies, Grade 7

Summer on the Farm

Down in the meadow
there was an
old fellow
who's hair was dark
and gray.

Out in the field
there was tons of cheer,
kids were playing
on top of
the hay.
Tania Ortega, Grade 7

Think

I can think about society.
I can think about school.
I can think about myself, too.
The thing I think about most,
Is what it would be like meeting you.
Just for five minutes.
That's all it would take,
To satisfy my hunger,
For meeting you.
For you Grandpa,
This poem is for you.
Sunnie Krutsinger, Grade 7

Hidden

Wake up,
Look in the mirror,
Time for drastic measures.
Concealing the blemishes
Disguising the bags,
Streaked below your eyes.
Blush brushing across your cheek,
Like the clouds covering the sun.
Hiding the true complexion.
Hiding the mistakes.
Makeup is a woman's best friend.
Megan Mullen, Grade 9

The Ingredients of My Family

My family is a gooey lava cake, unsure as to when the cake will fall and
see what goodness comes out from within.
My mother is the flour, the body of our family. She absorbs all her
children in and helps to keep us strong.
My father is the eggs of the lava cake, binding the family together and
making us work together to form something wonderful.
My sister is the pure white sugar. Sweet as they come, and always
here to put a smile on your face.
My other sister is the bitter sweet chocolate. Sweet looking on the
outside, but once bitten, one can see that she is as bitter as
chocolate can be.
I am the butter, to help flavor and build the Lava Cake. I am slick and
wise, and everyone loves me.
Once all these ingredients are mixed together and baked, you have a
cake, but once you get to know us individually you may be surprised
as to what is really inside.
Alexander Baker, Grade 7

The Meadows of Nebraska

There is a place of vast rolling hills,
like a bright green ocean frozen in time;
A place where butterflies sing the smallest songs,
as they beat their wings to and from a vivid cluster of blooms;
A place where the trees dance in the crisp clear wind,
as the grass applauds the orchestra of nature;
A place where the sun shines down rays of melted gold,
like the sweet, glorious honey, peacefully dripping down the swaying honeycomb;
A place where the divine smell of a swift spring breeze,
can bring the tiniest chicks out of their glistening white domes;
A place where the shimmering brook streams through the canvas of rocks,
as the trout gallop around the cool and refreshing creek;
A place where distinct memories are made,
from the clouds of anonymous objects soaring above

A place I call Home.
Jack Burke, Grade 8

Just Because My Parents Are Divorced

Just because my parents are divorced
doesn't mean I have a hard life
doesn't mean I love one parent more then the other
and doesn't mean I wish that they weren't
just because my parents are divorced
doesn't mean my family is different from yours
doesn't mean I saw my parents fight
doesn't mean I struggle to pick who I want to live with
just because my parents are divorced
doesn't mean I should be treated differently
doesn't mean I love my siblings any different because we only have one of the same parent
doesn't mean I'm more likely to get a divorce
Am I any different?
Am I sad?
Do I wish my life was different?
I don't think so.
Kyler Behrends, Grade 8

Hurt But Hopeful

I've been hurt by the demons every day
I believed that every day just got worse
But no, It's two steps forward
And one step back
Even though they're coming for me
Others are here to save me.
Life is dark
But there's this little twinkle within
It's called hope.
That light will only grow stronger
Even when it gets gloomy and you take a step back
It's still there
Sometimes you just can't see it
Because it is behind you
For those times when you fall into the depths of your mind.
So know,
That every day when you're hurting
There is that light,
That's following right beside you.

Becca Petrie, Grade 7

"Worth It"

They lounge on the couch, those lazy folks —
munching on oils, fats, and salt.
They have not a care in the world —
Their progress has indeed come to a halt.

Just learn to be self-reliant!
Learn in your youth to work hard.
You won't go far without work,
Not even past your own backyard!

You can sit on your couch and idle away your time,
And watch as your working neighbors walk on water.
Off they will walk, deep and far away.
Watching off in the distance stands a proud father.

Get in the dirt and get your job done —
It may be nasty, but in the end a battle will be won.
You will grin from ear to ear and smile the whole day long.
'Cause hard work is worth it, now go and get some more done!

Audrey Pickering, Grade 9

The Touch of the Wind

The touch of the wind,
And the joy of sun,
The beautiful breeze,
That brings us joy,
The sun goes down,
The breeze slows down,
The grass is fluffy,
The clouds come down,
The colors change,
The sunset goes down and makes me feel the day is ending.

Mariah Martinez, Grade 8

Blasting Off to Deep Space

I always dreamt of going to space
Because the starry space is just a wonderful place.
Yet it's also so mighty mysterious it makes you go
In a mind-and-body-swirling adrenaline rush!
Thanks to some Unanswered Questions which pushed
The national space programs of the U.S. and Europe
Into a race to conquer the last frontier where
The Europeans were first to launch a pair of human eyes
To wonder at the world from outer space,
While the Americans zoomed out on top
With astronauts who, on the wings of Apollo 11,
Landed and planted the Stars and Stripes and
Scooped a little hole in that cheese ball in the sky —
Neil Armstrong, Buzz Aldrin and Michael Collins.
Thanks to these brave people and thanks also to
John F. Kennedy, a great president who said that we
Would reach the moon not because it was easy
But because it was hard, space became my destination
For adventure and my dream.

Matthew Israel, Grade 7

Family Thanksgiving

As dad begins plucking the traditional foul,
I see mom step inside the packed pantry.
Deep inside my stomach begins to growl.
Opening the refrigerator, it is a sight to see.

There are vegetables of every color and kind.
There is wine and kids drinks of flavor galore.
The peeling of potatoes, as usual I'm assigned.
Breaking-up bread is what I'd really hoped-for.

It will be a Thanksgiving to remember, I guarantee.
Grandparents are coming and other relatives too.
Three tables are all set, looking fine and fancy.
We will serve up the delicious dinner right on cue.

Each person will get a chance to say their prayer,
Giving thanks to whatever strikes them the most.
I am thankful for all that we have to share,
And for a wonderful family, that I have to boast.

Nathan Cibula, Grade 8

Depression Is...

Depression is like a big bubble
    filled with your sorrows and madness.
Depression is like people coming up to you
    and saying really mean things.
Depression is like a big raindrop
    falling from the sky all alone.
Depression is like a huge storm cloud
    over your head to ruin your day.
Depression is like a bully coming to you
    and hurting you so badly you wish you had never lived.

Heather Holder, Grade 8

Gingerbread Love
My heart lives in a gingerbread house
High upon a hill
Where the wind is crisp and the sun is warm
And you can always eat your fill

But there is a catch to this perfect life
In this confectionary home
No one ever comes to visit
And my heart's always alone

"The hill's too high" some may complain
"The climb is just too steep!"
And oh, how much the heart does ache
From the wounds they cut so deep

The walls of the house are held together
By a single line of icing
A sugary glue so sticky sweet
That once seemed so enticing

So if the wind ever blew too hard
Or the rains came falling down
The house would either fall apart
Or the heart inside would drown
Breanna Dittert, Grade 8

Millions of Words
Pages, pages filled with words
Are more beautiful than the songs of birds.
I love this book a ton
Dread the day it is meant to be done.

With every line
The book and my reality start to entwine.
I become more attached.
The next book I read will be severely mismatched.

Every turn, every flip
Many pages you wish to skip.
Read with great haste
Because there's no time to waste

Love stories occur
Some gone in just a blur.
Their passions still burning,
But other things more concerning.

The book is now done,
But it only feels as if it has just begun.
The last page was flipped, last word was read.
Now you only wish there were another ahead.
Vanessa Gutierrez, Grade 7

Family Collection
My family is the collection of candy
My dad is fun dip, he's fun to be around, always laughing
My mom is kisses, she's chocolate skin, always giving me kisses
My sister is cry-babies, she cries, even if we go get her fries
My brother is dum-dums, he is dumber than dumb
And I am smarties, I'm smart and intelligent
Diana Argueta, Grade 7

Me
My hair is as blonde as the sun on a sunny day
My eyes are as blue as a wave in the ocean
My fingers are like cheetahs when I type
My mouth is like as loud as a tigers roar
My heart beats like a bomb when I get excited
My skin is as soft as silk
Shania Graff, Grade 7

Sisters
Sisters have weird relationships
They can yell one minute and laugh the next
No matter what they will always be there
Just give a call and they will be there
They can be your best friend or worst enemy
No matter what they will love each other
Haley Farr, Grade 9

Waiting
Waiting
Candy red like a hot summer night
With the silhouette of a star engulfed by smaller capsules
It takes its place in the midnight blue water and cream colored sand
And the affection of a lost, lonely soul
It waits...
Andrew Eiesland, Grade 7

Basketball Game
Sweat dripping from your face
From the gall I got to chase
The shot you took banked the board
A bad foul that was called on you, you have to ignore
Your friends in the stands roar your name
Good game champ!
Caroline Nicholson, Grade 8

A Farmer's Life
H ard working in the field all day
E verybody counts on the farm operation
L ittle people not working late at night
P ushing and pulling the implements here and there
E verybody tired after a big day
R eplowing the fields season after season
Wyatt Hilt, Grade 7

Sunset

As the sun goes to rest on the horizon
it lets its beauty show,
the sky looks a magnificent red
as it goes to rest its head,
and as it says goodbye don't cry
it will soon come again

Akayja Reding, Grade 8

Silly Puppies

B ecomes a pup
R uns out the door
U ses a sock as a toy
S its on our laps
E njoys our company
R uns around the house

Bryce Raby, Grade 7

Winter

W onderland of snowmen in yards.
I ce is very slippery.
N othing is really hot.
T he weather is cold
E verything is really cold.
R eally cold everywhere you go.

Chanclyn Vestering, Grade 7

Friday

F reedom from school
R eady to sleep in
I t's a new day
D ays go by quickly
A lready Saturday
Y et, school is a day away

Kyle Cantrell, Grade 8

The Desert

Sandy
Plants flow in the
Wind, rustling softly
As the blinding sun shines on them
Brightly

Nicholas Son, Grade 8

Nightmare

All I can do is run
It's coming for me
It's in the shadows
I can't make out a shape
It is faster than normal things are

Javeir Berends, Grade 8

Witch

With the moon they fly
With broomsticks in the nighttime
Screeching and laughing

Aubrey Hageman, Grade 7

Someday I Should Be?

Someday I should be an astronaut.
Travel through the galaxy in a shuttle.
Discovering new exotic land.
Go as fast as possible, and not land in a puddle.

Or I could be a food critic.
Eat all sorts of fancy foods.
All of the world, without ever having to pay.
Putting me into good moods.

But, maybe I should be Minnie Mouse.
Working at the most amazing place on earth, Disneyland.
Having fun and taking pictures with millions of kids.
Dancing and fake singing with the Disney bands.

An astronaut would be cool, but I'm afraid of heights.
A food critic would be good, I do love to eat.
Meeting new people would be fun to, I've always wanted to go to Disneyland.
So when can we start?

Aubree Noble, Grade 8

Anchor

We hold some things inside of us
They pull us till we drown
Our fears, feelings and emotions
Keep us from reaching a higher ground
Others use us as their strong hold
They trust us with more than we can keep inside
We pull the strength onto our shoulders
And hope we can be their guide
The waves crash over us
We can barely see the shore
I thought being an anchor was good
When really it was no more
Anchors hold us back, instead of letting us fly
And that's when I realized we aren't the anchor.
It's the things we bottle up inside that keep us from reaching the sky
They drown us at sea
In the opposite direction of where we are supposed to be
So let go of your anchor, don't let anything hold you down
Free yourself of everything or else you just may drown

Libby Moore, Grade 8

Societal Strife

I don't get why they do what they've done, Do they get the feeling that they've won
With twisted words and deceiving smiles, I know their trouble isn't worth the while
Yet I'm forced to lie about how I feel, It seems the pain is to strong to be real
I'm aware that people are not to trust, Never to care and they're pitiful with lust
There is no love in a world full of lies, When we only do to better our own lives
I fear the future while caught in the past, I need to move on from what's happened last
When denied of luck and filled with sorrow, In yesterday I'm stuck, not thinking of tomorrow
To prove I'm strong and to prevail, I will move on from where I've failed
When I've lost all hope and things seem wrong, I'm not alone, I can be strong
Life isn't easy, I know it's tough, I'll believe in me when things get rough
I'll never know why they do what they've done. I do know that they haven't won

Bethany Lutz, Grade 8

Emotions

The emotions are aloof
I hate you, despise you
I want to throw you off the roof
Well you, you don't have a clue

I hate you, despise you
You make me want to cry
Well you, you don't have a clue
I want you to die

You make me want to cry
Why? Why? I say
I want you to die
Would you just go away?

Jayleigh Peuster, Grade 7

Holding On

I'm holding your light in my hand
Pretend the dark doesn't exist
I tried to push it away
But 'twas something I could not miss

Hold on to your fading silhouette
Wishing that you were here
I said I'd banish this shadow
I'm in love with my true fears

But should I stop wasting these tears
When I'm stuck in an endless drought
I've provided it oxygen for so long
Should I let the flame die out?

Alasia Williams, Grade 8

Lonely

Have you ever cried so much?
Has life ever seemed too tough?
You try to be strong,
Though you feel all has gone wrong.
No one hears your cries for help.
They don't even notice you're there.
Do the flowers seem to die out?
The voices seem to get louder and louder
Your heart began to beat faster
Then you realize it was all in your head.
It feels like you're alone,
But there are thousands near you!
How can you breathe?
When everyone is always suffocating you?

Shakeysha Collins, Grade 9

The Soc's

A ll the Soc's running around
B eing reckless without trial
C aught up in their own problems
D efining themselves as the better league

Erin Connolly, Grade 8

Safe Haven

Way out there
Back by the shallow, cold, creek
You hop on the dead, gray tree and make your way across the shallow creek
You can see to the bottom it's so clear, but you don't dare go in because it's too cold
A fence of barbed wire lines the creek bank
You stop and think —
Do I dare?
You make your decision and make your way over the fence
You've never been back here before, so you're curious
SNAP! You step on a branch
The wind is rustling through the red, brown, and orange trees
You jump when you hear something
You turn quickly
Nothing —
You forget about it and go on
You hear someone yell "Time for supper!" So you start back
The calm, cool, creek is smooth and untouched
You climb across on the tree and almost fall, but you catch yourself
It's over. Time to go.

Jenna Kramer, Grade 9

Growing Up

When I was little I always wanted to grow up
I always thought that it would be the best time of my life
But I was wrong
When you grow up everything becomes stressful
Friends, relationships, family, etc…
Everything
You learn who your real friends are
And the ones who are just pretending to be real
People will use you
You go from trusting them one day
To losing all that trust the next
You will also realize that when your parents give you advice
They are right
They have probably been in the same situation and they don't want to see you in it
You will always see the light
When coming out of the dark
You always have to remember that after every rain storm there is a rainbow
And that you can always learn from your mistakes
But that's just a part of growing up.

Kassy Tieman, Grade 8

All About JB

kindness, tall, athletic, hardworking
brother of Jacob, Jaylin, and Jasmin
lover of sleeping on the weekends, playing sports, and eating food
who feels happy on the weekends, and fun with others
who needs summer, weekends, and basketball
who gives happiness, caring, and gifts
who fears some people, sharks, and snakes
who would like to see the cubs win a World Series,
the New York Giants win a super bowl, and the New York Nets win a championship
who lives in a big, brown house
barr

Julian Barr, Grade 7

Civil War

Battles
Being fought here
On this cold and dark night
Soldiers giving up their young lives
For slaves

Kyra Olesen, Grade 8

Basketball

Basketball is like playing the piano,
The more you practice, the better you play.
Our coach is like a music conductor,
His job is to lead the way.

Carrie Sleezer, Grade 7

Night

The moon is a glowing ball
The stars are a million flashing fire flies
I wish I could watch forever
But I won't always be alive

Brylie True, Grade 7

Darry

Big muscles
Fighting the Socs
Loves Ponyboy and Sodapop
Father

Matt Huinker, Grade 8

The Sun

Light and heat.
You remind me of a lamp.
Brightening up the day.
I wish you were always out.

Hunter Baysinger, Grade 7

Books

Good books are a prison.
They trap you, and hold you.
Once you're in, there is no escape,
Freedom comes at the end.

David Keiss, Grade 7

Bee

Do you hear buzzing?
It's a bee flying, happily.
There it goes, rushing,
To its hive.

Molli Kmetz, Grade 8

Homeless

"Spare change" that's what they ask
Sitting on the sidewalk petting their cats
Pushing carts full of trash
Watching as people pass by in a flash

Hannah Collins, Grade 8

Jacob the One and Only

A friend to all, and unforgettable to all that knew him,
A curious person!
Never satisfied with what he knew.
Always wanted to fly in a helicopter,
And he did receive the chance,
Jacob always said, "My life is like a crazy roller coaster."
His life was as fun as a five year old on a sugar rush.
One thing he loved was being in charge,
He liked to see new places and things
Had a great sense of humor,
was able to laugh at himself,
Even if a joke hurt he could still laugh,
but that was Jacob,
He always enjoyed one joke even in a cemetery,
It went like this,
Thank you so much for caring to come and read my epitaph,
but mind your feet because at the moment you are standing on a dead man!
Were you born in a barn?
So please leave because you are as rude as a pig,
but remember, he is gone but not forgotten!
P.S. — Look behind you there is a ghost! ;)

Jacob Rottinghaus, Grade 8

My Life Worth Living

Here lies the memorable Sona RoseAnne Fokum.
She was brave, but also afraid,
A dreamer, and a believer.
She worked hard and exceeded,
and might have been a little conceited.
She was a follower to great leaders,
and a great leader to her followers.
She dared herself to have fun,
All the memories…
walking through the drive-thru at Mickey D's,
dancing in the background of Live News on CNN.
and giving meals to the homeless.
She was loud, she was clumsy, and she was annoying,
but she was a good person,
she loved and was loved for.
She loved her friends, even if they fought
She loved her family, for what they taught.
they taught her to work hard, not to care what others think, we run our own world,
nobody's perfect, things happen in life, be grateful,
and she, this wonderful child,
she was grateful for chicken.

Sona Fokum, Grade 8

Where the Water Meets the Shore

A place where the water meets the sandy shore is my favorite place.
We go there when the sun is at its brightest and hottest.
I see the waves crashing on the shore and people skiing across the water.
I hear the birds chirping and the fish splashing in the water.
I choose to sit around the campfire and talk with family.
I will go there when the summer comes back.
This is my place I go to when I want to forget about the world around me.

Coy Cassaw, Grade 8

Snowy Winter Night

Sitting happily, with my tea
Watching snow fall peacefully
The inside is nice and warm
I curl up under a blanket and watch the gentle storm

The wind blows, whistles and whips
So I stay indoors, where it is comforting and warm
Where the wind cannot bite
And I drink my tea with delight

Quiet, peaceful afternoon
Watching snow peacefully
The inside is nice and warm
So, I curl up under a blanket and watch the billowing winter storm.

Abbey Lindeman, Grade 7

Grow Up!

You get in trouble, but I get it worse.
You play me just like a song verse.
You drag me in as your understudy,
But when you get caught, I'm the one who's unlucky.

Win the battle, but win the war,
Pulling my sinking ship back to the shore.
Some of us have to grow up sometime,
And when I do, I'm leaving you behind.

Even though we are related,
That's always there, but respect has faded.
I drank the last drop of liquid in my cup.
Now, I believe, is the time to grow up!

Jillian Ross-Mason, Grade 7

The List

It comes out before homecoming each year
And when the girls see this list appear
Only one from each grade is named prettiest
And only one from each grade is named ugliest
Yes, it is sad and is very bad
But it will bring out secrets they didn't know they had
But this book takes you into the lives
Of the eight girls on the list at Mount Washington High
And tells their stories of how they will survive
This mind blowing time
As some girls may be in fame
And most will be in shame
It will be exciting to find out who put these girls' names on the list
For an exciting twist

Maddy Ljunggren, Grade 7

Reading

The end is all too quick
The pages turning each at a tick
The people go on until they say goodnight
Until finally I close the book and stop for the night.

Tyra Mohrmann, Grade 8

Turtle Tears

The rain lightly falls on the ground
The raindrops hit the turtle's shell and burst apart like my heart
The turtle slowly walks away,
Towards the creek,
Away from humanity.
I used to have a pet turtle
He is walking away from me now,
Not looking back.
His name was King; he belonged to me.
Not anymore, now he is free.
The rain lightly falls on the ground,
Along with my tears.

Gable T., Grade 7

Severus Snape

A dark man trudges down a path
Far away from Master's wrath.
He glares, and grumps, and seethes, and growls,
And graces all that lives with scowls.

He is the scapegoat, his trust betrayed.
He spies by night, but works by day.

He knows no rest.
He knows no peace.
He looks a mess,
Hair slick with grease.

Nicole Barnes, Grade 9

Friends

My favorite thing to do is to hang out with my friends,
You can never have too many friends.
Friends are one of the easiest things to get,
As long as you are yourself.
Friends will help you in many situations.

Friends respect you no matter what.
You can have as many friends as you like.
If you are yourself, then you will gain friends,
Who like to be around you.
People will become your friend, if you respect them.
A lot of people will help you when you need it.

Kyle Long, Grade 8

A Diamond in the Desert

I take a long look back and see my Dad's face turn to a frown,
It's going to be different without him around.
I feel the dry gust of dirt brush my face,
I know this won't be as happy of a place.
I know this will be a difficult change for my family and I,
I get out of the sweaty and smelly bus with a deep sigh.
Lefty is missed along with Dad,
They were the most important things I've ever had.
I hope everything will be the same as it was in the end,
Because I miss my original best friend.

Skyler Teegen, Grade 7

Decisions

Life is full of them,
They challenge us,
Can make us question everything,
They are never easy,
But they are our own.

They are our own,
That's what makes them so scary.
They leave us with nobody to blame, but ourselves.

We may regret them,
But we can never take them back.
We'll never know if we were right or wrong,
Until it's already too late.

They can ruin friendships and lives,
Or they can bring greatness and prosperity.
The choice is yours.

Erin Kane, Grade 8

Galactic War

Six creatures take to earth
To explore the new found beings
They will decide what it is worth
Just by what they are seeing

They will bring forth a galactic war
It is the first of many that shall come that the earth will win
The souls of men will be tore
And the earth shall be only scraps of tin

The human species shall rebuild
Earth will soon be back to its normal way
Many men will be killed
One man will upraise and save the day

The humans shall be known as a thing of lore
But only after the next four
Galactic wars.

Joseph Mollet, Grade 8

Dance

Dance is an escape to a beautiful place;
A place free of judgment, where I can just be me —
Where I feel an angel's beauty, a swan's grace;
A vibrant colorful world that I love to see.
It's the purest way to release emotion:
Beautiful energy with every motion.

The moment I hear the music,
I remember exactly why I fell in love:
A passion so deep, it's worth all of the bruises;
A feeling so rare to fly like a dove.
As soon as I hear a beat,
I desire to be on my feet.

Lauren White, Grade 8

Lie Amongst the Purple Flowers

Walk alongside the river,
And hear the sounds of the woods
Knowing that you're alone and free and
Everything you need is in your own mind.

Untie your hair and lie amongst the
Purple flowers, letting the birds laze with you.

Instead of being fearful,
Throw caution to the wind and make
Sure you are one with your true self.

And most of all breathe; breathe as if it's your last breath.

Try to fly, you might fall, you might soar.
Remember that you are your own best friend
And don't love anyone more than yourself.
Peace found within is the finest peace there is.

A. Mecklenburg, Grade 9

My Friend Music

My friend Music is quite bizarre,
Music is here, there, and a far,
Music is in my house and in my car.

Music is my best friend I hope you see,
Even if it can't be physically seen,
Music is always there for me,
It eats, sleeps, and cares for me.

My friend Music creates allusions,
And when I'm down has the solution,
Music has no habitation, or destination,
Because my friend Music lives all over the nation.

Music is my friend, who I will defend,
Because music never leaves my side,
But one day it will end,
And music my friend, will find someone else's side.

Justice Heinold, Grade 8

Spring

When the wind whips through the tops of the
Trees and the ground is slightly squishy
Beneath my feet, I know
Spring is here.
I can feel it beckoning to me from
The outdoors. So I grab
My bike and go on my
Way through neighborhoods,
Forests, hills, and lakes. But when
I finally find the perfect destination, I
Sit down on the grass for a
Picnic, before time is
Wasted.

Nicole Launius, Grade 7

Best Friends Forever

Best friends doesn't even describe what we are.
More like sisters.
We still feel connected even if we are far.
It has and always will be sisters before misters.

Sometimes we fight.
Sometimes we get mad.
But at the end of the tunnel there is always light.
And we both know that we don't like seeing the other sad.

We laugh, we smile.
We dream about Niall.
Endless phone calls.

In the road there may be bumps and bends.
But I know forever we will be best friends.
Best friends since seven.
Best friends even in heaven

Grace Kovar, Grade 8

Graduation Day

Graduation day is coming
Soon we will be leaving this school
This is where we grew up
Beautiful memories that will never be forgotten

Graduation day is always closer
I can already picture myself in a yellow or purple cap and gown.
The colors that represent our school
And who we are.

Graduation day is here.
Everyone's eyes are teared up.
Today we all go our separate ways,
But will forever remember all our experiences,
The ups and downs.
My name is called an I proudly climb
the stairs to the stage.
It's graduation day.

Yureysi Hidalgo, Grade 8

I Want to Be

I told my grandma
I want to be a writer
She said, "The only place you'll end up is on the streets."
I told my aunt
I want to be an astronomer
She said, "The sky never changes. That's boring."
I told my uncle
I want to be an actress
He said, "You'll never make it to Hollywood!"
I told my mom
I want to be a doctor
She said, "You have to be smart."
I told my cousin
I want to be a model
She said, "You have to be pretty."
I told my dad
I want to be me
He said, "Now that is something you can do!"

Eve Odum, Grade 8

The Closed Door

Once more, I stand at the closed door of freedom.
Tears on my cheeks.
Pain in my heart.
They say that when one door closes,
Another door opens.
So why do I stand surrounded by four walls,
And only one closed door?
Why?
Secrets, silence, and solitude fill my mind
As I stand at the closed door of freedom.
I hear the smooth bells mocking me.
Their cheerful song rings in delight.
The melody they are playing is one I used to know.
It is the tune of freedom.
I try to find the freedom bells,
But feel nothing but fear.
And so I stand at the closed door of freedom,
Wondering what happens from here.

Elise Hobbs, Grade 8

Ethan

Ethan —
Friendly, outgoing, athletic, and smart
Brother of Jaxon, Nicole, and Shane
Lover of sports and outdoor activities
Athletic since the day of birth
Fan of sports since the day I was brought to this Earth
Likes to hang out with friends
Works hard on things and doesn't give up until the end
Usually joyful with a smile on my face
Full of joy and full of grace
Don't take life for granted
Appreciate something if I have it
— Lambrigger

Ethan Lambrigger, Grade 7

Fire

The beauty of the colors so wild and free.
It moves in rhythm with the crackling wood.
The ending of such would be devastating to me.
Add to it and lengthen its life, I should.
I reach out my hand to restore its life.
I reach out my hand to restore its life.

Heat emanates from it and jumps out at you.
It releases a bite fierce and painful.
Not being cautious is a decision you will rue,
But without its light the night would be dull.
An astounding creation soon to die.
An astounding creation soon to die.

Jake Calendine, Grade 8

Blinded by Love
I figured he was meant for me.
But as it turned out,
Just was not meant to be.
I looked inside,
Cleaned out my pride.
And recognized the mistake,
That I had begun to make.
Then, I realized my state,
That included thinking of a soul mate.
My love for him had increased.
Blinded by his love, I fell.
Those Caribbean water eyes,
Them, yes them, now I despise.
That tantalizing smile,
I don't want to see for a while.
His slow, reassuring gait,
That I had learned to hate.
But now that I'm wiser,
I learned to be a miser.
A miser of true love,
That's only sent from Him which is above.
Sarah Moore, Grade 8

Nature Within
Running down,
Pink petal path.
Lined in red roses,
Green grass.
Passing brown tree stumps.
Orange shading,
Stand still.
Yellow sunshine,
Blue sky,
White clouds,
Purple streak,
Black night,
Can't dodge it,
Must embrace it.
Frozen.
Ice melting,
Off my nose.
Want to scream,
Holding in.
Love it,
Full heartedly!
Emily Bourne, Grade 9

Trapped
Trapped
In the darkness all alone.
Trapped
Behind the bars of eternity.
Trapped
In a lie.
Who will free me?
Bea Hartman, Grade 8

Soothe
The music keeps me calm.
Like I'm reading a psalm.
It keeps my mouth quiet.
Listening to a griot in tune.
Relieving my worries
If my mind scurries.
Songs alleviate my sores
And opening doors to relax,
unlike paying a tax.
My teddy bear comforts me,
As if I'm in Hawaii.
I lie still when a chill passes by
Lightening the mood.
My happy attitude softens my soul.
I am settled.
The notes pedaled across my mind.
As I awaken, not mistaken for I feel better.
Mereesa Valera, Grade 8

Music
The sound is charming
Guitars strumming in moonlight
It isn't so alarming
Just sit back and enjoy the night

The words stick in your head
All through the night
Even when you are in bed
It is such a delight

Writers share personal thoughts
On the bad times
Even on days they fought
All trying to get the right rhymes

Music relaxes you
And you know it's true
Alexis Bakken, Grade 8

Tell Me Why
Tell me why,
all things have to die
Tell me why,
babies have to cry
Tell me why,
change is high
Tell me why,
summer has to leave
Tell me why,
people have to grieve
Tell me why,
angels spread their wings
Tell me why,
men give women rings
Tell me why
Mariah Brotzman, Grade 9

Fall
Warm rain, thunder storm
Rain boots splashing in puddles
Approaching autumn

Heat fading away
Unpacking scarves and mittens
Crisp air around us

Sky getting darker
The trees getting colorful
Summer is far gone

No longer hearing
Any early morning birds
Only cars and wind

Walking home from school
Leaves crunching under our feet
Carrying our books

Halloween costumes
Doorbell ringing, cheerful kids
Out trick or treating

Snowflakes descending
The silhouette of bare trees
Fall is now ending
Maddie Perreard, Grade 8

Where Ever You Go*
Where ever you go
I'll be sure to know
Whatever you see
I'll always believe

Until eternity
I will be thinking of sweet serenity
Because you taught me to be free
To be all I want to be

You're a part of me
That I no longer see
But you're in my memories
It is still bittersweet

You granted me my wings
So that I can fly
Right up to the sky
Way up high

Where ever you go
I'll be sure to know
Whatever you see
I'll always believe
Cinthia Naranjo, Grade 9
**In loving memory of my loving father.*

The Snow Tree

Created from a small seed encased in a small fruit,
It grew and became tall just like its parent.
Blossoms appear and eventually fall,
Drifting down slowly to the ground.
Then the wind picks them and let them float,
Covering the sky with pink snow, it's a warm winter wonderland.
The leaves fall with the blossoms and the tree is now bare.
It goes dormant and hopes for the best.
As it tries to survive the cold harsh winter.
Cold comes with winter, engulfing it in cold silver blossoms and Frozen claws hanging from the edge.

Andy Kim, Grade 7

Autumn

Faded banana yellow, grass green, and clownfish orange misshapen tattered leaves fall from pale semi-naked trees, and flutter effortlessly through the cool, autumn breeze.
The morning and afternoon sky resembles light blue jean material, free of the cottony masses we call clouds.
The night sky is blacker than the darkest black hole in the deepest sections of space; the stars are like miniscule glowing light bulbs, varying in colors, yearning to never burn out.
The air is thin, cool and blowing harshly, as if it wanted everything in it's path to blow away.
Various scents waft through the breeze:
mouth-watering Thanksgiving turkey, and delectable pumpkin pie;
melting wax and odd varying scents of sugar.
This is truly autumn in Omaha.

Kai-Bryana Marshall, Grade 8

Life Is a Marathon

Life is a marathon that never ends. You first start off not knowing where you are, not knowing anything.
But then you learn, and you notice that you are only ten feet in.
You get hot, tired, and you just want to stop. You are now at one mile.
There is much to think about, and much to see, but in the end you will be king.

Half way there you hear the crowd. The crowd is your family, your motivation to keep going.
Your journey is almost over, everyone is gone.
You just want to stop, sit, and cry.
You are at your last step, then you say goodbye.

Grace Konchan, Grade 7

The Plagued Posie

Ashes blowing through the wind with the rest of the desolate air.
A piece of pasture once known for wildflowers and its natural beauty but now all that's seen is the sorrow and hatred left behind.
I see you looking right at it, bright yellow like nothing seen before. It aged before our eyes in 1923.
The soviets came past and trampled the land. What's now left behind is dirt and rubble.
Maybe the discriminating communists did know a thing or two about the posies, but they all fell down.
You discovered it in the light ahead of the darkness.
It's all coming back to us we can move on if you and I could just get a grasp almost taste it.
What's left day by day is going to be one step at a time if we don't have tomorrow what will we have today?

Katei Hunt, Grade 9

Summer Breeze

The summer breeze feels warm upon my face, gently pulling my hair back and forth.
The summer breeze is as light as a feather upon my hands, lightly touch my arms with care and trust.
The summer breeze slides upon my legs giving me goosebumps, wistfully just touching the tops of my feet tickling them.
But I know one day I will say goodbye to the summer breeze and hello to the sharp, unforgiving wind of winter.

McKenzie Todd, Grade 7

Ballad About Me

Hi, I'm Cassidy. I know a lot of you hate me or dislike me, and I don't know why.
Maybe I'm not meant to be liked. What I know is it's sad for you to bully someone to the point where they want to die.

Yes, I want to die sometimes, but being bullied isn't the only reason why. I feel worthless and like I'm a mistake.
But my friends say, "Cassidy you are not! You're beautiful! Stay strong!" So I write music for my sake.

So, I want you to know that you're all beautiful, no matter who you are because every person is their own star.
No matter what you do, this is what makes you. You are who you are.

But maybe I shouldn't be so nice to all you bullies who say we have no worth.
So remember stay strong for all those who are bullied. Because we're all part of this earth!

Just before I go I want to tell you something more. It's sad to know how many girls and boys
Think they're not beautiful and handsome. It's sad and scary to think how many want to die. So please don't treat us like toys.

Because no matter what you're all beautiful in your own way.
For those who are bullied like me, stay strong because you're beautiful. Now have a good day.

Cassidy Fletcher, Grade 8

Good Friends

Good friends can lift you up with both hands when life only gives you one.
They will give you wings when your heart forgets how to fly.
Good friends will understand your past, believe in your future, and accept you for the way you are.

Good friends can always be there for you.
They will never leave you behind, and don't leave them behind either,
Because the worst thing you can do is be angry at someone when you make the same actions.

Good friends can know they are liked, but until when?
Just like seasons, good friends can change.
Some can be amazing, some horrible,
But when it comes to that harmful side, they can no longer be a good friend.
If you lose a friend, there is one idea to remember.

Good friends can be hard to find, difficult to leave, but impossible to forget.

Megan Chwalinski, Grade 8

Flight 93

Sheila got on a plane, headed for warm San Francisco where her husband Joe was waiting, on a beautiful September morning.
Joe's sitting in the conference room awaiting her arrival. He should be thinking of work, but instead he's thinking of her.
So far the ride's been good, no turbulence or storms. But then there's a commotion up in first class, and she knows something's up.
Sheila hears screaming and crying, angry men are shouting. Passengers come back with injuries to the third class area.
Back in San Francisco with his conference finally over, Joe relaxes in his room,
when he hears the news that the Twin Towers have been struck.
Meanwhile on the plane other passengers are getting calls about the attack.
Sheila realizes the horrifying fact that her plane's part of it.
She makes a call to Joe to tell him the news about her plane's hijacking, but she has to leave a message.
Joe then hears on the news that a plane from Newark is missing. His heart gets a jolt. Is it Sheila's plane?
Other passengers talk on phones, realizing their plane isn't just any hijacked plane.
It's part of a bigger plan, the passengers must fight back.
Sheila gets the news. She joins them in the fight, knowing that she will die. The plane crashes down.
Joe tries calling Sheila and sees he has a message. The message she leaves lives in his heart forever.
I love you, but I won't be here anymore.

Alex Mortenson, Grade 7

My Happy Place

I know a place where no ones home.
I go there when I want to be all alone.
A quaint little house on top of a hill.
I go there a lot when I have time to kill.
In the yard there's a lighthouse tower.
I like to climb up there to sit for an hour.
I look out the tower and feel the sun kiss my face.
I never realized how much I love this place.
The clouds are balls of cotton filling the sky.
With this view, I wish I knew how to fly.
This place to me is as good as gold.
I would love to retire here when I grow old.

Tatiana Chance, Grade 7

Shining Star

Like a shining star,
you are going very far,
you are very bright,
like a star at night.
You make people smile,
like a shooting star going a mile.
Stars always shine,
like you did in 2009.
You are shooting very far and fast,
like a star always last.
Stars always burn out,
but at least people know what you are about.

Jaelyn Williams, Grade 7

Please Be My Friend

Just because I'm small,
    Don't call me short.
    Don't make fun of me.
    Still hang out with me.

Just because I'm small,
    It doesn't mean I'm weak.
    It doesn't give you the right to call me names.
    It doesn't stop me from reaching my goals.

Just because I'm small,
    Please try to be my friend.

Nathan Cown, Grade 7

The Lion

Rampage Jackson was a lion so strong,
Though he used it for fighting which was wrong,
He roared louder than them all,
He made others look very small,
He would strike and defend,
He would fight 'till the end,
He stood tall and proud,
His fans would shout aloud,
He looked scary with his head held high,
Yet his skills were not a lie,
He would stand and fight,
When others would run in fright.

Logan Barringer, Grade 7

The Book

He lays there waiting to tell his tale
he wishes to be heard
many people like him
he is full of secrets
his spine cracks a lot
and his face is full of wrinkles
he may be too wise for many people
his strong voice is echoing in people's minds
booming through the years
everyone crowds to hear his tale
and all is dark without his take
soon he sleeps

Analicia Garcia, Grade 7

Tree

The tree stands tall and proud
He never lets anyone get to him even the crowd
Even though he got smacked
He never fought back
The tree's sturdy and strong
Jackie Robinson never did wrong
He endured a lot
Like when that pitcher aimed for an eyeshot
He was very fast
He stunned the ones he went past
He made a great stand
His story is never bland

Dalton Eichholz, Grade 7

Life

Life is like a rollercoaster.
It has many ups and downs.
The steep climb up to reach your destination,
And the plummeting feel of the unknown end.
The days pass by so lightning-fast.
Sometimes it gets so hard that your world is upsidedown.
And it takes courage to get back up and ride the waves of life.
It plunges downhill fast.
At times stops abruptly.
But you will always climb back to the top.

Hannah Stewart, Grade 7

Things of me

Jon
Funny, skinny, and quiet
Brother/sister of no one
Lover of music, art, and science
Who feels anger, hate, and joy
who needs chocolate, candy, and soup
Who gives jokes, happiness, and life
Who would like to see gold, The surface of mars, and the unknown
who lives in a decent house on Hollylane
Williford

Jonathan Williford, Grade 7

The Holocaust
A war within a war
With many people lost
At the hands of the Nazis

People try to forget
This terrible act
But history has been set
Forever in our memories

We have seen the pictures
From this horrid time
The horrible pictures
Where this took place

So let us be forever taught
Of this time filled with sorrow
The long war the Jewish fought
And hope it won't happen again
Heather Simpson, Grade 8

A Graceful Day
There's not a cloud
today, just a sky of blue,
As the sun shines bright
it feels so new.

As you walk down the street
you can see smiles from all
around, it looks like everyone
came to town,
To enjoy the summer's day
and let time freeze,
for a little while just until
the hour is a breeze,
until the graceful day
is over, time is frozen and
people stand still but mother nature
is in a thrill.
Justin Espanol, Grade 7

Icons
Men of iron
Men of steel
They are icons
But they aren't real
Mutants and metas
Hybrids and aliens
Fast as cheetahs
Reptilians and mammalians
Incredible power
Spectacular might
Smile or glower
Dark or light
Comic books are a form of art
They hold a special place in my heart
Nate Hochstetler, Grade 8

Without
Books without pages
Theaters without stages
A winter without its cold
A title without being bold

Time without hours
A hero without powers
A bear without fur
A him without her

Fishing without bait
Love without hate
Bingo without spaces
Baseball without bases

A clock without its tick
A magician without a trick
Summer without heat
Bread without wheat
Emma Beardsley, Grade 7

Mother Nature's Florist Shop
Mother Nature
Presents her
Creations
In many
Different Styles.

Mother Nature
Shows her work
And thinks of more
All the while.

Flowers
Weeds…
Its all the same
Any Kind
Any Name

I can't remember all the names
That's Mother Nature's Favorite Game.
Erica Brady, Grade 7

In the Room of White
In the room of white
there is nothing
Words are broken down
into nothing
And into nothing
we are broken
down
And when there is
nothing
The room of white is
done
Maria Velazquez, Grade 9

Grandpa Angel
your smile was bright as sunshine
that smile never died
even in pain that killed you inside
you always put a smile to hide
tears rolling down my face
but i know you are in a happier place
my love for you will always stay strong
even though you are gone
so many memories these past years
but it's time to wipe off those tears
because even though you are gone
i know you want me to stay strong
i know you suffered
but you stayed strong
even though you died
don't say goodbye
we'll be together again when i die
Katherine Soto, Grade 7

Country Girl
I am country from
My T-shirt to my boots
To the mud I ride in
To guns I shoot

You can wear
Heels and Dresses
and
Fancy make-up too

I will stick to
Mud holes,
Gravel roads,
And my pointy toe boots

This is a cowgirl's life
Kyerra Townsend, Grade 8

The Cost of Victory
The wind howls like a lonely wolf
through leafless winter trees
As snow drifts downward from dark clouds
onto the battle scene.
The victory has been won at last,
but won with a great cost.
Lifeless bodies scattering the ground
are those who have been lost.
Those who did not live to see the long-
awaited victory
Are envied by those who lived to see
dead brothers at their feet.
They question whether the victory
is worth all the lives lost.
While the rest of the world rejoices,
they are grieved by the great cost.
Elizabeth Kijowski, Grade 9

A Million Words
A million words to say, to hide, to think.
The ones you say you're not afraid of,
The ones you hide run after you like a haunting shadow, the ones you think a constant speeding highway inside your brain.

A million words to say, to hide, to think.
The words you say out of anger or happiness, the ones you hide always threaten to come out,
And the ones you think speeding across your mind giving you barely any chance to realize you thought them.

A million words to love, to hate, and forget.
The words you love remind you that there is always hope, the words you hate tell you how small that hope is.
But the words you forget are the ones that made such an impact on you that you pay attention only to the now and forget how everything even started.

A million words to love, to hate, and forget.
The words you love remind you there is a good in the world.
The words you hate point out how hard it is to see them under all the bad.
And the ones you forget are the ones of advice you received from wise people trying to remind you the difference between bad and good.

A million words
The ones you say, hide, think, love, hate, and forget.
You say them without realizing their meaning, you hide them not realizing their beauty, You think them because they fill up your mind so easily, loving and hating them at the same time, you're unsure if they're right.
Finally you forget them dismissing these words and thoughts because you're not sure what they mean yet.
And then you realize…that with a little thought that can change.

Ashley S. Chavez, Grade 8

Crying Skies
Spring has finally had its homecoming.
The next morning gigantic masses of clouds cover the sky, and the sky began to cry.

Drop by drop, by drop, water came splashing upon earth's concrete floors, splish splash splish splash.
It created more of a peaceful feeling, with the gentle bellows of thunder, roaring through the skies.
The sky is crying.

Tears of joy filled my face as the cool breeze, seeped through my face and the cool liquid trickled down my hair.
It's what inspires me to write this poem, to show my appreciation and admiration to nature and its aspect.
The sky is crying.

Tear drops from heaven, as they trickle down the streets, splish, splash, splish, splash
The roar of thunder fills the sky, a beautiful scene, an inspired sight.
The sky is crying.

Birds chirp as they fly to their homes, tears from heaven fall to the dirt giving plants life
The gray clouds engulfs the sun, and begins to cry, showing its true beauty.
The sky is crying.

In the end, the gigantic masses begin to clear up.
As heaven releases its sunshine down to earth.
They crate glorious rainbows, as what is left of the water, trickles down to the ground.
It reaches your thoughts clearly.
Once again another beautiful sight to see and feel peace and harmony.
Heaven is no more, to show its emotions.

Oscar Gutirrez Jr., Grade 8

Great Granddad
Granddad
The man who fought
in World War II
for our lives
The same man who
was shot
in the shoulder
Ten years later dies
of cancer
and that
is why I love
my great Granddad
Deana Kearby, Grade 7

Successful Students of St. Mary School
I love St. Mary School

We have made new friends!
At St. Mary School the fun never ends,

In free time, you'll find me reading;
Before I eat, you'll find me praying.

Our colors are blue and white;
In sports we never give up a fight!

I love St. Mary School
Paige Deitz, Grade 7

I Don't Understand
I don't understand
Why people dislike me
Why reading is hard
Why math is easy
But most of all
Why I can't focus
Why people can't get along
Why people can't stay
What I understand most is
Why I help out
Why some people care
Why I baby sit
Kelsey Gosnell, Grade 7

Manatees
M ammal
A wesome
N ative to Florida
A dorable
T olerant
E xtraordinary
E ndangered
S pecies

Manatees
Lila Van Acker, Grade 7

This Is Me
Jaz —
Athlete, generous, sweet, and funny,
Sister of Jaylen, Austin, and Andre,
Lover of basketball, the smell of the ocean,
and the taste of food,
Who feels happy when singing, proud when winning, and sporty when playing,
Who needs Summer, weekends, and sports,
Who gives hugs, friendships, and gifts,
Who fears spiders, trusting people, and being alone,
Who would like to see a peaceful Country, happy faces, and perfect lives,
Who lives in a small town in Frankfort,
— Culpepper
Jaz Culpepper, Grade 7

Will You Remember?
Will you remember when I'm sad and lost my way?
The day that I won't know what to say.

When the bright sun creeps down and the luminous moon comes up,
And the times that I used to care?

Most importantly, will you remember all the pain and tears you caused?
Those were the days I really wanted it all to pause.

Will you remember when I'm sad and lost my way
Because my tears are here to stay.
Arowal Ajuet, Grade 8

I Wish
I wish I saw you standing there with your glasses and gray hair
Why did you leave me? I don't understand. When you could be here, hand in hand
I just don't get it, I miss you. Up in heaven, do you miss me, too?
Come back for a day please, oh please. I'm begging you, I'm on my knees.
I wish I could see you one more time, when I do the bells will chime.
I hope that you are glad because down here, I'm sad.
I really hope I see you soon I wish I was right there, with you.
I wish, I wish that you were here but without you I only fear
I'll forget you, and your face I hope I won't be a disgrace.
I wish that you are looking at me, wishing someday that I will be,
Up there with you. Wishing on a star, and then it will be far, far from just a wish.
Ciera Poulas, Grade 8

A Collaborating Catholic Community
I love St. Mary School.
Munchkin-like children to colossal teenagers attend weekly all-school masses,
While Mrs. Keehn educates us about Gospels in religion classes.
Our church asks for us to donate money in rice bowls,
And our very own teachers help us achieve our academic goals.
Every day, we learn Christian values,
So we are to refine our own attitudes.
We first practice to receive the bread and wine,
And learn how sacraments are forever divine.
I love St. Mary School.
Krystal Rodriguez, Grade 7

Just Because......

Just because I'm blonde
Doesn't mean I'm not smart
Doesn't mean I'm dumb
And doesn't mean I don't know what I'm talking about
Just because I'm a girl
Doesn't mean I can't hunt
Doesn't mean I wear make-up
Doesn't mean I wear short shorts
Just because I'm short
Doesn't mean I shop in the little kid's section
Doesn't mean I'm not athletic
Doesn't mean I'm a midget
Just because I'm blonde
Why should hair color matter?
Why is gender stereotyped?
Does height really matter?
Just because I'm blonde

Dadrianna Serres, Grade 8

Broken Beauty

From the rack he slid out the Italian,
"This one isn't worth it, hun.
Regardless of the rich hues of the Mediterranean...
It's scratched and scrawny, this one."

She curtly nodded, "Well, I'll still try her out, for fun."
She closed her lids, envisioning a symphony
Bow poised, hair taut, stretched to run
Eager to consummate melody with harmony

Eventually her cheery "Concerto in C" blew
Feeling the glee unfit, her fingers reverted to "The Swan"
Shoulders arched back became wings and flew
Bittersweet as she closed her swan song.

Stroking the lattice of shattered cracks delicately with her finger,
she paused to behold its fragmented charm and allure.

Emma Liu, Grade 9

I Want to Go Back

I want to go back to the endless summer days
at the house on Grover Street
When I had no cares in the world
and everything was so simple
The thought of school never crossed my mind
as I ran through sprinklers at dusk
Chalk creations on the sidewalk were my pride and Joy
The pavement warmed my back
as I watched fireworks explode in the sky
I chased the ice cream man
and ate popsicles in the sunlight
I felt nothing but happiness
But now all that's left are pictures in a photo album
And I watch this place change and grow
as I change and grow apart from it
This place is just a memory
and I want to go back

Tess Hart, Grade 8

My Pal Gum

My pal GUM is quite a chewer,
He makes people's mouth get tired,
Helps people concentrate on work,
Freshen people's breath and cleans their teeth,
Come in different kinds of color,
There's red, blue, white and even pink!
But sometimes loses flavor,
He is the best pal in the world,
I could take him everywhere I go
When people see him they ask for him,
It irritates me when people deprive him,
It's so bizarre how people chew him loudly,
Even though he's in my book bag I get bamboozled,
People sometimes go in my bag and deprive him,
I love him so much I could chew him every day,
I already do any way he the best pal in the world,
And his name is Gum I love GUM!!

Elihda Saito, Grade 8

A Cat

```
    *           *
A cat       can
meow        with
a loud but sweet roar,
eat and sleep most of
the day, but once he's
 up you better get
out of his way. He's
ready to go and ready
to play, a fierce little
animal ready to pounce
give him a ball and see it
bounce. After the day,
it's time to end the play till tomorrow then it's a brand new day.
```

Katie Deslitch, Grade 7

Best Vacations

Flying was a drainage of energy
Above the clouds and close to the starry space,
But the warmth and scenery was paradise
And was worth everything.
Swimming, surfing, and snorkeling
The colors were bright like summer sun shining.
We swam like the fish below us,
The never-ending waves as big as buildings.
Surfing was like a roller coaster
But snorkeling seemed relaxing to me,
The fish seemed to scream louder and swim faster
Every inch we got closer.
Vacation was one of the most exciting points in my life
Becoming one of the memories concrete in my mind.

undefined Pyrzdia, Grade 9

A Symbol of Freedom

Born from a revolution
Led us through a country divided
Everybody lives free
Under the red, white, and blue.

Born from a revolution
Through harsh environment
You stand for strength and unity
You are a symbol of freedom.

Led us through a country divided
You showed what we were fighting for
During all wars you stood high
Waving in the breeze.

Everybody lives free
Due to your services
But freedom is never free
We will always remember all veterans

Under the red, white, and blue
Means we live shielded by the flag
Our veterans defended the flag
That is why we are free.
Tristan Sablone, Grade 7

Music Is an Expression

Music is an expression,
To show original thoughts.
Music is an expression,
To show individuality.

Music is an expression,
To show devotion.
Music is an expression,
To show ambition.

Music is an expression,
To show determination.
Music is an expression,
To show progression.

Music is an expression,
To show love.
Music is an expression,
To show happiness.

Music is an expression,
To show anger.
Music is an expression,
To show emotions.
Kate Witthuhn, Grade 8

I Believe

I believe there is hope
when it seems there isn't any.

I believe there is light
even what all surrounds us is dark.
We choose which path to follow
whether it's light or dark,
it's a path of our own.

I believe there is a reason.
There is a reason for everyone,
for life there's always a reason.
For family and friends.

I believe there is hope.
There is always something to live for.
But you need to find your reason.
Genesis Bahena, Grade 8

Flying Away

Sometimes I wish upon the biggest star,
and hope to someday soar across the sky.
I want to never learn to drive a car,
though instead be like superman and fly.

When I fly I don't ever need to stop,
I will go to Australia with no boats.
There will never be need to have a cop,
Since I would be the only one that floats.

But what if I run into hurricanes,
then I will never make it home that day.
Or if I get hit by a giant plane,
my parents may not find me until May.

Maybe flying isn't such a good wish,
I really don't want to die with the fish.
Rose Pilakowski, Grade 7

Trinity Gossage

T alking is one of her many talents
R oller skates a lot
I s crazy with her friends
N ot nice to siblings
I nside is where she will be
T acos are her favorite
Y ells a lot

G ood is the least thing she will be
O ut of her mind sometimes
S ometimes bored
S uch a blonde sometimes
A t her dad's every other weekend
G ets good grades
E asy to make her mad
Trinity Gossage, Grade 7

Winter

It's
Cold outside
I don't want to go
Outdoors and play
But mom says
I have to
Anyway

It's starting to snow
And I'm going to freeze
I hate playing outside on days like these
But wait a sec, I've had the
Most amazing, brilliant idea
I'll cover myself up
With snow and I'll
Hide in here!
Kea Roppolo, Grade 7

Sunset

as earth and sun crash together
colors emerge shining bright
taking us from the light of day
into the darkness of the night
down to the earth the sun sinks
the colors follow at its heels
with the light becoming very faint
there is nothing like how this feels
how it feels to say goodbye
to the sun we see during the day
with its colors shining bright
already starting to fade away
it is a lovely sight to see
its beauty so strong and true
but when the colors start to fade
a different beauty starts anew
Michelle A., Grade 7

The Puzzle We Call Poetry

Poetry
Is like a puzzle
It is tricky
Forcing us
To think
Like words
On paper
They piece us together
When separated
They are confusing
But when combined
You see the
Big picture.
What you see
Isn't always exactly
What you receive.
Faith Kemper, Grade 7

Lost

Sometimes I feel lost.
Trudging through a forest of my mind.
Wishing to leave my problems behind.
But I am still lost.

Sometimes I feel lost.
Unable to understand the world.
And questions in my mind are swirled
I am still lost.

Sometimes I feel lost.
Like I want to give in
To every one of all the world's sins.
I am still lost.

Sometimes I feel lost.
Then I realize I am saved.
That in my mind, the future is engraved.
I am no longer lost.
Grace Johnson, Grade 8

Ode to Ghost

Why did you leave?
Where did you hide?
All the sadness
Has arrived.

I cry night and day
You brought pain to my soul
And it's going to stay
Until you come home.

I want you near
When my heart feels empty
My eyes fill with tears,
When you're not beside me.

My heart broke apart
When you had to depart
but I know you will be:
by my side.
Keila Abigail Nunez, Grade 9

I Apologize

I ate the cheese pizza
which was in the
refrigerator.

That you had been
waiting to
eat for lunch.

I'm sorry, brother, it was
so delicious
warm and cheesy.
Baran Tokgoz, Grade 7

Viola

Tears drip down my cousin's face,
The smell of incense fills the air.
Outside a deep hole takes its place,
For she'll be buried there.
My uncle's face is stained with tears,
Though I hadn't seen him cry —
A recurring thought rolls through my head:
Why did she have to die?
Soft songs sound around my ears,
Nobody says a word.
I hope and pray that someday soon
My prayers to her will be heard.
Sorrow tries to drag me down,
But I don't let it win —
She wouldn't want me to be sad,
So I give her a grin.
I know that she can see me there,
Wherever she may be,
And whenever I'm feeling lonely,
She'll still be there to comfort me.
Jilly Kornak, Grade 8

The Spot on the Wall

The spot on the wall
Like a little black hole
I try to imagine it gone
But where would it go

Maybe under my bed
Maybe in my blanket
Maybe on my leg
Maybe in my hair

So I think comforting thoughts
But it keeps coming back
It's eight legs and eyes
It's fur whooshing against my skin

So there I lay
Staring at the spot
It staring back at me
Hoping it's not actually there
Graham Nicholson, Grade 8

Wonders of Summer

The smiles on the children's faces,
The birds chirping in the trees,
The leaves blowing in the wind,
The shine of rays from the sun,
The barking of the neighbor's dog,
The rubber wheels of a bike on the street,
The crackling flames of the bonfire,
The splashing waves in the pool,
The bouncing springs of the trampoline,
The sweet smell of the summer air.
Grace Costello, Grade 7

Thank You

You sacrifice your lives
So it's safe for us to go outside
Every day you fight
So we can sleep at night
Even though you don't have to
You still fight for us
It was your choice
To help us keep our freedom
You are away from your families
While we are with ours
I know it's hard for you
To be away for so long
so I just wrote this poem
To say thank you for what you have done
And we love you all!

Thank you soldiers and veterans!
Makadan Henry, Grade 7

Dirt Bikes for Me!

As long as I ride dirt bikes,
Since that is what I love,
Although it takes some practice,
Wherever it takes me,
That is where I will go.

When I unload my dirt bike,
After I put on my gear,
So that I don't get hurt,
Unless I'm riding trails,
I finally take off and go.

Since the weather will be nice,
Unless that changes tomorrow,
I won't make any plans,
Unless we go boating,
I will not pass that up.
Lindsey Novak, Grade 8

Letting Go

Caught by the breeze,
one with the wind,
slipping away
in the gentle morning air.
Done with terror,
done with pain.
Leaving it all behind,
for something amazing.
A brand new life,
a whole new way.
Each uplift brings a whole new day.
From over the hills,
into the undulating sea,
on this gentle breeze,
that carries me.
Anne Roszak, Grade 7

Ten Little Morgans

Ten little Morgans were looking so fine
One tried to curl her hair and then there were nine.

Nine little Morgans ate off some plates
One got food poisoning then there were eight.

Eight little Morgans took the name of Devin
Sydney got mad then there were seven.

Seven little Morgans tried to make a mix
One slipped on the batter then there were six.

Six little Morgans tried to do a dive
One hit the bottom and then there were five.

Five little Morgans tried to open the door
One got hit in the head and then there were four

Four little Morgans tried to get something free
One got caught and then were three.

Three little Morgans tried to make a boo
One got scared and then there were two.

Two little Morgans had a son
One had a pain and then there was one

One little Morgan decided to be done
She decided to leave and then there were none.
Emily Elliott, Grade 7

I Hope…Someday

I hope that someday
My voice be heard and never be judged.
So that I can sing to the midnight stars.

I hope that someday
My shadow can be seen and never be unnoticed.
So that I can have my white roses with me.

I hope that someday
My dance can be learned and never be forgotten.
So that I can walk in peace.

I hope that someday
My dreams can be true and never be broken.
So that I can dream on forever without end.

I hope that someday
My strength can be stronger and never be weak.
So that I can fight off all of my demons.

I hope that someday
My true love can be real and never be fake.
So that I can be loved, without tears in my eyes.
Crystal Long Soldier, Grade 8

Into the Depths

Beware the calmness
of those sparkling pools of light blue and hazy green.
Although they appear beautiful and harmless
they can be quite dangerous.

They are easily captivating,
pulling you closer and closer,
until like an ocean current,
they sweep you under into their dark blue depths,
where there is no hope of return.

As you suffocate slowly,
from lack of air,
Becoming lightheaded and dizzy,
you begin to have fear,
that there's no escaping now.

You're lost in his eyes.
Hidden in your own little world.
You'll never be found.
Jesilee Riley, Grade 9

Imprison

All I see; Is never new to me broken hearts and slower paces
Tired eyes on worn-out faces
It'll never get better
Not now, not ever
A rat race is all life has become
So bite the steel with your hand on the gun
A sulken face with sulken eyes
All hello's end with goodbye's
No sense in anything anymore
You will never settle any score
All hope is gone, no sense in trying
Every second we live, we're slowly dying
I have lost all faith in humanity
I have lost my last bit of sanity
So I guess if knowing tastes so good
Then I assume the metal, better it should
So either pull the trigger back
Or keep your hands in your lap
But remember that happy, we'll never be
Since we're prisoners of ourselves and what we always wanted to be.
Haley Wood, Grade 9

A World Your Own

Sand on a peaceful morning,
paper before it has been touched,
the wind before it has rustled.

The paper like thousands of seashells stacked up,
the tiny dots forming a sea of letters.
stacked grass, the color of the beach.
Just before you open it to read it,
and enter a world your own.
Kara-Lyn Moran, Grade 8

Mountain Climbing

One tall mountain
Two rock climbers
Three days have gone
Four shoes climbing up
Five fingers grasping rock
Six zippers on a bag
Seven hours full or climbing
Eight minutes of catching breathe
Nine more inches till the top
Ten cheers for succeeding

Kristina Hart, Grade 7

The Eternal Flame of Love

Charity is a crimson flame
That burns within the soul.
Its endless fuel provided,
Consumed with rapid pace,
Spreads warmth from heart to heart —
The love of God and neighbor.
Sad is he who tries to quench
This ever-burning flame,
The beacon in this strife,
The golden crown of life.

Germaine Goldade, Grade 9

Don't Judge Me

Don't judge me on what I'm
supposed to be
Judge me on who I am
Don't see only the walls of my body
See what I truly can
See what I can be,
Not what you expect me to
Cause the one that can't judge me,
is you

Amery Barbee, Grade 7

Compassionate Lovers

T wo people forever
R ed is the color
U nforgettable passion
E ager to see each other

L overs and loyal
O verly dramatic
V itally important
E ternity together

Alexis Burke, Grade 7

The Pastry Pickpocket

There once was a girl named Kalea Liesse,
Who stole a doughnut from the police.
They chased her 'round town,
Till the doughnut turned brown,
And the pastry was snatched up by geese.

Kalea Liesse, Grade 7

The Other Side

As I walked along down my street, the strangest thing my eyes did meet.
Among the Ritz of the towering estates was an abode that seemed out of place.
The roof concaved, the windows shattered,
Aside all the villas it seemed not to matter.
In my own curiosity, I wandered inside and gazed upon a divergent way of life.
No roads, just filth; an extinction of green,
No mansions, no diamonds, no limousines.
A vile smell filled the moist air around me, and litter was heaped as far as I could see.
Mangy creatures crawled through the streets,
When suddenly, I realized they're humans, like me.
I'm approached by a boy, unnaturally lean,
He brushes my hand and cries "Oh please help me!
I'm aware of the luxury you've always had—enough on the table, a mom and a dad.
You have what you need, and quite a bit more,
So why, I must ask, do you have a closed door?
Why don't you aid? Why don't you give? With your support a new life I could live!
So how do you sit behind a closed door
with all that you need, and quite a bit more?"

Madeline Siebert, Grade 8

The Big Game

It was the day of the Tournament, a day of fun.
In order to go to state, this game had to be won.
I was the star player on the basketball team;
I was the kind of person you would picture in your dream.

We got on the bus on our way to the rival town.
Everyone was cheering, "We are going to take them down!"
We arrived, got changed, and went down to the gym floor,
And that's when the rival team marched through the big, wooden door.
We shook hands with our rivals and the game began.
I looked at the crowd; foam fingers said, "#1 fan!"

We got the ball, and I was dribbling down the court.
I went in for the lay-up, but I was just too short.
I felt it, heard it, the crowd saw it…the ball missed.
The pain went through my body, and I knew I had broken my wrist.
The game was still going as I lie there in pain.
But I wasn't going to quit, and we won that game.

Kaysha Unruh, Grade 7

The Ballad of Cosette

Where are you, my greatest friend?
I heard you were sick last night
So I came to find you, yet came upon a dead end.

Where are you? You're not lying in the sunlight,
Nor are you curled up on the chair,
I hear a loud sob to my right, and now I'm filled with fright.

I yowl your name throughout the house, but I can't find you anywhere.
Here I am now, what can I do?
You are gone, all that I can find is your shed hair.

Oh dearest Cosette, where are you?

Joseph McMillan, Grade 9

Yesterday
Yesterday I saw you for the first time after two months.
It was like falling in love all over again.
Memories of the times we shared had come rushing back,
I was breathless.
And, I don't think I stopped loving you, it's just I had to stop showing it.

You were so breathtaking,
I was breathless.

I saw you yesterday, and I walked past you like I had never met you.
Our eyes connected for only seconds, but within those seconds came the realization that all those feelings I thought had left
had been there all along.

I do love you.

Autumn Papakee, Grade 9

Mom More Like a Guardian Angel
My mom is as bold as a tiger.
My mom is good at sports when she plays volleyball all you hear is POP when she hits the ball.
My mom, she protects me and my brother like a mama tiger.
My mom feeds us every day like a parent bird feeds its baby birds.
My mom cares about me like I am an expensive piece of gold.
My mom is as wise as one of Jesus disciples.
My mom watches over me the same way angels watch over us.
My mom is like a best friend to me, she is there through my ups and downs.
My mom is someone who knows me very well, she's been with me since day one and she will stick by me till the end.
My mom and I create a stronger relationship every time it's my birthday because just 13 years ago I was born.
My mom is out-going, she is fantastic, very caring and loving to my brother and me.
My mom, I hope you and me will stay by each other's sides no matter what circumstance we are in and that you will stay in my life
to the very end.

James L. Barrera, Grade 7

Somewhere Beyond the Darkness*
Don't dare go into the dying darkness, where the demons are haunting every soul. Demons will burn the torn and shaven in the weak and weary. Upon the shadows where the densest demons burn in hell. Rage, rage against the horrors of the densest burden. That gets tossed and torn throughout the shadows of darkness. In the deepest levels below the graves is a soul that is very lonely. It wants to come into the blaze of the light. It can't because blind eyes could blaze, with a single blinding sight of the light. Curse me now, with your fierce tears gazing at me in the shorn and shaven shadows. Why must you make old age burn and rage at the close of the day; Rage, rage against the words forked upon the burning thunder and lightning grieved that it's on its way. Grave men, near death, who see blinding light that will blaze like a meteor shower that brings fierce tears of death. Wild men learn, it's too late, burning of dead flesh in the dying sun. Wise me at the end of their line know it's time for them to go into the light. Because their words are broken into an unmerciful disaster of horror. Their trail deeds might have danced upon the light of the green bay. Good men, the last wave bye, crying how horrifying the brightness of the rage of death is. And you, my father, there on the sad height, cursed with fierce tears, all I have to do is pray that everything will be okay. Rage, rage against the horror of the densest burden. Don't dare go into the dying darkness, where the demons are haunting every soul around and you are NEXT!

Racheal Harris, Grade 8
*Based on Edger Allan Poe's creepy words from "The Raven," "The Black Cat," and "Tell-Tale Heart."

My Beautiful Location
My favorite place to go is fishing at a pond. Every time I fish my mind gets cleared.
I go there every summer when the grasses are bright green and the warm nights are peaceful.
I love to see the reflection of wildlife in the water; it is beautiful.
I hear the birds chirping, the fish splashing, and the casting of my fishing pole.
The sight of this beautiful location is like none other, and it is away from everyone.

Trayton Doyle, Grade 8

My Adventures

Deep in the woods I run and play
this can take me all day
Deep in the woods I listen to the birds
and see the trees glisten

I forget my past as long as it lasts
I see where the water runs free as a stream should be
Little falls look to me like little Niagara Falls

When I watch the deer
My dad is probably drinking a beer
Far away from me, my past, my life, my worries

I love watching the squirrels scurry up a tree
fast and free
This is my own little world to explore, find and imagine
of things not like dragons

Things really there not in your mind
those false realities can bind us
where we think there is nowhere else better
But when you find your adventure
That is your own little world

Alex Dwinell, Grade 7

Just Because…

Just because I'm shy
doesn't mean I'm stuck up
doesn't mean I have no friends
And doesn't mean you can push me around
Just because I'm shy
doesn't mean I can't have fun
doesn't mean I'm not obnoxiously loud when no one's around
Just because I'm shy
doesn't mean I'm not strong
doesn't mean I don't want to make friends
Just because I'm shy
Do people think I'm a freak?
Do they think I read books all day?
Do they think I have no life?
Because if they do then they're wrong!

Renee Redfern, Grade 8

Lines

Emma
Smart, funny, responsible, unathletic
Sibling of Harper, Brooklyn, and Brynlee
Who cares deeply for art, kids, writing, and animals
Who feels smart while drawing, and excited with my friends
Who needs empathy, love, and trust
Who gives advice, donations, and kindness
Who fears broken hearts and hatred
Who would like to see Hawaii, Paris, and Washington
Resident of Sioux Falls
Salzwedel.

Emma Salzwedel, Grade 8

Injury Season

It's my seventh grade year and I'm scared
Because I'm 4'9" and light as air
My mom says I'm fast and shifty
My coach says I'm clever and nifty
But it scares me when my parents say
"If you get flattened, it will be OK."
One hour till practice so I get ready
I pack my bag along with a medi
I put on my pants and my compression shirt
Just hoping that I don't get injured or hurt
My mom takes me in as I prep for death
My heart pounds so loudly that I go deaf
I put on my cleats and strap my pads
I wear a jersey that was my dad's
I walk onto the field about to fall
Ready to play a game called football

Jack Olson, Grade 7

Poor Old Man

Poor old man why do you sit there all alone in your chair?
While you sit there with that blank stare
When nothing…is sitting there.
Not a sound or breath is ever found
When you sit with that sad frown
While you sit on that old old chair
Death death DEATH is sitting…
Waiting there
As he sits and waits with the poor old man he picks him
Up with his frigid hands…
No longer will the man sit and stare or be in that old
Old rocking chair
Oh no he is not there he is with death now…
Somewhere…somewhere…somewhere

Matthew Foss, Grade 7

Dreams

Webs of clear paint drip down my face,
I listen to my heartbeat,
Needing sleep,
The angel choir helps me endure,
And erase the hate as the black dissolves in the season,
In denial reality is unknown,
Dew on the mountains and the jungle's leaves
A symbol of a tangerine twilight over the cliffs and streets,
Tides of hate
I mourn dreams.

Ashlynd Stout, Grade 8

Favorite Music

My family is a collection of music.
My mom is country music always wanting to go out in the country.
My dad is rock-n-roll always ready to be strong and protect others.
My sister is hip hop always listening to hip hop music.
My brother is old school always ready to go to classical concerts.
I am the new age music I'm always out going and strong.

Anthony Bonebrake, Grade 7

Stopping by My Memory at Any Time

My mind and memory loves to drift.
Sometimes it gives me gifts.
But it loves to deceive.
It goes around and shifts.
It loves to make me grieve.
It makes me naive.
I want to go and hide away.
But some don't believe.
So I just stay.
But don't run away
My mind likes to play tricks
It plays shows like Broadway
Plays and lies to me like politics,
Making me act like a lunatic, I hold
A crucifix.
It's my toughest conflict.
It's my toughest conflict.

Adrian Varela, Grade 8

My Family Is Awesome

My family is important to me
Especially my nice little brother.
Me and him are as happy as can be
Even though sometimes he's a bother

Even though we fuss about weird things
He is an awesome little brother
He is very awesome and lovable
Not to mention my parents who help us.

Me and him like activities
Such as movies and games
Even though they're games for kiddies
I happen to be the one he blames

Parents give us food, clothing, shelter
Even though we fuss over things.

Bernabe Chavez, Grade 8

Ode to the Moon

The big yellow moon
Lying within the landscape of the stars
Like a golden coin tossed into the fountain
It is the cheese of the sky
A smile and a night on the town
When nighttime falls, It rises
Glowing on the pavement
Shadowing strangers outside
and the young couple lying on the grass
Coyotes howl
The man on the street looks up
And dreams of a better life
It is a desert land with craters
A rock in the vast universe
But hope for the lost in the dark

Alyssa Ricken, Grade 9

Attention

There is a window between us.
A wall.
A door.
The glass won't shatter.
The bricks won't break.
The door won't open.
No matter how hard I scream,
You won't hear me.
No matter how long I wait,
You won't find me.
No matter how much I jump or wave,
You won't see me.
I'm trying to get your attention.
But I can't.
Because the glass is too thick.
The bricks are too bold.
And the door,
Was meant to hold.

Alexa Soto, Grade 8

Perfection

Perfection,
is imperfection.
The world,
is demonization.
And broken,
with damnation.
In a colorless world,
of desperation.
We all strive,
for realization.
To find our,
own salvation.
In a place,
full of temptation.
Why can't we,
become perfection?
It's because we are,
Enslaved to simulation.

Amber Bullock, Grade 8

Harvest

The sun is rising
The rooster crows
To the field I am arriving
The crops grown in rows
The tractor comes to life
Even through all the strife

The harvest is coming to an end
The sun is setting
Turning round the last bend
The last pass is ending
The moon is rising as I return
Now it's next year's turn

Alexander Delaney, Grade 8

Spring Is Here

Feel the warm breeze through the air.
What does this mean?
Can it be that spring is here?
Yes, it may be
Spring is here.

People start to run outside,
Soaking up the sun.
Kids can try to run and hide
Just for some fun.
Spring is here.

Smiling faces see the sun,
Glad for the weather.
Water splashing, daisies dancing,
Now, we are better,
Spring is here.

Flowers peek out from the ground.
Now, they see the sun.
Pretty colors everywhere
Now that winter's done.
Spring is here.

Abbie Borgstrom, Grade 7

Love of My Life

As I lay,
Not wanting to move,
The clock says seven AM.

Finding my dog,
Made of fabric,
Not of flesh.

Filled with life.
Through my eyes,
Stuffed with love.

As I lay,
Not needing to move,
The clock says eight PM.

Hugging my dog,
Made of memories,
Made of love.

As living as a real dog,
Through my eyes.
Stuffed with cotton.

Gillian Hannold, Grade 8

Change

The sun greets the night
Warm meets cold and light meets dark
Everyone is awake.

Margaret Griggs, Grade 8

An Idea

Ideas are good,
Ideas are great,
Ideas you need,
Ideas you seek,

What should I do,
What should I draw,
In this white canvas,
That is my life,

Should I do or should I not,
Should I listen or should I talk,
Time is growing old,
As am I,

Standing here in this vacuum of space,
Wondering what will waltz in my way,
As I stand alone and unique,
An idea is what I seek.
David Santacruz, Grade 8

Train to Paradise

The tracks click
Under my feet
On my way
To paradise

I look out
The window and
Watch every place I pass
The sun beaming
In my eyes
Thoughts running
Through my mind

A smile on my face
I listen to the sound around me
People talking
Babies crying
Waiting to see
Where I'll end up
Stephanie Hawil, Grade 8

Love

It is a feeling.
People forget to love.
People want to feel love.

We love each other a lot.
It is a major part of history.
It is a part of the future.

When people do love,
Some love more than others.
Some love differently than others.
Jacob Grieb, Grade 7

Happy Family

My family is
Loving in times of need.
My family is
always there when I need them.
My family is
my other half.
My family is a
Kind and generous family.
My family has
a very loving, fulfilling heart.
My family always
makes me happy.
My family is
Funny, fulfilling, and fun-loving.
My family has
a great sense of humor.
Rylee Walz, Grade 8

When I Read

The sensation I get when I read,
Is unexplainable.
The worry, the tears, the amusement,
It's all from the book.

Sometimes it's gloomy,
Sometimes it's funny,
Sometimes it's action-filled,
The sensation I get when I read.

The feeling I get when I read,
Never seems to bore me.
I fall in love with the characters.
I even love the dialogue.
I love the story plot even more.
I love the sensation I get when I read.
Hannah Easterly, Grade 8

Dragons

Flying over mountains,
Over vast plains.
Through the harshest
And the nicest of weather.
Shining like the sun,
Never before.
Scales like armor.
Claws like razors
Sharp as ever.
Teeth like white, sharp pearls.
Gentle.
Yet powerful.
Wings as fragile as an egg.
Colors of every color.
These powerful creatures,
Are DRAGONS!
Destinee Vi Flesch, Grade 8

These Chains Are Oh So Cold

Reaching and stretching —
Pain —
Sharp in my wrists
Oh, how I long to reach you.

To reach outside this
Unending dream
Of cold and dark.

I feel the chains —
They burn me like ice.
I long to run free
To reach outside this dirty cell.

And these chains
That bind me
Are so cold.
I only wanted to love you.
Elizabeth Reiter, Grade 9

I Am

I am a reader and a believer
I wonder when people will stop dying
I hear the screams of the living
I see innocent blood being split
I want it to stop
I am a reader and a believer
I pretend I can't see or hear it
I feel the pain of the grieving
I touch a shattered soul
I worry that it won't heal
I cry for all of the sorrowful dead
I am a reader and a believer
I understand that war is in books and life
I say that it is all in life
I dream that one day it will forever stop
I try to stay strong
I hope I can make a difference
I am a reader and a believer
Brianna Conklin, Grade 9

When You Forget Me

One day it will happen.
You'll forget me,
And not look back on our memories.
When laughs were shared,
And tears were shed.
I consider you family,
Because family doesn't end in blood.
You're there for me now,
But I know you'll leave like the rest.
I've always known this to be true.
But remember,
When you forget me,
I will not forget you.
Kaylin Penninger, Grade 8

Football Game

Whenever it's time to ready up,
Wherever the game is played,
Even if the conditions are bad,
As I put my gear on, I hope for a win,
No matter how good the other team is.

After I'm suited up,
When we drive to the dead field,
I think about how we will own this game,
While listening to my banger music,
To pump me up for the game.
The game is on,

The kickoff has started,
We charge to tackle the ball carrier,
While I hope for a fumble,
It won't matter, because this game is ours.
Justin Rosche, Grade 8

Wishing for Spring

Warming sunshine of Spring
But all I see is the bitter cold snow.
Snow falling from the sky
Like a swarm of bees
Stinging my face.
Oh where is my
Warm sunshine of Spring?
I jump out of bed
Hoping Spring has come
But all I see is falling snow.
Oh Spring, where are you?
Once again here I go
Into the bitter cold
Shoveling snow once again.
Stop the madness of winter snow
Oh snow, I hate you so!
Oh Spring, where are you?
Stefano Positano, Grade 7

The Bruised Heart

A single teardrop is brought down,
Thanks to the bully.
Do I deserve this treatment?
Does this person have issues with me?
I'm being torn from my pride.
I have a bruised heart.
How do I heal?
The bully is hungry.
I am its prey and
A vulnerable one.
Cyber bully, verbal bully, sexual bully
So many to sneak up on me.
Scary.

— Now read it backwards
Jadin Mershon, Grade 9

No One Should Be Judged

No one should be judged,
By what they can afford to wear.
No one should be judged,
It's not very fair.

No one should be judged,
By the color of their skin.
No one should be judged,
If they aren't very thin.

No one should be judged,
By the vibe they project.
No one should be judged,
It causes an effect.

No one should be judged,
Is the message I am "hinting."
No one should be judged,
Always be thinking.
Jaidyn Buckingham, Grade 8

The Boys of Fall

Of all the sports, I must really say
I'd take football any day
It takes skill to be the one
To drill someone

The plays are called
The defensive of line is walled
Both lines push and shove
But they won't budge

The crowd is loud
When the team is proud
The game is coming to an end
As the boys of fall holds off 'til the end

The game comes to a close
As the wind starts to blow
The seniors shed their tears
As the field begins to clear
Kara VanMeter, Grade 9

The Strength of Charity

There is no virtue like charity
For melting hearts of iron,
Nor anything like cheerfulness
For making crosses lighter —
Everyone is capable,
Forgiveness is what matters,
Mercy and compassion
For even those who injure —
A few kind words
Will warm their hearts
And start this fire divine.

Catherine Peterson, Grade 9

Dad

Hard-worker
Bill-payer
Money-maker

Hug-giver
Care-taker
Twizzler-chewer
Burrito-eater

Construction-worker
Kitchen-completor
Tire-fixer

Light-sleeper
TV-watcher
Boat-driver

Amazing-cooker
Pizza-baker
Positive-trainer

Cat-hater
Puppy-lover
Opossum-trainer

But most of all, the best of them all,
My Dad
McKenzie Johnson, Grade 7

Soldiers

Ones who have sacrificed their lives—
Just for the sake of ours.
They hold their guns in their bare hands,
During the war for hours.

This is how they live their lives now,
Battles with other countries.
I'm sure they've got enough guts—
Enough to join the army.

They go and fight, giving it their all.
Blood stains, even nature camo.
Do you see what they've done for us?
Pride is what they all show.

They barely see their families,
All these passing days.
This is why we respect them
In every single way.

When you see one of these heroes,
Be sure to even say,
"Thanks for helping, stranger.
I know what you did—
To keep us all out of danger."
Aleximae Martin, Grade 7

Ode to Gymnastics

Twisting through the air.
It's super scary, I am aware.

I love to flip down the floor.
Especially when the boys score.

With broken bones and bruised hands.
Gymnastics will always be my plan.

I find it the best sport.
And love how it doesn't matter if you're short.

Competitions after competitions that's the way I go.
So watch as I perform my show.

Maddie McEvers, Grade 7

Sounds of Solitude

Outcast and alone…
　　　　never quite for sure where to go,

In circles I go yonder and far…
　　　　if I was to go anywhere at all,

Oh how joyful was the sound of their laughter…
　　　　yet it never reached thine empty heart,

With such bitterness and sorrow I left them all
　　　　no more shall pain and misery be felt,

Faces will be blurs and names will become letters,
　　　　as the memories of them fade away…

Elizabeth Blackmon, Grade 8

Change

The warmth pressing against my lips,
The gentle curving around my hips,
The thought makes my heart do flips,
　— but only on July 26th.

The memories were filled with pain,
The words I hoped not to hear again,
The tears felt like acid rain,
　— but only on September 26th.

The day was special, just for you,
The scars, they showed, you just never knew,
The talk of you just made me blue,
　— but only on November 26th.

Madeline Otto, Grade 8

Chaos

As darkness covers the world.
A storm of madness ravages through the town.
As the Underworld attacks the over-world.
The mound of chaos is all around

Damian Fayle, Grade 8

Summer

Summer is the best time of the year,
When the weather gets hot you know it's near,
Everyone is getting out of school,
And then heading to the pool.

Days at the river are the best,
Sun shining down and getting no rest,
Boating and swimming all day,
'Til there isn't even one sun ray.

I love concerts and county fairs,
Along with having no cares,
Sleeping in until one,
Waking up and having fun.

When the school year comes back around,
I want to head to some warm ground,
Making every summer day count,
Because the number of days is a small amount.

Brandy Thieman, Grade 9

As She Sits

She sits alone,
Drawing for days.
Her eyes are an inkwell,
And her skin like paper.
She is covered up with ink.

She has swirls on her
That look like the ocean's waves
She has words that mean something.

People stare in disgust
She looks back with her creative inkwell eyes,
And says it is art.

So with the bland world
She gets up,
Her eyes ready to design.

What is art?

Analisa Fandino, Grade 8

Understanding Society

I do not understand
　　Why people bring others down
　　Why people can't pull a smile from that frown
　　Why people live for war

I most of all do not understand
　　How people think of only themselves

But what I do understand
　　Is the smile you get
　　After making another person smile

Travis Ligon, Grade 9

Change

Bushes are growing
the birds have been chirping
grass is turning green
flags are waving on the pole
as the rocks sit still always.
Grant Blondin, Grade 7

Light

L ife
I n
G od's
H eavenly
T ruth
Alexis Berg, Grade 8

The Hunt

I went roaring down the hill
Going fast with a chill
I had my trusty gun
And I was having fun
With intent to kill
Seth Andrews, Grade 8

The Mouse

There once was an adorable mouse
Who lived in a big old house
He drove very far
In his little old car
To find his long lost spouse
Kamille Smith, Grade 7

Ocean

Crashing blue water
Sea animals living in
Salt stinging your eyes
Wet sandy beaches by it
Separating continents
Drew Holtze, Grade 8

Minds

wise minds speak innocence
sanity crafted by reason
lucid and fine
but intricate in design
full of riveting nonsense to be told in time
Odochi Akwani, Grade 9

Freedom

Freedom
What does it mean?
It is the right to vote;
It is the right to speak our mind;
Freedom
Tessa Beeman, Grade 7

The Midnight Journey

The air is still and bitter, pure white snow glinting in the moonlight.
Sullen trees shed old, papery bark, and carry the cold, heavy burden,
Resting on their outstretched branches.

My massive paws move me swiftly through the snow.
I keep a watchful eye and listen, catching the sounds of squirrels playing tag in the trees.
The snow grows deeper as I continue my journey,
So I begin to run, letting my nose lead the way.

Smells wash over me, damp earth, musky trees, and finally,
The smell like wet bark and fresh rain slices through the air,
Disappearing as quickly as it had come.
Now I know where to head, and I take off at a sprint,
Thankful for my paws' marvelous balancing act.

As I maneuver through the maze of trees, a howl sounds in the distance.
I tilt my head towards the starry sky, and answer back like an echo.

My tail swishes and I push my muscles,
The last little bit towards my destination.
Then, I see it,
A mass of silver, ebony, pearl, and russet.
At long last, I'm back with my pack.
Camryn Bird, Grade 7

The Faucet

I awaken to a sound, drip drop drip drop,
I get out of bed and go check what's making the noise.
The sound seems to be coming from the kitchen, I assume it's the faucet dripping,
So I turn it on and back off, and head back towards the bed.

Once again I awaken from my slumber, to the familiar sound, drip drop drip drop.
With a groan I get out of bed, and head once again towards the faucet.
I turn it on then off, and head back toward the bed.

I awaken once again, to the familiar, yet annoying sound,
Drip drop drip drop, but to my surprise it's coming from outside.
I go and peek out the window, it was raining very softly, as I head back towards the bed,
I shake my head in disbelief, all this time it had been raining,
when I thought it was the faucet dripping.
Carlos Perez, Grade 8

Rumors Kill

Listen close classmates; To what I have to say
I saw on the news that; A young girl took her own life today
She was talented and beautiful; Everyone said she was so sweet
Crazy how her life got changed; From one hateful tweet

Rumors spread like wild fires; She thought she had no place to turn
Standing among the bullying flames; Hurtful words caused her heart to burn
In a moment of desperation; She told the world goodbye
She just couldn't take it anymore; She thought her only option was to die

So think twice classmates; About what you have to say
Your words may be what makes; Someone decide to live or die today
Kayley Reyes, Grade 8

The Pains and Gains of Rain

When it rains
My mind wanders.
Does this rain create pain,
Or does it create gain?

The growers of life,
Their crops flourish.
The rain to them brings no strife.
The growing greens bring life.

For some, the rain cuts.
It comes from the sky slicing.
Through the wind it flies, but
Some will ask, "For what?"

When I look upon the rain
As it patters against the window,
I know what I am to gain
From this miracle called rain.
Brennan Browning, Grade 7

O' Thank You Mittens

Mittens, I want to say O' thank you.
You kept my hands so warm and snug,
You kept away the snow and the dew,
And every day gave my fingers a hug.

Now that springtime is coming,
And I've hung up my heavy coat,
But my mittens keep my heart humming,
And my wintertime joy afloat.

My mittens, my last surrender,
I hole onto you until it's too warm,
Tissue-wrapped I store you, so tender,
Until autumn brings a chillier norm.

Mittens, I must express my gratitude,
For warm fingers and cheerful attitude.

O' Thank You Mittens
Hunter Bates, Grade 8

School Buildings

I am in school every day,
When I leave school I yell hurray.

P.E. is my favorite class,
More fun than playing in grass.

The lunches are really tasty,
On pizza day I go crazy.

Eighth grade year was the best,
Oh great! High school is next.
Zeb Huseman, Grade 8

Life

From the day you were born
To the day of your first steps,
I don't want to grow up

From the first words you say
To the first bike you rode,
I don't want to grow up

From the first day of school
To the first hard assignment
I don't want to grow up

From the first time you took a fall
To the time you got back up
I don't want to grow up

From the last day of 8th grade
To starting high school
I don't want to grow up

From going to college
To being on my own
I don't want to grow up

From the day we die
We are done growing up
Gianna Corban, Grade 8

I Hear They Call It Love

Of glowing cheeks and soft smiles,
A feeling grows that will not be denied.
Bells of laughter and tears of joy,
Brighten the eyes and loosen the soul.

Hands clasped in pure mirth,
Toes wiggling with anticipation.
Heart beaming with rays of light,
Mind filled with thoughts so jubilant.

Happiness blooming and feet dancing,
Legs shaking and stomach flipping.
Arms tremor and lips curve,
Hearts so divine as bodies entwine.

A feeling that seeps in,
And embeds itself in the mind.
Makes the wise foolish,
And the evil weak.

Only one feeling can bring,
Such destruction and agony.
Only one feeling can bring,
Men of strength to their knees.

I hear they call it love.
Tehreem Chaudhry, Grade 9

The Pond

I told him not to move
I said I would be right back
I knew that pond was dangerous
And that's the last time he'll disobey
Slowly bending down
He picked up the stick
I was 200 feet away
At the top of a hill
Then, BOOM!
The world exploded
Debris was everywhere
I felt as if I was in a sand storm
I rushed down toward him
My heart filled with horror
I told him it would be okay
But then I saw the blood
I pulled out the stick
And sewed him up tight
With fire and bottle cap in hand
I regretfully sewed the wound
And I told him not to move
Isabella Dimitriou, Grade 7

Salute to Spring

To walks to my cousin's house
To downtown trips
To hanging out at the park
To swimming on a hot spring day
To rainy afternoons
To stormy nights
To the sun shining bright
To the flowers blossoming
To trees growing fresh green leaves
To the smell of dirt
To the scent of coffee early in the morning
To the smell of freshly cut grass
To the sight of dogs playing
To kids having fun
To the sound of birds chirping the morning
To the sound of dogs barking
To the first bite of watermelon
To freshly baked M&M cookies
To watching Netflix all day
To those sleepless nights
To spring.
Andrea Armas, Grade 8

24 Hours

Day
Bright, happy
Shining, swarming, comforting
The sky's turning black
Menacing, darkening, chilling
Scary, animals
Night
Andrew Perez, Grade 8

Waiting

A heavy feeling on my chest
All I can feel is my heart racing
Breathe in, breathe out
My eyes survived the drought

I am trying to control it
I'm trying to hide it
People stare like I'm on display
I want to run away

No one can help me
Just leave me alone
Give me space and time
I'll be all right

Waiting for it to pass like a storm on a cloudy day
Waiting to breathe
Waiting, waiting, waiting
Waiting to be okay

Jewel Heubner, Grade 8

The Marine Corps Memorial

A tribute to the men who went down that dreadful day,
"It was an honor to serve with them," the survivors say,
The statues of the men crying,
Just shows how much they were trying,
To raise the flag that made them say "No dying!"
The men who went down that dreadful day.

The men who were so brave,
Were like damsels in distress that couldn't be saved.
Die-Day on Iwo Jima they called it,
The medics didn't have left one medical kit,
Most just started a fit.
The men who went down that dreadful day.

Some remember that day,
Like it was just yesterday,
Some remember it was horrible,
Expressed through this memorial,
Of the men who went down that dreadful day.

Giorgio Laudati, Grade 7

The Chair

During the day, he holds you up,
But most of the time you don't notice him.
When you sit down, he is always happy and sturdy.
He is excited and warm.
If you listen closely, sometimes you can hear his heartbeat.
But when the day is done, he is not so perky. He always gets lonely.
He sighs and cries but no one listens.
Soon he forgets and falls asleep.
But when the day comes back he is alive again.
Someone sits and makes him happy.
If only we understood the life of a chair.

Hannah Joseph, Grade 7

Silent in the Night

Flowers bloom in the dark of the night.
Birds screech while in flight.
Neighborhoods sleep.
The world is silent, not a peep.

Cats run through streets,
Dogs close on their heels.
The dogs hoping to get a little treat.
The cats refusing to give them a meal.

The world is lit by moonlight,
Giving the sun a time to rest.
Families sleep in this night,
With their blankets tucked tight up on their chest.

Soon the sun will rise.
The sun will rise and the people will open their eyes.
The night will be over.
And the world will no longer be silent

Caitlin Walsh, Grade 7

Fishing

School is over;
It's a warm summer's day
By the shore I see some fish cover,
There's no where I would rather be than in this bay
This is great!
Every time I say I love to fish, my sister gives me a weird look,
But she still helps me find worms for bait,
Which I set on the hook

My hook is ready;
I cast it out
I try my best to keep my pole steady;
All of a sudden I see a lake trout —
It takes the bait! I set the hook;
The line is as tight as a bolted seal
My pole shook;
I kept it still like welded steel
I have landed the fish!
This will make a great dish

Jason Taylor, Grade 8

Through the Forest

I am walking through the forest
past all of the lakes and trees
as I hear the crumble of
the autumn leaves beneath my feet,
I follow the path oh where oh
where will it take me, I must wonder
as I travel more and more
seeing the animals, that are amazing
and talented, hoping I don't get lost.
I take a long pause to see
My surroundings, but they all went away in reality.

Weston Jones, Grade 7

Freedom Has a Price

When I walk outside
I think of all the people
Who fought through their lives
And for those who have died
For us
To live
In the United States
Some people have gone places they hate
But still they stay
So we can be called

Citizens of America!
Christine Griggs, Grade 7

Baseball

I step to the plate
My team watching nervously
The sound of the ball hitting the bat

The crowd cheering
I run to first base
My team yelling and jumping

I hit the game-winning run
And running back to the dugout
I realize
This is why I love baseball.
Mark Fry, Grade 8

Cancer Cells

C ancer
A ttacking
N erveless helpless bodies
C an
E rupt
R uining lives

C anceling
E verything
L iving
L ife
S trives for
Amelia Sayer, Grade 7

Blank

I sit and stare
At the bare
Paper in front of me
I try to think of a word to write
With all my might

I try to use my imagination
But nothing seems to come
So I guess I'll sit here and wait
Until I can think straight
Jenna Ebbers, Grade 7

Motherly Care

Mothers are always there
For you or others —
Be it a helping hand
Or a loving hug.

They give hope and comfort,
Encouragement and joy,
As well as criticism if needed —
Be it brutally frank or tenderly truthful.

My Mother is
Strong and courageous,
Caring and loving,
Among all things, she is the one who does all of these things the most.
Jeremy Kolasa, Grade 8

What Is the Meaning of Family to Me

Family is not about if you are related to them by blood
It is about how much you love them and how much they love you back
Family is a group of people that stick by your side during hard times and good times
Family sets a foundation of morals and values
They help you learn what's right from wrong
Sometimes they let you learn the hard way so that you won't fall down in life
Families are an unit that share feelings of love, happiness, sadness, and anger
Most of us hold on to the feeling of love and happiness
You can feel their love for you by everything they do
When you are sad, they lift up your spirit
When you are mad, they leave you alone to calm yourself
When you are happy, they share it with you
When you are alone, they stay by your side to you let you know that they are there for you
For me Family is a place where I find love, happiness, and peace.
Preethi D'souza, Grade 9

The Violin

Life is like a violin.
One day, you can play the most inspirational song,
    lifting your heart,
    lifting you soul.
The fiddle make a graceful, smooth sound as you slide into third position.
In an eighth rest, you've changed keys,
    drowning your spirits,
    drowning the joyful memories.
The bow slides slowly across b flat, vibrato making the tone even
    more eerie.

The strings will snap, the bridge will fall.
But the fiddler keeps on fiddling,
    and the audience keeps on listening.

Lauren Raimbault, Grade 7

On the Mountain

In the winter on a mountain, you can hear the gentle wind follow the storm.
As the butterflies erase danger, the frost is dissolving off an evergreen tree.
When it's dark, you build a fire.
Time is honored with giggles, love and smiles to mask the sour misery you endure.
Morgyn Bordwell, Grade 8

Poetry/Snowflake

Poetry
Is like
A snowflake
Which flies
With the wind
Just like a poem
In your head
Like all snowflakes
Are different so are
All poems

Eric Diaz, Grade 7

My Sports

B eat the other team we're playing
A ttack the basket with the ball
S eventeen is my jersey number
K nock the other players out
E ngage into the game
T all people blocking my shots
B ruises are battle scars
A ttendance is important to the game
L ots of pressure at the last second
L ast game of the year was the best

Joslyn Ketzner, Grade 7

Soldiers

S tupendous things you do
O bstacles you have been through
L ove of the United States
D angerous duties you did
I ncredible fears you have faced
E xcitment that you bring
R ough things that have happened
S ongs we sing to you

Thank you for serving our country!

Alleya Williams, Grade 7

Team

B ecause of
A ll the hard work and
S weat, each and every
K id has managed to
E xceed all expectations others have,
T he team always stays humble and
B attles through every obstacle that
A ppears in its way; the feeling of
L osing only builds character and
L eads each player to the path of greatness

Cherokee LeBeau, Grade 8

Leaves

Green leaves dance on wind
Skittering in bright colors
Across large blue skies

Hunter Hawk, Grade 8

Out Foxed

Once upon an even' weary, while I brooded, dark and dreary,
Over many a faint and unbiased newscast of invented lore,
While I listened, TV granting, suddenly there came a panting
As of someone flustered ranting, ranting 'bout the Afghan war.
"It's all Obama's fault," Sean swore,
"Only his, and nothing more."

Ah, distinctly Megyn said it, "health care kills," and to her credit,
She blamed Obama for all who died from lack of insurance too.
"The blame lies with the Femi-Nazi — Hill'ry Clinton caused Bengazi!"
To a rapt'rous Teapot Party, Bill O'Reiley next did moo,
Having scored a broadcast coup,
Never was there such ado.

Oh, the sly FOX, never caring, ever airing, always blaring,
On the flickering flat screen just inside my safe room's door,
How it's eyes have all the seeing of a daemon that is dreaming
Of foul lies for'er misleading, throws it's shadows 'cross my floor,
Shadows one dare not ignore —
'Tis just the "truth" — and nothing more.

Thomas Hosford, Grade 9

An Unexpected Experience

Change, it's something we all experience.
From age, seasons, height, lifestyle, even our appearance.
Change, is to create a difference.
It might scare you a whole lot, or reel you in with interest.
Change, a six letter word but a variety of ways to explain.
Going from sick to healthy or from modest to vain.
It can give us a different point of view,
Or it can even give us a life lesson.
At the end of the day, change will lead us to the right direction.
To think change is coming, sounds pretty frightening.
But change is good, it's interesting, it's quite enlightening.
To change for good, will make a better place.
To change for bad, is something we shouldn't embrace.
Change, is to be refined.
In many ways, it will help you stay unconfined.
Change, is to revise.
Don't think of change as something alarming, because it's a life prize.
Change, don't think of it as a disaster.
Because I promise,
When Change comes, you will live happily ever after.

Agustin Martinez, Grade 9

Winter Day

Waking up on winter day is always fun
Kids think snow or snow days, adults think no work
Drinking hot chocolate and spending time with the family
Christmas Day, waking up feeling the joy in the air
Everybody smiling, laughing
Family not nagging or arguing
Being thankful,
Surprised by seeing presents that you hopefully haven't already seen yet
Please winter stay here and don't go away

Anna Wilson, Grade 9

Forgot

I walk into my room
I feel like you're still here.
"Hey! Where are you hiding?"
My laugh rings loud and clear
I forgot.
You're dead.
I sit down on my bed
Horrible thoughts run through my head
Why did you leave?
Did you forget, too?
I'm still here. Waiting for you.
I still hear you running in the halls
Your silly phone calls
I'm trembling — shivering in this pit
It's dark in here…
You left me behind. But friends shouldn't do that.
We stick together like glue.
But you dried up and fell off. Like a leaf off a tree.
My falling words come down with me.
Join me.
I don't have anywhere to be.

Mercedes Maglio, Grade 8

Cloey

Love has caught my heart for good,
I know it's love because my heart burns,
Love is the feeling I get when we hold hands,
I love her more than anything in the world,
I'm happy and proud to say I'm dating her,
She's so many things; smart, beautiful, nice,
Her eyes sparkle better than the stars,
I think about her all the time,
I want to be her everything,
When I'm with her nothing else matters,
She has what I need,
Every time I look at her,
And our eyes meet it's like the world stops,
Whenever we're together I don't want it to end,
I'm not complete without her,
If I didn't have her the world wouldn't make sense,
Her eyes sparkle better than any diamond on the planet,
My heart aches for our lips to join together,
Everyone has something to live for,
My thing is her,
I love her, and forever will

Kezery LeBeau, Grade 8

Night Hike

When I'm on a night hike we turn off the flash lights.
We don't stir, or move, or make a sound.
We listen to animals moving about.
We listen to mice scurry.
Then of a joke, someone makes a coyote howl.
Then a coyote returns the message.
We leave in a hurry.

Aidan Witthoff, Grade 8

Mirrors

She stares at herself in the mirror on the wall.
Long dark hair and stormy gray eyes.
But her reflection doesn't tell her story at all.
Her face doesn't give away her troubles.

She's never thought herself beautiful.
She's never been clever, or athletic.
Her dark hair doesn't seem impressive, even dull.
Defeated gray eyes meet the mirror girl's.

And deep inside, sparks begin among the coal.
Because she doesn't need beauty, she has a beautiful soul.

Natalie Ruckman, Grade 7

The Concrete Ocean

And so we fell straight into a concrete ocean
And sunk to the bottom of a cement sea
And the realization took a moment to sink in
There was nobody else to care about me
Because as you swam away and left me to drown
You took my life jacket and went on your way
Left me to be bait for sunken-eyed sharks
As you went towards an island of ethereal mermaids
I sunk to the bottom of a titanium bay
For I couldn't swim without your help
You went happily on your own way
And took with you my severed heart

Olivia Popovich, Grade 7

Basketball

Basketball season is right around the corner.
Basketball is one of my favorite sports.
On my team I am the point guard.
I dribble up and down the court,
I shoot and make a lot of three-pointers,
And I pass the ball and get the assist.
The feeling when you make a basket is so amazing.
It makes you feel like you are the star of the game.
Even though the practices are very hard,
It is all worth it when you can pull off the win!
I am as good as Lebron James at basketball.
Basketball season is the best time of the whole year!

Hunter Breske, Grade 8

Welcome to the Good Life

Welcome to the good life
Where tall corn grows
And cattle roam fields
The ground is vast and brown
But the sun will smile down at you
Giving you hope and happiness
Surrounded by dry towns
You will still feel welcome
Ready to take on what this state will throw at you
This is Nebraska. This is home.

Ava Macke, Grade 8

After All*

You can trash talk me and ignore me,
and exclude me from you're conversations.
You can make sure my heart breaks apart,
Hearts will mend after all.

You can yell out all of your hatred,
Throw all of your words into my face.
You can scream at me until you're gasping for air,
Words are just sounds after all.

You can punch me and pummel me,
Kick me and shove me to the ground.
You can torture me until I beg for mercy,
Wounds will heal after all.

You can do everything in your power,
To make sure my life will be miserable,
To make sure I cry myself to sleep,
Tears will dry up after all.

You will do anything you can,
To try to break me,
But you don't understand, you can't.
You are just one person,
After all.

Prachi Patil, Grade 7
*Dedicated to all victims of any type of bullying. Stand tall, Keep your head held up high,
and remember that there are more good people in this world than bad.

Perfect Imperfections

In the deepest corners of her heart
Lie the secrets she never told
The thoughts that crossed her mind
But were unacceptable to the people that she loves.

Within her biggest smiles
Lie the biggest heartbreaks of her life
The deepest pain she ever felt
But no one knows about it.

Behind her laughter
Lie all of the lies she has ever told
The things that she's done and said
Just to protect herself from the cruel world that she has to call home.

Underneath the long pants
Lie the scars that are almost impossible to hide and impossible to bear
Lie her weakest, most vulnerable moments
All because of the girls that thought they were being funny.

Underneath the perfect girl that everyone else knows,
Lies my best friend.
The girl that makes mistakes, but still has the most genuine heart of anyone that anyone has ever met
But most of all,
Lies the perfect girl, all because of her imperfections.

Kaylee Ramaeker, Grade 8

If Only I Were Cinderella

If I were the one to do the chores,
Would you think of me the same?
If I were the one to sweep the floors,
Would I be the one you were to blame?

Could I have a fairy Godmother?
And go to the ball for my wish to come true.
Or would I have a controlling stepmother,
Betray her and lose my shoe.

Would you try to find whose foot fits the shoe?
And search all day and night for me.
Would my evil stepmother have a clue?
And learn I am the girl, your mystery.

Would I hear your presence at my home?
Would I open the door and run to you?
Or would my stepmother trap me in a dome,
So I could not try to fit my foot in the shoe.

The shoe fits it's true.
You'll be my favorite "fella,"
I know this came out of the blue,
If only I were Cinderella.

Allison Arview, Grade 8

Cinderella

Oh, Cinderella, poor lil' girl
Her only friends; mice
Mean sisters and their dress that twirls
They can never be nice

She's stuck sweeping by the fireplace
Sisters are getting fit
To go to the ball; in their case
Nothing but screaming fits

Hopes; she can make a dress in time
Oh my, look, she sure can
She's happy as if she found a dime
Until her sisters came.

Boom! Crash! They destroyed her masterpiece.
No, ball for her anymore
Unless magic can some how cease
Gee, it's fairy godmother

She makes it; but has till midnight
A dance with the prince fun!
The clock strikes, and her shoes not tight
They then get married; done!

MiaKayla Koerber, Grade 8

Malaysian Flight 370

"Good night Malaysian three-seven-zero," they say
Then fly for hours more,
"Oh, God, what's going on?" we scream,
We're frightened to the core.

We don't know why the pilot did it,
Perhaps he wasn't sane,
Either way, it won't mean much,
For the radar lost our plane.

The air smells hot, like burning metal,
We dive straight to the ground,
The lights, they flicker, on and off,
There's screaming all around.

I clutch the seat, I beg for life,
I curse, I scream, I yell,
We fall and fall, 'till no one's left,
'Till no one's left to tell.

"Good night Malaysian three-seven-zero,"
We know we're gonna die,
We hit the water, sink way down,
Where no one hears us cry.

Meghan Bloom, Grade 8

Cherokee Rose

Blistered feet brand foreign soil
Obsidian hair whips faces of toil
Moccasins long since broken
Cries of protest yearn, unspoken

Ladled from their "Melting Pot"
Poured out, left, abandoned, forgot
Nu na da ul tsun yi
Bearing shadows of ignominy

Silt and clay so lachrymose
Lamenting the moribund Cherokee Rose
White petals plucked from xanthous core
Sorrow-soured song twangs a dissonant chord

Crimson tears stain crooked ambition
Silenced horror stays unwritten
Is deliverance still worth fighting for
When your home isn't yours anymore?

Herded like cattle, spurred by pain
Deemed benighted, savage, unfit to reign
Demagogues crying, Manifest Destiny!
Sealing our sepulcher in the Land of the Free

Sydney Kohl, Grade 7

A Noteworthy Memory

An icy gush of wind sweeps through me.
Hundreds of people in the crowd are silently judging the quality of our music.
My heart pounds as I lift my metallic horn into the air, the crisp sound echoing through the room.
Her baton begins to rise and move swiftly through the air, creating patterns in the sky.

An icy gush of wind sweeps through me.
Trumpets have started blasting, trombones are blaring, and drums are booming. Our first piece has begun and I feel the adrenaline pumping through my veins. It is now or never, time to come in.

The sound carried through the auditorium filing the audiences' hearts with pure joy.
The sound of the saxophones warmed their hearts.
The music danced across the walls, giving off a feeling of radiance.
It was our solo and we exceeded the limits.

The crowd rose to their feet and proudly gave us a standing ovation.
Their faces were contorted with happiness and emotion;
For their children had just performed with the best players at the school.
The symphonic band ruled all.

An icy gush of wind sweeps through me.
It gives me goose bumps and sends feelings of relief, excitement, and sadness through me. My first concert in Symphonic Band was a success! The memory will last with me forever; I was recognized as one of the best musicians and given a throne.

Emma Dickenscheidt, Grade 7

Me

I can be shy yet out going.
You may see me smiling like a crazy person or keeping to myself in a crowd I don't know.
My hair is kind of boring and plain because it's straight and brown.
I'm a kind of short but I try not to worry about it.
I usually don't wear anything very extravagant or interesting mostly just sweaters and leggings.
Sometimes I like to dress up but other times I feel too weird.
I love my family very much, they help me get through a lot and go through a lot with me as well.
They are crazy and fun to be around, I don't know what I could do without them.
I have two sisters and a brother; they are just like my best friends. Sometimes, well a lot we fight
and argue but I think it's just because we are so alike.
My friends are like my other family, they are hilarious and helpful. We share plenty of laughs and
secrets, they are like my other half.
I have a kitten and a dog and I love them very much; they are so cute and funny.
They can cheer me up almost all the time. I really like shoes; they are so fascinating to me.
Even though my shoe collection mostly consists of converse and boots sometimes I like wearing heels.
School isn't as easy for me as it is for other people.
Even though sometimes I struggle I still try to push through and try harder.
Summer is my favorite time of the year because, I can stay up as long as I want and then sleep as
long as I want.
I can go to friend's houses and not have to worry about school or home work.
You may think that my life is simple or even boring but to me it is anything I could ever ask for.

Sara Swank, Grade 8

Raindrops

Rain is necessary for life.
Without it there would be no puddles for the little kids to jump into.
There wouldn't be spring it would only be a season that it could be snowing or it could be warm.
With out it, it would be as dry as a desert.
We wouldn't be able to watch two rain drops race down the window.

Guillermo Angel, Grade 7

Where Are You?*

I don't know how long I've been here trying not to bite my nails
An hour? Two?
I lost track of time, but not of the little sailboat on the horizon
Getting bigger and bigger, and the clouds getting darker and darker
I hope you make it back home before these clouds burst into booming thunder and crashing rain
Where are you?

My legs hurt from standing and pacing
So now I'm sitting on the yellow grass and the sand and dirt, mostly dirt
My pretty little blue dress that you loved so much is ruined
Where are you?

Thunder crashes and a bright crack in the sky follows
Rain is tickling my skin
Where are you?

The little sailboat is now docking
There you are, my husband

Michelle Soltys, Grade 8
*Based on the work "Girl Seated by the Sea" by Robert Earle Henri

Just Because I'm a Cop's Daughter

Just because I'm a cop's daughter
Doesn't mean I'm good
Doesn't mean I'm the best kid in the world
And doesn't mean I'm perfect all the time
Just because I'm a cop's daughter
Doesn't mean I'm a perfect little angel
Doesn't mean I'm not allowed to do fun things
Doesn't mean I'm a person who doesn't have fun
Just because I'm a cop's daughter
Doesn't mean I'm a goody two-shoes
Doesn't mean I'm against all bad
Doesn't mean I'm locked up at home every night for my life.
Just because I'm a cop's daughter
Why do I have to stay away from certain people?
Why do I check my surroundings at all times?
What's so bad about being a cop's daughter?
I'll tell you.
It's not being sure you will see your dad the next night because he might have been shot and killed.

Ricki Hickstein, Grade 8

Finding the Light

Lightning crackles overhead, and I snuggle deeper into my bed.
Thunder will accompany it soon, echoing throughout my room.
Rain will splash upon the ground, making a distinct dripping sound.
Clouds will block out the light, making it seem like it is night.
It may seem like a dreary place to be, but after the storm you'll have to see.
When the sun parts through the cloud, quietness will drown out the loud.
Sounds of nature will once again fill the air, birds chirping noisily without a care.
You will bolt out of bed so you can play, in the streaming sunlight you wish you could stay.
Everything that you might view as bad or frightening, like thunder booming and crackling lightning.
Always must come to an end, and from its remains something new will begin again.
Everything has more than one side, you'll just have to see where it takes you and enjoy the ride.
Even if something like a thunderstorm makes it look like night, glance between the clouds and bask in the light.

Kara Prorok, Grade 8

Fear

Fear is like butterflies in your stomach.
Fear is like your heart beating so fast
 it's like a butterfly's wings flapping.
Fear is like a scream that startled you.
Fear is like when you throw a ball
 into the woods and birds fly away.
Fear is when the phone rings and no one comes
 home.

Lynly Bridwell, Grade 8

You Are

You are my new kitten,
Your soft, fluffy fur, I can tell it's you from a distance,
Your black caramel fur,
You are small but cute.
You are always scared, but one of a kind,
Your soft purring soothes my being,
You are rare amongst them all for no one can replace you,
You are my new baby kitten.

Jennifer Paz, Grade 7

Summer Sounds

In summer I hear
Cheering for me
At the softball tournament

In summer all I hear is balls hitting the mitt
Balls hitting the bats
Balls hitting the fence
Woah there goes a HOME RUN!

Kristina Adams, Grade 8

Backwards

I cooked my teeth and brushed my toast
I chewed my sucker and licked my roast

I answered my sock and put on my phone
I sat on my flower and smelled my throne

I blew my nose in my desk and sat in my Kleenex
I flew like a pizza and ordered a phoenix

Zachary Zimmer, Grade 7

Smiles

Jumping around from face-to-face
Smiles brighten everyone's day
Bringing happiness to every place
Jumping around from face-to-face
The joy inside, let out of its case
Letting people know you enjoy what they say
Jumping around from face-to-face
Smiles brighten everyone's day

Alyssa Voytko, Grade 8

Getting Ready for School

At the crack of dawn, I try to get ready
I rush to get my lunch bag so I won't be late
But then I remember to brush my teeth, steady
At the crack of dawn, I try to get ready
I sing a song and feel very heady
I pack my bag, as if it were a crate
At the crack of dawn, I try to get ready
I rush to get my lunch bag so I won't be late

Dawid Worwa, Grade 8

Freedom

We honor the flag of the United States
To remember our veterans who gave us freedom
The veterans who risked their lives for us
Our brave soldiers are sacrificing their lives for us
As kids are at home enjoying their freedom
Some of our soldiers are dying to defend our country
We thank our veterans for giving the United States
Freedom

Alyssa Rosborough, Grade 7

Many Lives

The horse gallops wild and free in a field full of blossoms.
While a cow looks, searching for her lost calf in a wide open field.
The tiger growls in a dark forest stalking to it's prey.
While a little mouse squeaks in fear of being found.
A stray cat meows softly; a sod purr from a lion.
While a lynx roars; telling the kingdom who's boss.
A person reads a book as if it were nothing.
While a young boy writes a circle on a clean-cut piece of paper.

Julie Davis, Grade 8

Darkness

Darkness is a vast world with fear locked inside
It holds all bad memories.
When you sleep it releases horrible dreams.
We can learn to fight Darkness
But after the battle we must learn to use its strengths and powers.
Can we use it for good or for bad?
It's society's choice
OR maybe you can choose for yourself!

Ayanna McCoy, Grade 7

Him

All of these thoughts run through my head
I miss him so dearly, that my heart aches
So many words were forgotten, or left unsaid
All of these thoughts run through my head
In the mornings, it's hard to get out of bed
Why can't he come back, for goodness sake
All of these thoughts run through my head
I miss him so dearly, that my heart aches

Aubrey Frederici, Grade 8

Poetry

Poetry is Poetry,
There is truly nothing equivalent to
Words mixed together forming a
Group of unity,
Poetry is Poetry.

Poetry is Poetry,
Nothing can't be poetry.
It is dangerous, yet harmless,
Calm, yet ferocious,
And silly, yet meaningful,
Poetry is Poetry.

Annika Graber, Grade 7

Happy Summer Time

H appy every day during summer
A lways outside
P laying different things
P raying for no rain
Y ou always are doing something

S unny every day
U ntil it rains
M e and others are glad it's sunny now
M ight be a good day
E veryone is happy
R eady for our summer

Latrell Vance, Grade 8

Life

Life is a confusing rollercoaster
Full of ups and downs.
I have spent my ride
Wondering its meaning.
What's my goal, what's my purpose?
Am I supposed to just exist
Or really be something?
But then I have to realize
It's all up to me
What I want to do.
I decide my fate
And my fate decides me.

Quinn Mullally, Grade 7

Ode to Bacon

Look at the freshly cooked bacon.
Oh, how long I've been waitin'.

Oh, how it sizzles in the pan,
And how it pops, oh man.

You can eat it all day,
Any time of the day.

Oh, how I love to eat bacon.

Gracie Young, Grade 7

Monsters

Someone turning into a monster,
Not knowing what they are.
Something everyone goes through,
But people rather come to accept it then deny who they are.

They unravel,
And become who they said they never would be.
But in order to survive in the world,
You need to become what everyone else sees.

But it's real when you play the role of a monster,
Just to keep others happy.
Because who's really happy?
The people who you wish to inspire or turning into the ones that inspire you?

Viviana Vazquez, Grade 8

The Pencil

The pencil
Painstakingly paints the paper
Constructed of pine
And could possibly be painted purple and is partially permeated with graphite
Pushing down places particles of silver
That precisely puts down parts of a personal parable
Or a public paper used to persuade people to purchase
A partially pointy yet perfect Peruvian pencil
That the police could use
To prosecute protesters protesting medical practice on penguins and pink parrots
After perceiving this poem that is permeated with propaganda
You can see that the pencil
Is possibly the most practical piece of processed wood
Ever

Joey O'Connell, Grade 8

Images*

The boy is dressed in his nicest clothes.
He wears a sea blue and snow white striped sweater,
Covered by a coat as blue as new jeans.

He sits politely in an old wooden chair,
Looking forward with ice blue eyes.
His hair is combed nicely to the side,
And cheeks red like a tomato.

His sand colored hands are connected,
Held one over the other.
The blue cabinets behind him,
Remind me of the light blue summer sky.

Francesco Campanella, Grade 8
*Inspired by "The Boy in the Striped Sweater" by Amedeo Modigliani

Has Winter Ended?

Green grass and new leaves like no other before.
Lots of rain and quick puffs of fresh air.
Is it here? Is it finally here? The time, has it come?
The thing I've been wanting for all of these cold winter days has come.

Ethan Olson, Grade 7

The Olympics

Whenever I watch the Olympics,
After I have watched the opening ceremony,
Before I can even move,
Where I finally see,
The U.S. hockey team score.

As much as I enjoy watching,
Even though the U.S.A. is not winning,
Until we come together,
In order that we win as a team,
We will always be cheering

Whatever the medal place might be,
When one of us wins gold,
Even if we might not have a chance,
As long as we cheer on,
We will give the strength to the U.S. Olympians.

Jayden Reed, Grade 8

My Night Family

Why is the night feared so
The moon has been my companion since forever
The others do not seem to know
That the stars have left me never

We cannot see in the dark
Thus many scare
Because they can't see their mark
They cannot see what's there

The moon has been my mother
With me at all times
And the stars have been my brothers
Ready to come help at the drop of a dime

In the dark I can see
Family love for the first time shown to me

Molly Nelson, Grade 8

Votre Jour

For today is the day that you will live and be glad in it.
For today is the day you will seize, and see it is amazing.
Your time on this earth is not long, but very valuable.
Living this time on earth is not easy, but watch as it unfolds.
You're days on this earth are a treasure to be found,
Or a mountain to be climbed,
Or a creature to be discovered.

Now is the time you need to understand your precious time.
Now is the time to want to live.
Now is the time to understand your time to live is slight.
Now seize your precious time on this terrestrial planet.
Fill your life with happiness.
Surround yourself with wonderful things.
Your time will come!

Gregg LePlatt, Grade 7

The Sunset

The sunset is dim but yet
luminous enough to light up the world.
The sunset is the sensation
of warmth and coolness to my skin.
The sunset is the feeling
of calmness and the tranquility within.
The sunset is saying farewell
to the earth and kissing it goodbye while it leaves.
The sunset is glorious orange
colored light, lighting upon us and lighting the way.
The sunset is dim but yet
luminous enough to light up the world.

Alan Rodriguez, Grade 7

Black and White Keys

Like day and night, the black and white keys
Let off musical sounds;
I play them with ease, For all around.
Playing every day for family and friends,
Makes me think I will never end.

As I practice each night
Playing lots of songs,
I try with great might,
With the help of my mom.
I love to play; I must stay so.
This passion I have, is playing the piano.

Megan Goodhue, Grade 8

Friends Forever

When you're with your friends you laugh, cry, smile, fight, joke.
You can't live without each other.
You trust each other with your darkest secrets,
Share the funniest memories,
Never leave their side, you're friends forever.
You tell each other your problems,
Help each other out, laugh at your funny videos.
You're friends forever.
You grow up together, watch each other change,
Keep each other from doing something stupid,
And do stupid things together.
You're friends forever.

Tala Barnett, Grade 8

Treat Me Normal

Just because I don't have a good Dad,
Doesn't mean I am not smart.
Doesn't mean I will be like him.
Still care for me even though he didn't
Just because I don't have a good Dad,
It doesn't mean I will treat people like he did.
It doesn't give you the right to make fun of me.
It doesn't stop me from being who I am.
Just because I don't have a good dad,
Please treat me like a normal person.

Cordie Kelly, Grade 7

Winter Weather

W atch the snow come falling down.
I can't believe it's coming again.
N o sun, just snow and sleet.
T ry to stay inside if you can.
E ven though you need something, it's best not to leave.
R ed lights are flashing everywhere!

W atch out! The cars are sliding!
E very car is off the road.
A mbulances are all over the place!
T here is so much snow you can barely see.
H ey the sun is coming out!
E veryone thinks it's over…
R ethink, because it's just the beginning.

Katie Cochran, Grade 8

Thoughts from My Sole

The darkness fades as I'm lifted to the light.
Then a giant squeezes into me;
Pulled and stretched, she yanks me tight,
Knotted before we are set free.
A sharp noise causes fear as I quake;
Then I see others like me are all around.
I start to wonder what this will take,
While being pressed into the ground.
The hard terrain is smashing at my sole,
And there is crunching under me.
I wonder how much longer I can bear this toll;
Moving so fast, I feel like I'm free.
Suddenly with one last smash, I know I'll be fine,
For I'm the first cross country shoe across the finish line.

Justine Rosburg, Grade 8

My Great Uncle

My great uncle fought in World War II
He fought for our red, white, and blue
Returning home with a crutch at his side
Though they tried, they could not break his pride

My great uncle's name is now on the wall
Because of him, I stand tall
I can't imaging how scared he was to go
On his way home, did he know he was a hero?

Every veteran should feel proud
For all of you, we cheer real loud
I wonder if the sky would be so bright
If you weren't so very brave to fight

Tabitha Brown, Grade 7

Tears

They don't understand why I cry.
It's not because I'm a baby, or sad.
It's because I've been too strong for too long.
I cry because I'm broken, afraid, frustrated, and angry.

Madelyn Calease, Grade 9

Forgive You Not

You wonder why I do not sleep,
Curious as to why I grow suspicious.
It's because my own heart I wish to keep
After what you did to me, I do not believe in us.
You broke my soul,
You ripped it to shreds.
Your hate finally began to take its toll.
It pulled me apart until I had nothing but threads.
You ask why I do not forgive,
You act as though you know nothing.
The one thing I will never understand is your motive.
Your name hurts my tongue and leaves a sting,
You're the one thing I try not to relive
Because you're the one thing I cannot forgive.

Kristen Dethloff, Grade 9

Rematch

Shall I compare thee to a summer's day?
Perhaps an automobile would be more accurate.
Both belch black smoke when not okay,
and, well maintained, the latter is more temperate.
For love, a cat shall make me whole,
and though thee should outlast it,
the feline's speech may soothe my soul,
where thy complaints shall blast it.
Let this poem tell, I pray,
that with thee, I am done.
To seek to best a summer's day —
of creatures vainer there are none.
So give me cat and automobile, and free me from thy gaze —
and let me trust instead my happiness to summer's faithful rays.

Adam Quinn, Grade 9

El Santiago Bernabéu

What is there to say about this fantastic stadium?
Home to the best football club in the world.
In the central of Madrid
It stands out of every other stadium.
With its astonishing lights
And buzzing atmosphere
It's an amazing spectacle to be a part of.
Every person in the world would want to be there.
This stadium seats almost 82,000 people.
All of them came for a reason.
To watch a beautiful game of football
And also to be in the home of every Madridista.
Home to Los Blancos
This is el Santiago Bernabéu.

Abel Naranjo, Grade 7

Missing You

We walk through the halls like we've never met in our lives.
Broken promises and unwanted goodbyes.
I wish you could see,
How much you meant to me.

Taylor McPhail, Grade 8

The Farmers Theory

When you rest, a farmers hand burns
the heat pressing the close of the day
still working when the sun starts its rays
when you double in laughter, hurting another
not knowing the knowledge you could gather
needing to know what really matters
do you not see his rough hands?
do you see the defeat?
do you not see the light in his eyes?
do you see the patience?
do you not see the good in his heart?
do you see the care!
when the sun sets on a beautiful view
a world of fire and destruction moving out of sight
the man covered in piercing and tattoos
saves a child from fright
how strange it is, for one to be another
when it is not that at all
its an idea, that its not that at all
The Farmers Theory

Jennica Boardman, Grade 9

My Daughter Bess

My Daughter Bess
Turned into a bloody mess
She was me
From Blood to flesh

The world is cruel
You cannot play it for a fool
Or else you will become
A bloody mess, just like my daughter Bess

The king was cruel
His men took her life
Putting a musket, pointed at her chest
Why would they do this, to my sweet little Bess?

No one plays fair
I wonder if there is such a thing as share
Who caused them to go here
I shall never know
I shall never know…

Joey Cermak, Grade 7

The Hurricane

she started just a spout
but slowly she got bigger
roaring destroying everything in sight
she dashed through cities leaving
only little left
she is nothing but death
they still have not repaired what she has done
there are huge buildings torn to shreds
but all we can do is pack what's left and move on

Tony Cotton, Grade 7

Traveling the World

There are many different places I'd like to see.
At the top of my list is beautiful Hawaii.

Glaciers, whales, polar bears, and snow,
Alaska is another place I'd like to go.

Thinking of hot sun and sand between my toes,
Makes me want to go to Mexico.

Shamrocks, castles, and fields of green,
Ireland is where I'll go in between.

Prince William and his wife, Kate,
Will surely make London, England great!

Fashion, models, and the Eiffel Tower,
Makes Paris, France a place to scour.

Artwork, museums, churches, and fine food,
Rome, Italy will certainly brighten my mood.

Germany is where my family's from,
Beer, brats, and sauerkraut, yum!

Egypt is also on my list.
Pyramids with mummies won't be missed!

Parthenon, Acropolis, and the city of Athens,
This is where it all happens

Katie Hemmersbach, Grade 7

Time

It starts in the womb, where we wait nine months
for a miracle that only happens once
we waited to be born, only to wait
for years until we all have to face our fate
Time is something that is not worth to waste

The early years we learn the basics to life
without these teachings we couldn't suffice
all the sounds, shapes, and colors we need to know
these are the proudest things kids want to show
These are the times where we think life is nice

Then it is almost time to go away
the time that you put into your work all day
you won't need it now for time is gone down
your off to a great place, no need to frown
You haven't wasted your life here anyway

The time has come, go back to the Father
the life that you lived hasn't been a bother
back to where you came form, a better place
you lived a good life, so be filled with God's grace
Your new life; be blessed with holy water

Charlie Odom, Grade 8

Turtles

Their shells as strong as gold,
Which I do not wish to melt.
The click clack of its claws on the rocks,
Searching for flies, fleas or fire bugs,
The turtle lurking in the dark waiting to devour its next meal.

When will spring return?
No one knows as the turtle slowly progresses forward.
Wishing time went faster than the turtle,
Making things harder and harder to get done,
Will it ever reach this far?

Red, blue, green, or orange,
The shell of a turtle as mysterious as the aurora borealis.
How will the turtle ever be forgiven?
As it moves forward without the slightest of knowledge,
Waiting for the day the turtle arrives.

Sophia Valverde, Grade 9

To Just Be

I miss when dreams could not fit in a box
When I swore I would be a superstar
For birthdays all I asked for was a fox
And wanted in my room a stocked snack bar

I miss when front doors always got knocked on
When friends stopped by without a plan to play
We would run and run free on the front lawn
Good times measured by how we spent the day

I miss when we were knights, and queens, and kings
When it wasn't silly to mess around
Being "fake" wasn't really a bad thing
And from a blanket I could make a gown

I long for times when as a child free
My only job was simply to just be

Claire Watson, Grade 9

Just Me

I am creative
I value the creator in me
I write what I feel and believe
I trust my instincts
I honor the people who care
I give voice to what is right
I write and just get boisterous
I am always getting inspired
I make a home out of nature
I hold the outcomes in high self esteem
I listen to what will help me
I turn a paragraph into a detailed book
I can be very inspirational
I write a lot of alliteration
I turn simple writing in an adventurous journey

Jada Tate, Grade 8

We Were There

We were there,
When he-who-must-not-be-named
gave you the scar that will
forever mark you as "the boy who lived,"
when you defeated Tom Riddle for the 2nd time
and realized you spoke parseltongue,
when you found your godfather; your only relative,
when you saw Voldemort return

We were there,
when you fought the Death Eaters alongside the Order
and saw your only relative die,
when you saw the only person Voldemort feared
and you started your hunt for the remaining horcruxes,
when you found the rest of the horcruxes
and realized Snape was only protecting you,
when you defeated the most feared wizard of all time.

Alejandra Morales, Grade 8

The Stars

A truck bed full of friends
A broken dream,
The forgotten past returns
A single memory…
My mind turns to the future

The darkness creeping in
Falling with the sun,
I feel like floating away
The whoo of an owl in the distance
The grass swaying on the hilltops

A brisk wind rolls in from the east
Then it goes dark and the stars come out
One, two, three, and then a whole skyful
A story written in the stars as words in a book
Slowly, becoming aware of the reality of life

Brody Voichoski, Grade 9

I Am an Actress

I am an actress.
I live my life through the stories of others.
Our lives merge until I become one with them.
I become that person.

I am an actress.
I speak the words that they are thinking.
I see through their eyes.
I share their emotions; one heart, one mind.

I am an actress.
I live in another world; nothing is the same.
Each time, each character, is different.
I have new friends, new conflicts, new opportunities.
I am an actress.

Karlie Sines, Grade 9

The Tears of Winter

The Summer is a time to laugh and to play
The Summer is the time when all my leaves stay
My beautiful leaves, so colorful and bright
Cannot stay without the sun's light
The pretty blue flowers blossoming on me
They glisten so bright like the sparkling sea
My firm and long branches are so good to me
But without them, what would I be?
My tree trunk so strong, it holds me year long
But where have all my leaves gone?
A change in the weather, and we're no longer together
The leaves fall like the tears on my face
Without them, I feel like I am a disgrace
My precious leaves have once again left me
But without my leaves, how can I be a tree?
The Winter is a time to mourn and to grieve
The Winter is when all my flowers leave
I see the first snowflake fall from the sky
I feel the tears rushing from my eyes
Uh oh…blizzard.

Francesca Rugo, Grade 7

My Amazing Grace

Life is a long, tiresome road,
that one must respect, and follow its code,
A friend is someone who walks alongside,
and helps bend the laws that one must abide,
Through Rain and Hail, Floods and Droughts, Fire and Ice,
you always bless me with your advice,
When I hit a bump,
you hold my hand and help me jump,
When I stray off the path,
you tell me to come back with a merry, little laugh,
And when at last the path shall end,
we will part there, my dear friend,
But that journey is for another day,
the day we both die away,
Today you are my dearest companion,
who helps me through Life, with love and compassion,
Today you are to me a dear sister,
who tells me the truth, and is a great listener,
Today and forever, until the bitter end,
You are my Best Friend

Ana Georgescu, Grade 8

Words and Purrs

Poems are like cats.
The calm words make you tired.
The striking words come at you.
The sweet words sound like a soft purr.
The surprises stop you as you try to continue.
The different words show the personality,
Just as if it was fur.
The suspense scares you like an attack,
But the slow movement calms you.

Julia Kwiat, Grade 7

Perspective

I can't seem to recall which had hit me first —
The blur or the hit.
According to my logic,
I infer the hit was prior.
I had been on the wall when a giant walked in.
In its hand laid a slapper,
or that's what papa had told me to beware of.
The giant moved slowly.
Step by step it inched near me.
Suddenly, the slapper came down on me.
No time to fly so I stumbled a few steps and landed on the window.
Once again, the giant tried again.
Suddenly, the slapper came down and whacked my leg.
I laid on the wall counting to ten waiting for it to leave.
I was a fly,
Not a rotten piece of trash.
I have a life as well as yours.
Spare me.

Kristine Xie, Grade 7

When the Time Comes

The future embraces mysteries,
All of dynamic curiosity.
Such to leave one restless,
Endlessly conjecturing, fantasizing.
The curse of bewildering ignorance
Leaves a ravenous craving of enlightenment.
The hunger and thirst for valuable perception,
Induces a forceful desire.
This lack of understanding,
No different from aimlessly wandering through darkness,
Is exasperating, holding eerie significance.
Fears multiply the burdens I carry,
Composed of violent anxiety.
Intense pressures oppress my tenuous frame,
Congesting my consciousness.
This life I lead, of such uncertainty is all but transparent.
Though I believe that I will see,
And I will know… when the time comes.

Jenny Deng, Grade 7

The Penalty Shot

I grab the ball and set it in the penalty spot
The rain washes the sweat off my face
I can hear the cleats 10 yards behind me in a muddy pot
I step back from the ball and breath at a steady pace
I am getting nervous, I can feel my body starting to shake
I start sprinting at the ball then slow down to try to fake

The goalie falls for it and dives right
I gather my momentum and finally kick the ball
Everything is in slow motion in the dim sunlight
I hear the ball hit the back of the net like a wall
All my teammates including me start jumping and screaming
I try to seem cool and calm, but on the inside I'm beaming

Emily Branson, Grade 8

Maze

Turn a corner and you're lost
Come back the way you came
Only to find that it's the same
For hours on end you search and search
And find a crow in its perch
It flies away
Leaving a key
That opens the door that sets you free
You race back to the door
Turn the lock and push on
Only to find more
You said it would be easy
But you were wrong
You sit down on a bench
To dazed to go on
Telling yourself
This truly is an
Impossible maze
Mason Tharp, Grade 7

As an Angel You Fly

It was a normal day,
Nothing really to say.

I came to check on you,
But then I saw you already flew.

As an angel you fly,
That night I cry.

Just a dream I thought,
But it certainly was not.

I think about you,
Remembering all of the things
You would say or do.

It's hard to say goodbye,
But now as an angel you fly.
Alex Hansen, Grade 7

Dogs

Dogs so warm and furry
Guard you, protect you
Help you
Best friends
To you
Stay by your side
Are so very loyal to you
Comfort you when you are sad
Smiles as big as a watermelon
Like a brother or sister
Stay by your side
Bark loud like a siren
And they will forever wait for you.
Maegan VonEye, Grade 7

Mr. Barr, the Writing Teacher

Mr. Barr the writing teacher
funny and exciting teacher
hardworking man
responsible and understanding
Mr. Barr the writing teacher.

Mr. Barr the writing teacher
always laughing with a big smile
ocean like eyes
Mr. Barr the writing teacher.

Mr. Barr the writing teacher
inspiring to write and be free
encouraging and never let's
you give up. a role model
Mr. Barr the writing teacher
Julia Lopez, Grade 8

Grandma

When I touched
the knob I could see
a bright shiny light
The sound of the knob
was like the sound of
bells when I first stepped
into my grandmas house
all that I could smell was
fresh roses that had been
in her garden I am so
lucky I have a grandmother
like her.
My grandma is so outgoing,
she's cool, funny and her
food tastes really good
I LOVE MY GRANDMA!
Emily Estrada, Grade 7

Four Walls and a Roof

I love the scorching summer days
The wind blowing in my face
And sparkling water blinding my eyes

I love the relaxed atmosphere
The sun tanning my skin
And the slanted cottage

I love the fish nibbling at my feet
The seaweed filled water
And the warm sandy beach

I love the joyful feeling
The endless laughs
And the happy memories
I will never forget
Brooke Pieroth, Grade 8

A Warning Message to All

I step into the light of day
which fell into the rain;
What I can feel of skies affray
I only feel as pain.
My one true wish: a day untold
when warheads will not fall,
But now the black and liquid gold
oh, how they hear it call.
Everyone knew of the war
that was so soon to come,
Riches blinded them before
but now we stood there numb.
Swallowed up into a void
never to see the day,
And then our world will be destroyed
and everyone will say,
"Oh, where did we go wrong?"
"Oh, where did we go wrong?"
Nathan Schmidt, Grade 8

Anchor

The waves were crashing,
thrashing, and splashing
against the dark, jagged, rocks.

It was dreary and dull,
the oceans were full,
and no one was out to play.

The anchor was pulling,
pulling down to the ocean floor.

No one could see,
how deep it may be,
and maybe that's why its so dull.

The sky may be gray,
but there's always a way,
to brighten someone's day.
Katie McKee, Grade 7

Forever With You

Things without you are very different
Things without you are very hard
The only thing I can think about is you
And the fun times we have had together
Everywhere I go I wish you were with me
A day without you is no day at all
But I know you are with me
Every hour
Every minute
Every second
You are by my side
So in all reality every day you are with me
So our fun times can go on forever
Abby Wetzel, Grade 9

Silence Has a Sound

It's never quiet
There's always sound
I can't ignore it
It's always there, that shallow pound
Complete silence, there's no such thing
Into my ears the pounding will creep
I can always hear its shallow ring
But I guess that it's my burden to keep
It's my fair share
For, others have it far worse
Some don't know, and they might not care
But I don't mind, it's my personal curse
I can't ever escape it
My torment I cannot sell
But I still hate it
And it's my personal Hell
Silence has a sound
A sound you probably can't hear
It's like a constant pound
And it's a sound you will fear

Cheyenne Nikolaus, Grade 7

Corset Strings

I draw back the corset strings
Cloaking my withered soul
One more day, one more step
The hole draws so near
In one more day, in one more step
My soul may disappear

I draw back the corset strings
Constricting my wretch'd tongue
Tie the knots, tie the strings
Thread is spread so thin
I'll tie the knots, I'll tie the strings
My tongue is nigh its end

With every word you read
My life you thought was grief
Read the words, read the stanza
Need you any clues
I wrote the words, I wrote the stanza
But just about my shoes

Jadyn Lovelady, Grade 9

Prosperity

H ope everywhere
A pparently time files
P laying in the yard
P eace and tranquility all over
I nability to be sad
N o anger anywhere
E xceptionally exciting
S o much fun in the air
S miles fill the air

Alex Queen, Grade 7

Love

Love Blossoms within the core of a person's heart
Pulses rapidly through the veins, as it spreads pleasure.
With its joy, love can also bring tears of sorrow.
Tears of sorrow that have the power to put two broken hearts together.
From the coldest icecap to the wild, blazing fire,
Love has the power to tame the soul and make it a whole.

Sibani Ram, Grade 7

Poetry Soaring

Poetry
Is a bald eagle
soaring through the sky.
An eagle soaring, creating motion.
A poem is a fierce eagle.
A bald eagle soaring through your mind creating thoughts in your mind.

Jordan Eskew, Grade 7

Shoes

Many styles and shapes, colors and sizes. It is filled with many surprises.
Keeps your feet from the muck on the street. Boy! Aren't they sweet!
Fitted to fit perfectly tight, they are a friend that is filled with delight.
Accompanying you while you're running. They sparkle and shine, they are stunning.
With them you can run or play in the sun or mud all day.
Always with you to help you out, that's what it is all about!

Grace Vavrik, Grade 7

Sweets of Easter

E at lots of chocolate bunnies
A fter the church service
S earching for Easter eggs
T his is a fun time for children
E ating lots of marshmallow peeps, then
R ound and round their stomachs go, "Ooo…, I think I'm feeling sick."

Mason Schmid, Grade 7

Symphonic Jukebox

My hair is like a giant mess, not curly or straight
My eyes are like Auto Correct, they see all wrong doing
My fingers are like a symphony, playing everything from F. Seitz to Bach
My mouth is like a jukebox, it sings and hums all day
My heart beats as a source of care for family and friends
My skin is as German as possible

Miranda Ruesch, Grade 7

Puzzle Poetry

Poetry is like a puzzle.
You scramble to find the words that fit in perfectly with the others.
The picture it makes is like the finished poem staring into your mind.
Yet, for those who seek attention,
It is nothing but a dumb puzzle.

Isabel Schultz, Grade 7

Book

Some see me as insignificant.
Some see me as a life source.
Some treat me with care.
Some throw me around.
My pages are clean and crisp.
My pages are damaged and hard to read.
I am full of stories that many like.
I am full of information that many need.
Sometimes I'm uncypherable.
Sometimes I'm well known.
I am the dream that many wish.
The land that many think they deserve.
I help many but I am loyal to only one.
My author is the definite one.

Katie Tasich, Grade 8

Volcano

I roar with the power of the sun
Bringing down the fire's rain.
Nothing is safe from my fury
Once I am wakened again.

I am with the blood of the Earth
Until my furied strength fails.
Lifting my head I thunder
Down the rocks the Earth's blood sails.

I am a sleeping giant
Conquered only by the sea
Pray to the gods of volcanoes
That never will you encounter me.

Evelyn McEwen, Grade 7

Water Wars

I hid on a roof
with water balloons
that were stuffed
in my arms.

He approached
where I would
throw.
I lock and load.

I aim
and throw.
Forgive me for soaking you.
But it is a war, after all.

Dan Ryan, Grade 7

Wind

There is silence throughout the forest,
WHOOSH!
The wind blows rapidly through the trees,
Silence again.

Jerrika Williams, Grade 8

My Life Advice

Coming from a good home, with many things that are unknown
Growing to become who I am
Learning not to scam the people who actually care about if I am in despair

The ones who care about me and the ones who can see who I am inside
I've cried, everyone has, it's what you do about it that makes it right

Whether you remain sad or forget about the past and don't stay mad
Because the ones who always struggle, will be the ones who get stronger

You have to go after what you want or you will be taunted
By the choices you did not make
And for your own sake, go after what you want

You can't let anyone tell you who you are
You need to find who you are, 'cuz life is a blur
And you have to be your own entrepreneur,
Build your own life, be your own boss
Don't let anyone control what you need to,
Because in the end, you are your own you

Amy Zhang, Grade 8

Three Drops of Color

In a boring world, all black and white
That had not a color to be seen
And everyone who lived there liked it that way
Or at least they didn't complain
Black and white clouds drifted in
And deposited black and white rain
Amidst the dull 3 droplets stood out
That were colored and oh so bright
A red droplet, pure as blood and a bright sunny yellow one too
With a blue one as deep as the ocean itself
These three colors so small and tiny
In a big big world that they would soon change
Blue dove in a river and it lit up in color, while yellow gave the sun a kick
Red kissed all the apples up in a tree
But there were some things that did not fit
And the colors had noticed it, too
Blue on the leaves did not seem right, nor did red on the moon
So the colors joined hands, a big flash was conjured
Out of the bright came orange and green
Along with every other color, to make the world complete

Matthew Kovich, Grade 7

Blue

Blue is the slick ice, the clear sky, and water.
Blue is the taste of ice cream.
Blue smells like fresh blueberry pie and sweat.
Blue makes me feel sadness.
Blue is the sound of splashing water and crashing waves.
Blue is the vast ocean, a water park, or your favorite ice cream stand.
Blue is staring at the different shapes of the clouds.
Blue is always cold as ice.
Blue is a melted snow cone on a hot summers day.

Devin Knust, Grade 9

I Like That Stuff

You can lay all day on it
You can play all night on it
Beaches
I like that stuff

There's no snoozing with it
You sometimes lose from it
Running
I like that stuff

You can spend it
You can lend it
Money
I like that stuff

You can learn from it
You don't yearn for it
School
I like that stuff
Lily Steffen, Grade 7

The Race

I fell in love with the feeling
of the track underneath my feet;
with butterflies swarming in my stomach,
scared to the bone of getting beat.
My feet up against the block,
hands trembling on the ground;
waiting patiently and anxiously
for the starting gun to sound.
Ready, set, bang!
I throw my weight forward,
feet moving as fast as they can.
Air rushing onto my face,
like it was the fastest I've ever ran.
The crowd roaring all around me,
the finish line coming so near.
I kick it up to full speed
and at that moment it was clear.
With a smile plastered across my face,
I realized, I had won the race.
Abi S, Grade 7

Spring's Arrival

Snowflakes cease to fall,
Frozen waters flow again,
New flowers will bloom;

Nature springs to life,
Hibernation can't exist,
A soft breeze will fly;

Animals return,
Pretty petals will now fall,
Spring has found its way.
Stephanie Shoaf, Grade 7

Aqua Joy

Water
Going through cracks,
People taking showers,
Making beautiful waterfalls
Droplets
Raining
Rushing down rocks,
Animals drinking out,
Of a pond by my house outside,
Drizzle
River
Animals live,
Swimming happily in,
The nice warm water playing joyfully
Pond
Ocean
One of the world's
Act of God that has very,
Wondrous regions such as the coral reefs
Seaway
Dillon Gottschalk, Grade 8

Art

It begins with an idea in mind
And starts to come to life,
With your canvas and a pencil
And a little bit of light,
Your pencil begins to sketch
And looks like a mess,
But when it's all finished
It relieves a little stress,
That's when you begin to paint
And take a little break,
From the creativity
That you create,
This is towards the end
When you have to finish,
You clean up all of your lines
And your mistakes diminish,
That's when you stand back
And look at it afar,
And that's when you feel
A little less bizarre.
Samantha Duve, Grade 8

Teardrop

A tear drop in your eye
To others may look small.
But looked through,
It stands high as China's thick brick wall.
While it rolls down your face,
It leaves a long trail,
Like a clear plastic paste,
And hits the ground like rain
On a rail.
Jovan Williams, Grade 7

Fighter

She stands alone; her battles fought,
But nothing is gained,
Much is lost.

They tore her apart;
Conformed her soul,
Stole her dreams,
Crushed her spirit,
Shook her courage,
And filled her with fear.
She builds up walls to block out love.

She blends in now,
Just a twin of the crowd.
All that's left is a cold, empty shell.
Just a tomb of yesterday's joy.

She moves on,
Glimmers of hope long forgotten.
She joins the enemy…
A relentless, heartless group.
Converting life's bystanders,
Trampling the weak,
And destroying the inferior.
Michaela Marcy, Grade 9

Rain

Dark clouds make up a horizon.
A cool wind blows on past.
The weatherman, for once, is right.
The sunshine will not last.

A single raindrop falls on down
And splatters on the round.
It's followed by a thousand more;
They make a pitter sound.

Then from the clouds there comes a flash
A booming sound is heard,
And yet someone is in the rain,
And walks on undeterred.

Two feet splash through deep squishy mud.
Their owner plays no mind.
Two eyes look back and see a trail
Of footprints left behind.

The droplets come down slower now.
There's only a few more.
It all dries up and now the world
Looks like it did before.
Meg Gile, Grade 7

Awake in Silence

I am woken up by silence.
I lay, still
Unable to move,
until something breaks the silence.
The silence is broken,
shattered by the ongoing sound of a beep.
Beep.
The only way I can fix the broken pieces,
is by pulling the plug.
I pull.
but instead of silence,
my room is filled with thoughts.
My thoughts and others.
I wait,
expecting the clock to sprout wings and take off
Zooming by so fast,
I can't see it pass.
Thoughts take over.
The clock has made it around the world.
And I still lay.
Woken up by silence.

Sara Vucic, Grade 7

The Highway Man

I think I could be happy since the Highway Man is dead
But all my hopes and dreams to Bess were never said.

I weep for you my sweet Bess
Don't know what I'll do without you, I confess.

Losing you to another man was like the world's end.
But losing my love for eternity is more than I can fend.

When the Highway Man came riding…riding…riding…

I heard the Bang! of your gun
My breath was instantly done.

Though I thought you would stay,
I sit here and pray

That you could be
right here beside me.

No more the Highway Man came riding…riding…riding…

Josh Ralston, Grade 7

Flashing Lights

Sorrow seems bright red
Like the color of the lights on the ambulance I am driving
I see a boy lying on the floor in pain
I hear a mother crying for her injured son
I smell exhaust as I run to the back of the vehicle
I touch the ambulance's door handle as I help the boy inside
I taste the tears which I cry for this poor child

Ryan Grover, Grade 9

The TV Remote

The TV Remote

I sit here in someone's hand
Quietly waiting for my next command.
It is my duty to select their next desire
Whether it be a soap opera or the latest news on a forest fire.

They push and hold one of my many buttons
Until I select the show they have just summoned.
Scrolling, selecting, stopping, and showing.
I'm the man in charge without them even knowing.

Over the many nights I've been worn down and used.
But yet I am still able to stay somewhat amused.
Every day is a different adventure.
So many different movies and shows to venture.

I'm the most popular because everyone wants to use me.
But I have feelings too as no one ever sees.
One night I'm tossed and thrown against the wall.
But like an outcast nobody seems to care about me at all.

Nicholas Svoboda, Grade 8

How You Survive

I am a speck of darkness
In this hateful and involving world
A little flame
In this frozen land
I am the creature
That is hunted with hate
I am split into groups
One is the cool type
The other is the ones who keep to themselves
I am the one who keeps to himself
Tears make these creatures want to hurt me more
I am breaking free
But doing the wrong things
I am in the bad groups
I now…
Steal
Hang with gangs
Do drugs
and deal them too
I spend all night with my members and wonder
is this it?

Jovanni Castro, Grade 8

The Perfect Victory

Triumph seems gold
Like the sweet victory of winning a competition
I see the medal that will soon be hanging from my neck
I hear the trumpets in the background blaring proud music
I smell the sweat and blood I have shed over the years
I touch the medal and its shining glory
I taste the success I have accomplished

Taylor Rogers, Grade 9

Shining Stars in the Night Sky

This distance between me and you feels as long as a black hole.
It feels like the night sky without a single star shining bright.
It feels as though the sun is not shining on the Earth itself.
But the distance I can handle and I hope you can too because I'd rather be with you then without you even if you're still far apart.
I'd rather see the sky on a stormy day then a day where the sun's brightly shining if it means that I get to see you.
I'd rather see the world turning then to know that it's in place if it means I still get to be with you.
I'd rather walk the distance just to be with you then to let it stop me and you from being together.
I'd rather do a lot of things to make this distance feel like a footstep or a blink of an eye, but I can't.
I can't make the walk feel like a drive or the hard times feel like a plane passing by, but I can love you till there is no longer anymore love I can give.
I hope you can love me till this distance becomes no more.
Till the walk is right up stairs and our love will always be there.

Angela Richards, Grade 9

All About Me

Connor
Fast, funny, lazy, talented
Son of Steven and Paterice Sowell
Who cares deeply for WWE, NFL, and my video games
Who feels amazing when he wins a match, successful when he gets an A on a test, and excited when I open my laptop
Who needs video games, food, and movies
Who gives money to charities, 100% on my tests, and happiness to my siblings
Who fears snakes, spiders, and poisonous things.
Who would like to see his sister go off to college, be successful in life, and one day have a great career
Resident of Sioux Falls, SD
Sowell

Connor Sowell, Grade 7

Cora Maynard

Cora
loving, caring, sweet, gentle
Daughter of Mark and Krystal Maynard
Who cares deeply for her dog, her best friend, and her iPod
Who feels sad when family dies, loving when she babysits, and gentle when she helps a small child
Who needs more babysitting jobs, shorter school days, and no gym class
Who gives joy to the kids that she babysits, presents to her best friend, and concerts to her dog
Who fears spiders, snakes, and gym class
Who would like to see Carrie Underwood live, Rio 2 and The Smurfs 2
Resident of Sioux Falls, South Dakota
Maynard

Cora Maynard, Grade 7

Emotions

If ecstatic was a color,
It would be pool water blue.
If ecstatic was a taste,
It would be warm chocolate chip cookies that
just came out of the oven and classic New York cheesecake.
If ecstatic was a smell,
It would smell like spouted daises, fresh cut grass, and something yummy cooking in the kitchen.
If ecstatic was a feeling,
It would be like a surprise vacation that you haven't known about for months.
If ecstatic was a sound,
It would sound like bees buzzing, the car honking, screaming, and feet running around.

Bhavya Jasthi, Grade 7

Music

People can get addicted to music, like a drug.
Songs express feelings that words cannot.
The lyrics of songs enwrap like a warm hug.
People can get addicted to music, like a drug.
Lyrics get stuck in your head like a bug.
In lyrics of songs, you find something you'd sought.
People can get addicted to music, like a drug.
Songs express feelings that words cannot.

Wes Jolly, Grade 8

My Safe Haven

Relaxation seems crystal blue
Like the ocean waves rolling onto my favorite beach
I see the clouds drifting slowly through the sky
I hear the tune to my favorite song
I smell the morning air after a refreshing rain
I touch cold, silky sheets on my queen bed
I taste a cherry popsicle on a hot summer day

Sophie White, Grade 9

My Hair Is As…

My hair is as curly as a corkscrew.
My eyes are like the deep blue sea.
My fingers are like a fast race car when I'm texting.
My mouth is like a lawnmower when I'm talking.
My heart beats like a million rabbits thumping
their back legs against the ground when I am up to bat.
My skin is as soft as a teddy bear.

Miranda Flenard, Grade 7

The Girl With Long Fingernails

I find it kind of funny how she chews her pen when she gets bored
Or how she laughs at the stupidest things
Maybe it's just how long her fingernails are
Her nail polish chipping away just a little
I find it kind of funny how her hazel eyes dance when she smiles
smooth as pearls
I wonder if she knows how beautiful she is.

Faith Harton, Grade 8

My Family

My family is a collection of household objects.
My dad is the vacuum always picking up trash form the floor.
My mom is the phone always calling out to me.
My brother is the clock always on time.
My sister is the couch always comfortable about anything.
And I am the refrigerator always cold and freezing.

Blan Meshessha, Grade 7

Thunderstorm

Thunder rolls
From booming clouds
Hanging overhead, growling
Flashing brilliant white fangs
Crash

Courtney Miller, Grade 8

Bow Equipment

A lways dependable to use
R eliant when the time comes
R eady for any task or problem
O ut runs any animal, no matter what the speed
W anting a target or animal to become a new victim
S cavenges for another target to take down

Cody Baxter, Grade 7

Halloween Night

On this very Halloween night
People run and scream in fright

As you know on Halloween
There are things you've never seen

Like your tasty stew
May turn into a witch's brew

You go in with a broom
To sweep the floor of a room

And you happen to see the empty space
then coincidentally trip on a lace

You may think the room was wider
Then you may notice a giant spider

Then you will think this whole night over
And wished you had a 4-leaf clover

Now I shall tell you to sleep tight
And stay under your covers tonight

Because there are creepy things out there
That may crawl and get stuck in your hair

Now thanks to me you can dream
What will happen to you this Halloween.

Smriti Barla, Grade 9

Game Point

We're up by one:
This is our chance.
"This could be fun!"
I think in a trance.
I'm behind the line
Waiting to serve
When I get the sign —
I'm getting the nerve.
So I serve the ball
And it lands on the ground;
We wait for the call
All gathered 'round.
We leap in the air!
We won fair and square.

Brianna Richard, Grade 8

I Don't Know

It's what you say...
When you can't remember
When you can't think why
And you choke on your answer when asked how, when, where
When you're in shock and feel stuck
It's what you think
When the future turns the corner
When you just can't be sure
It's what they say when you ask why
It's these three words
Can they define you?
Can three words change you?
It's what you say when you lie
Isn't it just easier that way?
When nothing seems right and you're drowning
And in a lie these words have power
You use these three words in countless number
Typing "IDK" when you really do know but choose to hide
These three words
But do you ever really know?

Jessie Houghton, Grade 8

In Front of a Crowd

I walk up to the front and take a deep breath.
Taking my time, trying to put it off,
hoping that it all goes well.
Trying to stay calm, as I prepare to start.

I grab my cards and turn toward the crowd,
and when I look the world is frozen like an iceberg.
I see everyone staring at me,
I am so scared it even seems like the wall is staring at me.
The teacher gives me the cue, and I begin.

I start off quiet, but then I get louder.
I start off racing, but then I slow down.
I can hear the clock counting down, like a bomb behind me.
Hoping that I don't go over time.

I finally come to the end, and the applause begins.
All I can hear is the tapping, snapping, and clapping of the crowd.
I had finally faced by fear,
and it turned out not to be so bad.

Erica Gorden, Grade 8

Springtime

As spring comes near, winter disappears.
Children laugh and play, obviously enjoying the day.
Soon they are tired out, and look to the sky.
They all soon dream they could fly.
Then one older child exclaims, "Look what I can do!"
He leaped from a hill, a marvelous jump!
But landed upon his rump.
Everyone laughed for a while, and the boy just smiled.
For this is springtime, the time of regrowth and birth.

Brenna Fisher, Grade 8

Stop and Stare

No matter how much we argued,
No matter how much we disagree with each other,
I will always miss you,
I made the mistake,
Of not treating you with respect,
I should have done what you told me,
I should have told you I loved you every day,
I should've said more before you left that day,
Only if I knew it was the last time I would see you,
It was only a day,
Before I knew you passed,
But I tell myself every day,
That you're in a better place,
I will always miss you mom,
I miss the memories,
I hate that we can't make anymore,
I miss every moment I didn't spend with you,
But I didn't know one day I would lose you,
I know I can't have you back,
And I hate that fact.

Cloey Dooley, Grade 7

The Inevitable Event

It is like just closing your eyes,
Not being able to open them.
Or is it an endless stream of dreams.
Everyone will eventually know.

Is it painful?
Or pleasantly peaceful?
Do you know what's happening?
Or like you're trapped in your mind like a caged animal?

Will I go to heaven?
Or sent to burn?
Will it come soon?
O later on down the road?

Heart attack or cancer.
Drowning or a fire.
Are ways this could happen.
Situations can be dire.

Jarid Olson, Grade 8

On the Track

My favorite place is on the track
This favorite place is located behind the St. Francis High School
I am going there in an hour
I do hurdles, run, and be my athletic self
I see people hard at work, running, jumping, and throwing
I hear "runners to your marks, set, go"
I have chosen to do hurdles and run
Sometime today I will go back there
This is my place because I can be myself

Jylian Laten, Grade 8

Rainy Day

Rainy Day
The heavy droplets of water fall to the ground
Making distinguishable pops each time they make contact
When they land, bonding together
Making puddles galore
The water starts slipping down the street
And being stomped on by thousands of feet
The rain is getting too abundant
It is almost becoming redundant
But now with roofs soaked
And the whole street cloaked
The rain has dominated
And now the church has flooded
And all of the people act cold-blooded
But then the priest
Came out due east and said
"Do not worry, for you are destined for great things."
Alex Colbert, Grade 8

Summer

although the summer nights will always fade,
the memories will never leave my mind.
and those summer days were so greatly made,
the hot days and the cool nights silver lined.

the beach is perfect with the waves around,
and catching fireflies that glow brightly.
with rays that turn my skin so lightly brown,
and the stars that shine in the sky nightly.

but now we've reached that time when summer's gone,
the air is cooler as the leaves fall down.
and lessons start so free days are withdrawn,
the holidays now take over the crown.

there's sounds of celebration in the room.
though summer will be back in time to bloom.
Sophia Mitra, Grade 7

Fall

Fall is a season of change,
Like people each one is different.
Like snowflakes each one is unique,
Fall is a time where leaves drop down from their abode.
And rest on a carpet of grass.
Fall is a time of colors,
Leaves let loose their gaudy hue
Nature turns into a painting
Splashes of red, gold, and brown;
They trim the soft green grass
Birds leave their dwellings,
Embarking on a pilgrimage they travel south
The ones that stay behind
Beware the winters might
Fall, a season when nothing stays the same.
Riley Baum, Grade 8

Ray of Forgiveness

Rising sun, glimmering ray,
Greeting us warmly every morning, every day.
As we rise from the comfort of our dreams in sleep,
To a waking world of love so deep.

Every sin, every lie, every secret kept,
Oh, how we burdened ourselves and wept!
But now we know that the Lord will forgive,
Never stop to judge, just open up and live!

The care the compassion, the efforts unseen,
The ones that are known only by God up above;
Our sins, our lies, our secrets, all our faults are redeemed.
Forgiveness falls on all who desire and love.
Francesca LaMantia, Grade 7

Pursuit of the Ghillie

The outfit of the shadows,
Impossible to see,
Who confronts it meets the gallows,
Those who possess it remain free,
Not easy to obtain,
Failure after failure I heard the mocking refrain,
Day after day, I got closer to my prize,
Like waves upon the beach,
I knew the Ghillie was about to rise,
It was well within my reach,
I now wear it with pride!
The great Ghillie of the Deep!
Now I can hide,
For it must be mine to keep.
Kenny Blazer, Grade 7

Sleep Tight

Sleeping in a brown crib made for him.
He looks like an angel that fell from heaven.
Hearing a cry makes me sad.
"Don't cry my little angel, sleep."

Holding him until he sleeps, his skin is soft and smooth.
Waiting for my love to make him sleep.
"Don't cry my little angel, sleep."
An angel he is, he is my little angel.
Charlotte Kirchner, Grade 8

Lack to Notice

Wild things
Magic spells
Capacity to notice the suffering for kindness a shallow performance
He is strictly alone
He desires, hurts and lacks
At no point does anyone return the kindness,
that we assume has been shown to him
Harming, healing so beautifully portrayed
Many parents lack to grasp
Victoria DeMarrias, Grade 7

Vivid Lastings

You are Barbie dolls
with long blonde hair
waiting to be loved
by others — not just me
even after my childhood years are gone.

You are Dad's car
on a bright, sunny day
with dirt covering every inch
just asking for a wash
from the little girl inside me.

You are my baby sister
so many years from me
needing a bottle, a reading
I chose her book
and bored her until the sun slept.

You are all my memories
so vivid in color
so happy and playful
so new and adventurous
so long remembered.
             Taylor Lang, Grade 9

Castaway

Castaway at sea,
Alone for eternity.
The clouds come nearer,
And bullets of rain pound upon my ship.
Leaving me, lost at sea.

Food runs low,
As my hunger grows.
The engine breaks.
Now the motor's gone.
I start to row.

The fish splash by,
Catching my eye.
Taunting but untouchable.
All hope seems lost,
And I let out a sigh.

Little did I know,
where I'd soon go.
Instead of sigh I gasp.
My eyes fill with tears,
As I scream, "Land Ho!"
             Dominic Vilatte, Grade 7

The Jungle

Green, dark, and spooky
Monkeys swinging from the trees
Still is the jungle
             Kaity Hixson, Grade 8

My Haiku

This is my haiku
My name is Umair Syed
I am very fun

Mostly, Jokes aside
This poem is so serious
I am nearly done

In my class right now,
I ponder for ideas
For my dear haiku

My mind is empty,
As the sky, my mind is clear
Looking for ideas

Pop! An idea came
A bubble floating in mind
The idea, it holds

Finally, I grasp
Holding on to it firmly
It flows through my hand
             Umair Syed, Grade 7

I Am

I am a boy,
I'm a trustworthy friend,
14 years of age,
normal teenager,
but not he same as all,
I want to be different,
depend on myself and only myself,
I work pretty hard,
to go far in life,
it would not be easy,
but possible.

I am student,
I complete work,
do homework, try most of my best,
to receive the best grades I can,
I soon will be grateful for my
A in writing and good grades,
in every class,
I goof around quite often,
but do pay attention,
and know what's going on.
             Christian Morales, Grade 8

Trees

Looking down on us
Skyscrapers of the forest
Stretching out of sight
             McCoy Bila, Grade 8

Easter Glory*

Man and the world in glory began
But with sin and guilt
Glory diminished
And became
Most pale.
Christ's life
Repaid our debt
With perfect obedience
Merited grace, our strength
To battle the devil, flesh, and world.

With snow white petals the lily blooms,
Then slowly begins to droop
Decaying more and more
Till it withers, wilts
Then dies.
In spring
The lily triumphs
With Christ's resurrection
Easter's glory, His victory
Over the world and death and sin.
   Mary Elizabeth Lapushinsky, Grade 9
        ***Inspired by George Herbert.**

Softball

I love to play my favorite sport softball
Every time I go to bat a hit
The outfielders will have to chase the ball
But they never get it inside their mitt

Every time I run I get to home
I score all the runs for my team
Even though I'm very very slow
I make it all the way to home it seems

I run around the bases with my speed
I pass the infielders with my big grin
All the players miss the ball with greed
And I make it home for the big win

When I'm behind the plate I get the signs
When they get up to bat they are cowards
I caught a foul ball in the air one time
And then I got the MVP award

I love to play softball it is my life
I always play the sport with great delight
             Lauryn Jones, Grade 7

Roses

Gorgeous
Green leaves and thorns
Such a lovely sweet smell
Beautiful rosy red flowers
Roses
             Allie Bonitatibus, Grade 7

Softball Ambitions

I step up to the mound to pitch the ball,
I have to be sure to give it my all.

For some this may be just a game,
As for me, it's my chance at fame.

Other girls' dreams are to grow up and become a movie star,
I just wanna be skilled like the best college pitchers are.

It's a game of strategy, accuracy, and speed,
A love for the game is all you're really gonna need.

Softball players will never quit,
We commit and are built with grit.

Bruises and scrapes we don't mind,
That is how we are defined.

We back each other up, and have each other's backs,
But still you will see no one on that field relax.

There is no 'I' in team and we have to work together,
It all begins with picking the ball up in the leather.

Everyone is beginning to shout,
Because it's strike three and batters out!

Maria Howard, Grade 8

What Is a Poem?

What is a poem?
Well you're asking the wrong person,
But I know you can rhyme,
Or be yourself, write what you want.

What is a poem?
Well there are many different kinds,
But my least favorite kind is haiku,
Or love poems, too mushy.

What is a poem?
Well it's lines and stanzas,
But essays, now that's the stuff,
Or poems, why that's what you're asking about,

What is a poem?
Well your frustration won't hurry me along,
But a kind please will get your answer,
Or a pleasant smile to sugar coat the cookie,

What is a poem, please?
Well that's how you ask,
Just start at the top of this paper,

And ask yourself then,
What is a poem.

Jamie Houser, Grade 8

The D Word

Here I am now lying in my bed,
trying to find sleep,
so I lay down my head.

Yet, I cannot sleep;
there are voices outside,
yelling, shouting out loud,
a screech and a scratch, I start to cry.

The voices grow louder,
and repeat in my head,
those words of anger,
hatred, and mean instead.

I plug my ears and scream out loud,
But nothing will work the voices still ring out.

My mom and my dad,
talking about like two birds without doubt,
could they be these voices?
had they spoken out?

The voices have stopped,
so I close my eyes once more,
but I cannot sleep;
I keep on thinking evermore.

Sam Royer, Grade 8

Dirt Bikes

Oh dirt biking
What a wonderful thing
So many different styles
You can do so many wonderful things

Hill climbing where you race to the skies.
Racing where you can go as fast as light.
Trail riding where you and your bike are one,
Like a ballerina.

Freestyle where I go and fly like a bird
But you have to land as smooth as butter
If you don't you fall hard and bad

Some falls don't hurt but some can hurt a lot
Some times your ribs get hit.
You get the wind knocked out of you.

Oh so much talent out in the world
Feel the wind going through our helmet
Your tires lifting off the ground to fly through the air
All the adrenaline pumping through your veins.

So many brands so many choices.
The god of all of them,
Honda

Zach Bell, Grade 7

Happy
Sun
Summer
Sand
The beach
The blue sky
Fresh baked apple pie
Out with the family
Swimming
Playing outside

Now that's what makes me
HAPPY
James Grant, Grade 7

The Humming Bird
Nelson Mandela was the humming bird
Where ever he spoke he was heard
Sometimes he would get smacked
But he would never fight back
There was a war against the whites
But Nelson Mandela never fights
When he was in prison
The good Mandela was risen
Once out he was just as resident
Sooner or later he was president
Even the humming birds' last word
That word was still heard
Will Shanklin, Grade 7

Your Heart Gets Erased
Poetry is like a hug
As soon as you read you
Immediately get
Taken in, embraced, you have
Great emotion pour our of your
Heart, words that have never been
Spoken, erased because of
The love that you feel
And you never want to let
Go of that feeling of being free
At the heart but embraced
By arms around your warm body
Dalys Helgren, Grade 7

Sunset
Out on the distant horizon,
the sun,
reaches out
with its yellow touch, like
ichor
flowing through the veins of the gods.
It turns everything
as far as the eye can see,
into molten gold
just like King Midas himself.
Kelly Christensen, Grade 9

A Lot More Than Honorable Mention
You're gone daily from lifelong dreams, and all you hear are deadly screams
You're gone away during holiday fun, most of the time in the beating sun
We celebrate Christmas, Halloween, and Thanksgiving
While you're in a different country making a living
Right now I say, to veterans today
When you pass from these days, your memory will still be praised
Throughout our brains as a memory that is sustained
You will long live in our minds, as the men who were brave and kind
Veterans you are not conceited, your time in war has been completed
You stand here today, with nothing in your way
You have fought long and served well
Today we will honor you with a loud yell
You've served us well throughout the years
Today you will shed well earned tears
This is not just another celebration
it's a day to honor your dedication
To me and everybody else
Veterans, you should be proud of yourselves
When you were in the dreaded fight, you were gone day and night
Veterans, even through the pain and tension
You are a lot more than honorable mention

Nathan Meese, Grade 7

Rain
Oh, here's the rain again,
As it was here yesterday.
The rain appeared the day before and again will come tomorrow.
Droplets of cold water hit against my face, then I think,
Oh here's the rain…AGAIN.

Oh, here's the rain again,
On a Saturday where I'd rather be shopping than sit here bored to death
Looking at the rain fall and hit the cement,
There's nothing to do.
Oh here's the rain…AGAIN.

Oh, here's the rain again,
It is now Monday, the sun is out.
I head to school when suddenly I have been tricked,
The rain comes pouring down,
I run, run, run as fast as I can
Yet, I am too late!
I arrived to school soaked
Then I think,
Oh, here's the rain…AGAIN.

Lesley Garcia, Grade 8

My Acting Family
My family is the acting equipment.
My dad is the Director he tells us what to do.
My mom is the clapboard because she tells us when to stop when we do something wrong.
My sister is the roses that the actors get after the performance because my sister is nice.
I'm the main actor who's the good guy in the movie because I'm good at acting.
My dog is the laugh track because my dog always makes us laugh.
My tortoise is the movie because it will live on.
Cameron McAleer, Grade 7

Dancing

As I dance across the stage
like no one is watching
I feel a brush of wind
SWOOSH!
I begin to smell the sweat of
my dancing.
Moisture.
We collaborate with our eyes
still listening to the sound of the
fast tempo music.
People can see us dancing
as if we are professionals.
Our dancing is over the roof
I can feel the nice breeze
blowing across my skin
as we dash off the stage.

Trinity Ragland, Grade 7

Hope

Kept and kindled yet attacked
Destroyed but never sustained
To be locked up away forever
In the heart of Spartacus
In the eyes of Lincoln
Being the key to Martin Luther's success
The ammunition for the Allies
In times like the Battle of the Bulge
But like a gun used for both good and evil
Living in the heart of Hitler
In the times of his imprisonment
And in the stone cold heart of Kenghis Khan
Wreaking havoc to all who pass
Yet still being there for all who care
Because that is hope

Andrew Kim, Grade 8

Cake

The singing starts
The candles glow
The cake is coming
And that I know
As it is set on the table
And the candles are blown out
The cake is ready to be served
As I take a piece
And put it in my mouth
There was nothing else
That I could think about
It was so delicious
Perfectly moist and sweet
There was nothing I would rather eat
Cake is my favorite treat

Milijana Franco, Grade 7

Salute to Spring

To warm weather
To buds on trees
To green leaves on trees
To flowers in the dirt
To rainy days
To wearing rain coats
To wearing rain boots
To feeling rain drops
To using an umbrella
To walks
To taking long strolls
To hearing the birds
To the feeling of joy
To playing outside
To softball season
To seeing the sky change colors
To seeing the animals go away
To seeing the sunset go down
To dark skies
To sleeping
To spring

Delilah Juarez, Grade 8

Breathe

Feel the fresh air fill your lungs.
Release the toxins.
Life is good.

The sun is shining.
The grass is wet with dew.
It's a brand new day, and
I can smell the flower fragrance.

Can you smell it too?

Breathe in the sweet,
sweet smell of the rose.
The daisy. The tulip and peony.
So fresh it was born yesterday.

Already, you have forgotten
about the storm-cloud day
of yesterday.

Because you know how to breathe...

Carrington Curphy, Grade 9

My Goal

I have lots of goals I want to accomplish,
To improve myself as a student.
I would like to improve my math grade.
I would like to be better at math.
One way I can do this is to ask questions.
I need to participate more in class.
Goals are a very important part of learning.

Stacey McAllister, Grade 7

That's Right!

Sitting quietly in the room
Which is an extremely soundless class
A question no one knows
Except me
Tick...Tock...Tick...Tock...
Goes the cranky cracked clock
Everyone's keeping their heads down
I deliberate what was told
The teacher gawked at our frown
Think...Think...
Jotting down the answer
Again. Wasting time
Should I give out the answer?
Heat rose in my body as I thought about it
Forcing my hand to stay down
I wait...
Glancing up, the teacher noticed me
"Do you have an answer?"
She caught me, nodding my head quietly
I answered it
And it was, right!

Macy Olson, Grade 9

Words

I get up and start to speak
The words sound right to me,
But come out wrong
I hear someone laugh
And I want to scream
The students say repeat, repeat
But to repeat would mean
To make a fool
I sit down and hear once again
The mockery spins around my head
Again I know I will never change
And the tears start to flow
Before I know
I am out again alone
But something starts to click
Click inside my head
And I know it no longer matters
Once again here I am
Presenting and speaking
The mockery begins
And I sit down with a smile on my lips

Jordan Fashing, Grade 9

Fire and Ice

Ice
Freezing, Skating
Cold, Sparkly, Hard
Winter, Ice Cubes, Humidity, Heat
Hot, Damp, Big
Burning, Camping
Fire

Kaitlyn Sopko, Grade 8

No Title to Explain My Hurt, Just Read

When I go home some days
I cry
I cry 2 maybe 3 hours
I cry because of the struggles I go through and I am so young
My zodiac is an ARIES
They are confident, adventurous, and speak what's on their mind
But I don't feel like none of these characteristics
When you die
You lay in a casket BY YOURSELF
Just face it
The world will never be like it once was
When I go home
I go in my room and think
Think about life and the struggles I go through
My friends DYING left and right
Family not being supportive or considerate
It's just me, this is how I FEEL
When I go home I cry
I cry for 2 maybe 3 hours
I cry because of the struggles I go through and I'm so young

Maya Mills, Grade 8

Tick Tock

Tick tock, Tick tock
I look at the clock every few minutes

Tick tock, Tick tock
Waiting for myself to get out of this business

Tick tock, Tick tock
It's almost here
It's very near
I think about it all the time

Tick tick, Tick tock
Keeping me in here should be a crime

Tick tock, Tick tock
I imagine myself in that cap and gown

Then finally the clock stops ticking,
And that day has finally come,
And I will not frown.

Lauryn Cummings, Grade 8

Time for Good Cheer

C arolers who sing
H anging bells that ring
R eindeer pulling sleds
I magination that is spread through our heads
S now that fills the air
T rees are put up with great care
M anger above the fireplace
A ngels around us spread grace
S ongs we embrace

Giulia DiMarco, Grade 8

Heavy Rainstorms

H ard winds rip the roof off of the house,
E ntire family cowers in basement,
A ttic torn to shreds above us,
V ery frightened little sister prays to God,
Y ou must stop this storm now, Lord.

R ain pounds the sides of the house,
A n apple flies through the air,
I n seconds, pieces of straw are stuck in wood,
N ow the house is destroyed,
S ave the family, still alive,
T ornado tears through the neighborhood,
O mitting only our neighbor's house,
R uined houses and debris litter the streets,
M ama staggers out, in torn nightgown and slippers,
S obs into father's sleeve, ordeal is too much.

Alex Mahnich, Grade 8

Warm Weather Fun

W hen the sun comes out,
A round us, everything gets a little better,
R unning outside in the hot sun,
M aking the best of the day you have.

W hen the sun goes down after a long day,
E verything settles down,
A ll the kids are in their house,
T hey could be watching movies,
H anging out with each other,
E ven sleeping,
R eally long days really wear you out.

F un in the summer is a piece of cake,
U nder the sun, who isn't happy?
N ever take for granted the hot summer days.

Reilly Martyn, Grade 8

Sense of Sight

Darkness, such a stark contrast to light.
What is black compared to bright?
Black is the emptiness of one's mind,
without an ending of ever present fright.
Black is the loneliness one feels,
in the dark of the night.
Black is the pain,
bigger than the host's own might.
Black is the anger one hides,
to save from an unnecessary fight.
Black is your own personal bully,
one with a much greater height.
Black is like being submerged into water,
fighting for a last look into the light.
But without the black,
no one could appreciate the delayed return of the sense of sight.

Kathleen Wood, Grade 9

Hanging with Friends

R iding a bike with my friend Shalyn
O ver the hill, we go laughing
L anding at the end with a thump
L aughing even harder than before
I n comes Shalyn, rolling behind me
N ot knowing she was coming so fast
G one, we are like the wind

Christina Frink, Grade 7

Football

Football is a time flyer
Football is a sport just like basketball
Football is a violent sport
In Football kids don't get hurt
When I play I hear crack of our helmets
Super Bowl Sunday is a silent
I can see the green grass glowing

Jacob Smith, Grade 8

Accomplish in Achievements

B elieve you can accomplish anything
E nter anything which challenges you
L et tons of blood flow till you're energized
I nherit what you and your family hope in
E xtend the belief for yourself
V enture yourself into trying anything
E xtend your hope inside yourself

Seth Mosee, Grade 7

Children/Teenagers

Children
Naive, playful
Laughing, jumping, asking
Toys, naps, cell phones, clothes
Confusing, aggravating, growing
Unique, immature
Teenagers

Nina Vo, Grade 8

Sitting on a Swing

Poetry
is like sitting in a swing on a summer day
swaying back and forth—
in a fluent motion
sometimes relaxing, other times rhythmic.
Poetry is a wonderful thing.

Emma Moulding, Grade 7

Sadness You Say?

Sad makes you feel down and all alone
Like you can't do anything at home
It's all around you
Surrounding you
Depressed in stress
Is such a big mess

Zoie Nichols, Grade 8

Triathlon

It was the hot summer of 2012,
When I had just delved
My hand into the freezing cold water
Swimming, swimming, for I could not falter
Finally reaching the white sandy beach
Knowing I definitely was out of reach.

Now it was time to pedal so fast,
Right over the black roads to be exact
Steeper and steeper the road had become,
But I could not stop, for I would be done
Racing and passing others so quick
It was challenging, I will admit,
But I was hardworking and began to run
Through the blazing heat that came from above.

Eventually the giant finish line,
Could be seen by all of mankind
I pushed and pushed ever so harder
Determined to prove that I was no giver-upper
Step by step, I ran and ran, past the finish line, which was my game plan
To this day, I will always remember,
That challenging time in the heart of September.

Catherine Cabrera, Grade 7

Friends

Friends are like the money you make.
Hard to earn, but easy to throw away.
The time it takes for a friendship to develop is like the time it takes to develop your voice.
It may take a while, but the result is something truly amazing.

Friends are like flowers.
With them, it's amazing how time seems to fly.
You can talk on the phone for hours and hours.
That's a great way to help the time go by.

In the end, friends are priceless.
They can bring joy in your life, if you let them.
Screw something up, it could be a mess.
And you must admit, we all like having a friend

Morgan Ramet, Grade 9

Music

I like it when you dance
I like how I can make you smile when you are sad
You don't have to listen to me
But when you do, it makes everything better
Beyond my notes are stories
Some of my stories are easy to understand while others might not be
Sometimes I am just loud annoying noise in the background
I don't always just make people happy
Every once in a while I am sad and I let others join in being sad with me
I'm usually not sad for very long though
I get over it and I'm happy again
And when I'm happy, usually you are too.

Hannah Kennell, Grade 8

Nebraska's Hail Mary

Nebraska was playing Northwestern in football.
We were down by three, but not ready to fall.
Two of Nebraska's quarterbacks were hurt,
But our senior, Kellogg, was still alert.

Abdullah made an incredible run.
If he didn't make it, Northwestern would have won.
Now it was second down and ten.
On the forty-nine yard-line were our enormous men.

Kellogg was about to back out,
But then he hurled the leather ball with no doubt.
He knew his throw was worth gold or cash,
When it fell into the hands of the man with the 'stache.

The crowd shouted and roared with all of their might,
When they saw that the catch was just right!

Lauren Klingemann, Grade 8

My Future

a hazy silver mist clouding the future
what will happen? what will I do?
overlapping paths, which should I take?
what should I do? money or happiness?
needs or wants? am I choosing for myself?
or am I choosing for others?
is it even worth the effort?
what if I make a wrong decision?
what if I regret something?
what if something goes wrong?
wait a second, stop that
bad or good choices may be made, so what?
you may be stretched to your limits, so what?
if I spend my life worrying
will I ever get to actually do anything?
stop worrying, the future is now
don't wait for it, make it happen

Jessica Prus, Grade 8

Roller Coaster

Roller coaster, roller coaster, you look so tall,
I'm regretting this decision after all.

We get into our seats, and the seat belts lock,
As we go up the hill, the car starts to rock.

We stop at the top and I'm screaming out loud,
They can hear me real well, beneath in the crowd.

We're picking up speed while heading downhill,
Throwing up, throwing up, I'm certain I will.

We come to a stop, right where we began,
As scared as I was, I'm going again!

Maddie Baker, Grade 8

My Dearest Feet

Thank you for bringing me up when I'm down.
You are always there for me when I fall to the ground.
You help me walk, you help me run.
You have always outdone.
You support me each day,
In every possible way.
You have always been there for me,
Now I can see,
The specialty you have brought to me.
You always lead me on the best path forward,
To reach my goals I'm going toward.
Even though I stumble and fall,
You always help me get through it all.
Forever there when I look down,
Even when I turn around.
I know it's hard sometimes to see the path ahead,
But we'll keep on going right up until the end.

Lauren Salit, Grade 8

Thine Eyes

Thine eyes they show your sorrowful heart's truth
Your eyes seem to bring to sight thy painful song
Your song played to a miserable flute
This pain; making a young girl an old crone

For you see, look to me and see our pain
Thine eyes they seem to me, a reflection
In pain we gave ourselves the mark of Cain
Cursed to wander the earth; no direction

In black night, thine eyes they light grievous fires
For at your last bed, you set your last blaze
And thine black fire did bring relentless ire
May I find friendship in thy steely gaze

If I could I'd wonder what was in thought
For with your death; pain and sorrow you wrought

Abhay Adhyapak, Grade 9

In the City

In the city I hear the bangs
Of violent gunfights brought by gangs.
I hear the calming voices of the sane,
Without a sign of messed up ways.
I see poor, broken faces that are filled with unsought pain,
All the while I still see the warming smile across your face.
In the city there are poor but by the looks on the brochure,
There are rich and there are stars,
That fill the shining, gleaming cars.
In the city is the world.
A world that's great yet filled with hate.
So make this world a better place,
And throw away every trace
Of any world that's filled with disgrace.

Julia Silver, Grade 8

Courage

Facing your slightest fears,
Conquering you greatest terrors,
Both force you to do the same — be courageous.

Courage: not just given but earned,
When fear knocks on your door, answer it.
Don't pretend you're not home.

Courage, bravery, dauntless,
Different words, similar meanings,
Everyone has some degree of bravery.

Countless ways to show courage,
Standing up to a bully to staying true to yourself,
Not giving into peer pressure — be you own person.

Courage means many things to things to different individuals,
Doing the thing that terrifies you the most,
Or trying the little frights that shocked you ago.

Attaining courage every day,
Working towards the special day,
The day when you conquer your fears.

Fears get in the way,
So beat them,
Be courageous.

Darissa Overweg, Grade 8

The Apple Tree

Life is an apple tree.
It produces apples to eat —
soft, sour, hard, and sweet.
Tart are some apples, while others are delightfuls.

Light showers and storms
help them all to grow,
and from this, a person can learn and know
how to find the good in bad
like an excellent expert and pro.

The winter wind and flakes of snow challenge the person, yet again.
Remember the saying, "After the rain comes a rainbow!"
People learn to savor the flavor of the fruit.

Some are ours, they are the ones that we share.
Others are dedicated to people we care.
And everybody loves the sugary ones.

Though not all of them are red delicious,
most of them turn out quite nutritious.
Life gives you fruit to make apple pie,
apple sauce, and apple juice.
But the important thing that matters
is how they are used.

Jennifer Guo, Grade 7

Circle of Life

Life is a winding road that leads back to the start
Smooth, slow, scary, fast, frightening, and fun memories.

Your first heartbeat
Your first step
Your first day of school.

Your first true love
Your first real passion
Your first day of work.

Your first fairytale dream
Your first child
Your first struggle.

Your last struggle
Your last child
Your last fairytale dream.

Your last day of work
Your last real passion
Your last true love.

Your last day of life
Your last step
Your last heartbeat
Life is a winding road that leads back to the start.

Kelly Swindell, Grade 8

What's Real Love?

What's real love?
Is it true?
Is love what we define,
When young and old too?
It creeps up on us from out of the blue,
Just for 3 words "I love you!"

Love is a passion.
Love is a lie.
Love can live on.
Love could also die.

We experience love,
Every day and night.
Loving someone, feels so right.
The warmth of love, exaggerating feelings,
It's what many want to be feeling

We love many
We don't trust any
The one you love might loose your trust.

Fighting and fussing.
Crying and cursing.
Is that what love does to a person who's hurting.

Shawnnika Williams, Grade 8

You and Your Heart

I can't read your heart, just like my favorite book.
Yet you have me hanging, like a fish on a hook

Why can't you see? Why don't you understand?
All I've ever wanted, is the touch of your hand.

Your eyes how they glimmer! Yet all I see is me.
In your reflection, but I know it can't be.

Your heart is dark and filled with fear.
I keep trying. Please! I'll always be here

The secrets you keep hidden away.
With a smiling face, you say, "I'm okay."

I know there's something, deeper and true.
Give me the key and let me on through.

I love your laugh and your pearly white smile.
Such a shame, not seeing them for quite a while.

When you ignore me, the pain strikes sharp.
Nothing can comfort me, not heavens, nor harp.

You read my story, understood my fears.
You laughed at me and shared my tears.

You make me feel so happy and free.
My love and care? I wish you'd see.

Miranda Bendig, Grade 9

The Best Kind of Rain

The best kind of rain is summer rain,
The kind that is unexpected and surprising,
The kind of rain that asks you to stay outside forever.

Drip, Drip, Drip

Warm rain soaks the sidewalks
And falls from the trees above.
Raindrops race each other down car windows
And patter against sides of houses.

Drip, Drip, Drip

Sunlight starts to peak out behind clouds
And attracts children to jump in leftover puddles.
The air feels refreshing and carries an earthy scent.
It is silent except for birds calling to one another.

Drip, Drip, Drip

The best kind of rain is summer rain,
The kind that is calm and runs slowly,
The kind of rain that begs you to stay outside a little longer.

Natalie Barta, Grade 8

The Ones That You Need

They think you are the weirdest person alive,
And find you quiet strange,
But they love you anyway.
They are your friends.

They are people you can rely on,
They are your shoulder to cry on,
They are the only ones who understand you,
The ones who bring out the best in you,
And ignore and try to help you overcome the worst in you.
They are your friends.

They are the rainbow after the storm,
The sunshine in your day.
They are your friends.

They are the ones that believe in you,
More than any other person.

Many people come and go, but they are here to stay.
They are your friends.

Julia Block, Grade 8

Remembering Strangers

Visiting the war memorials and cemeteries
Brings a sadness for these people
Who you never knew
But who made a huge difference in your life.
Whether it is one person or one thousand people
Each and every one
Named and unnamed
Made a significant contribution
To your life as it is today.
Seeing those paying their respects
To mothers, fathers, sisters, brothers, friends.
Even strangers.
You stand in a silence.
Not only one of sadness
But one of respect and admiration
For these strangers
Who gave their all for all of us.
So live your life
And do what you can
To make these unknown people
Proud.

Katie Johnson, Grade 9

Country

C ornfield after cornfield,
O nly light from the pole in front of the barn and the moon light.
U nderstands the true meaning of farming and hard work.
N o easy way around the dirt and gravel roads.
T rucks and tractors are a common sight.
R eal people with rough hands and faces.
Y oung kids grow up to be farmers.

Caeden Pierce, Grade 8

Beautiful Savior

When I pray at night
I feel a healing hand
Come upon my heart
As if I can't stand
I kneel in honor
With no words to say
And praise my Lord
For being there every day
I bow my head
And call His name
And just like that
My prayer is made

Kerrigan Kelly, Grade 8

Hunter Hayes

H eavenly looking
U nderstands music
N ever backs down
T reats people right
E ntertaining
R eveals his true side in music

H onest with everyone
A ward winning smile
Y outhful
E nergetic
S outhern accent

Keagan Newberry, Grade 8

Basketball

Nobody ever said it's easy.
It's aching muscles,
Twisted ankles,
Battered and bruised knees.
It's hard work and determination,
Running suicide sprints,
Lay-ups and free throws.
It's believing
In yourself and your team,
And going hard every second.
It's not about winning or losing.
It's the love for the game.

Michael Wolfe, Grade 9

Love

Hearts are the   symbol for love.
Love is the   knot that holds
The ropes of life: If we didn't have love
Together: would we just have hate?
Love is the bubbly feeling inside,
When someone makes you
Feel really blissful.
Love is the true
Magic in
Life.

Kaylee Lowe, Grade 8

Equality

I do not understand
why men tie the knot and lure more bait
why men believe women belong to the office, kitchen, and the personal daycare
why men hit, bruise, and whip the fragile body of women they loved long ago

But most of all I do not understand
why women chase cruel abusive bad boys with the 6-pack and the height
why women expect loyalty by playing a role of a flimsy Disney princess
why women believe love comes from revealing their sacred bodies

But I do understand
that men need to change
that women need to change
that men need to be kind with words and hands
that women need to be honored
that there will be a day
where the scale will almost be balanced

Kristine Yim, Grade 9

Escape from Reality

Some write because it is away to earn money or fame
The same people who only knew writing as an escape from reality
Something they could turn to when they were hurt, lonely, or upset
When they wrote the world changed
It became like moldable putty they could from to their liking with only a pencil and paper
The only limit was their imagination
Their ticket to a better world with no racial hatred or other prejudices
A land without evil
The closest thing to heaven we could experience on earth
A place where all are loved and all are accepted, it was their friend in hard times
It brought them peace like nothing else in their broken life could
Now they have forgotten that
It is only a tool for money
They write what people want to hear and not what they themselves feel
They are famous and accepted by most everyone
They forgot where they came from
What got them to where they are today

Sawyer Good, Grade 8

In a Perfect World

In a perfect world there is no agony or pain
No damaging words said can break you
The future ahead would be something to look forward to
Not something holding you back
The world would be like living in a dream
A fairy tale with a happy ending
No darkness or shame
No hate
But there will be laughter,
People overflowing with joy
The light will be blazing through the darkness
Forgiveness will always be found even for "the least of these"
Sympathetic, affectionate people helping you when you are caught in the midst of trouble
When you reach out they will grasp your hand, and guide you down the right path
Always helping, in love

Abbi Taylor, Grade 8

Spring

Mother Nature calls loudly
While birds chirp proudly
And animals run wildly
All is well
Spring is here

Rain pouring down from the sky
While fish swim deep in reply
And the fox creeps very sly
All is well
Spring is here

Great flowers start blooming
While the ducks sit back grooming
And the speakers are booming
All is well
Spring is here

Robins sing with amusement
While ducks quack with excitement
And eagles soar with judgment
All is well
Spring is here
Danny Borgstrom, Grade 8

Spring

Winter is finally packing up
Spring shows through the crack
First to emerge is a tulip
Birds are flying back
Warm weather is here

The world turns colorful
The buds come out
Trees turn green and get full
The birds chirp and shout
Warm weather is here

Grass becomes green again
Outdoor sports are beginning to start
The children no longer build snowmen
Warmth of the sun melts a heart
Warm weather is here

A gentle rain falls often
Increase moisture in the air
Making the ground soften
The sun produces a warm glare
Warm weather is here
Nolan Feeney, Grade 8

Trees

Trees softly swaying
To rhythms of the warm wind,
All is very calm.
Cody Madsen, Grade 8

Talent Show

Stepping on the platform
Light warming me inside
The butterflies are trapped
With nowhere to hide

It's finally time
To let go and let free
Watch the butterflies fly
With the cicadas and bees

I hear myself play
Music overwhelming my heart
Telling stories through song
My life from the start

I hear
A herd of animals unknown
Howling with excitement
From what I had shown
Hayley Zoiss, Grade 8

What Is Love?

Love is home
My family
My friends
Love is a smile from my best friend
To brighten my life
Any time
Any place
Love is a warm hug
When the cold cruel world
Has turned you away
Love is walks with my mom
Laughing and bonding
Love is breakfast with my dad
Talking about anything, really
Love is lying on the floor with my sister
Watching Netflix on her laptop
Love is the small moments in life
That warm fuzzy feeling inside
Love is what we live for
Sydney Larson, Grade 8

Winter

Chilled wind falling down
Making white glisten on ground
Winter is now here

White on trees like milk
I go outside and see snow
Everywhere it is

I look out window
And see the wonderful sights
Of snow falling down
Dylan Horner, Grade 7

A Decision

Running, running, running
Sobs ringing through the air
Samantha knew she couldn't leave
She was stuck at this miserable castle
Forever

Bittersweet as that may be
She knew it was true
It was to protect her
Why then,
Did she feel so trapped?

She tried, tried, tried,
To bang against the wretched gate
More force than she could muster
And it opened

Samantha stopped dumbfounded
Her decision could change things,
Forever
Abigail Torres, Grade 7

Cries

They tell you it's okay,
They tell you it's fine,
But in reality,
It's all just a lie.
They crush you,
Break you,
Mess with you,
Defeat you.
You are stressed,
Depressed,
And overly
Messed.
You are hurt,
Distraught,
Pummeled by your
Thoughts,
Excluded,
Hurt,
Maybe one day
You will be heard.
Jessalyn Galvin, Grade 7

Sunrise

The dark slowly fades to light.
The stars wink out one by one as
Light seeps through the trees,
Making a fluffy golden rainbow of clouds.
The leaves rustle a good morning.
Grass, flowers, and spider webs
Collect clear dewdrops, creating a
Sparkling world of a hundred diamonds—
Stealing the stars
Caroline Welte, Grade 7

Soccer

When you step into the field
you feel thrilled, and pump up,
when your running back and
forth you hear people screaming,
you hear your coach screaming
and your parents are screaming to
make a goal, when you are holding
a soccer ball you just want to kick
the ball, when you are sweating and
having fun you want to go drink water
and relax after that game.

Jesus Ayala, Grade 7

Dylan

Some things about me
I am Dylan Baumbach
I have been to the Grand Canyon
I play football, baseball, and basketball
I have never had ice cream
I have been to California
I live in Chicago
I love Under Armor and Nike
I love fishing
I love football
I am Dylan Baumbach

Dylan Baumbach, Grade 7

Beautiful Spring

Bright sun
The wind blowing
The smell of flowers
Walking through the grass
While eating your ice cream
Blue sky
The leaves rustling
The smell of the lake
Swimming with your friends
While diving on a hot sunny day
Beautiful Spring

Priya Oliver, Grade 7

Fruits

Bright beautiful colors.
Looking perfect mounted up together.

Each one is different
Each one is unique
Different feels,
Different taste.

But all are the same.
Bright beautiful colors,
Waiting for me to enjoy!

Estephanie Garcia, Grade 8

Keep Your Head Up!

Why does it have to be me?
The one they make fun of and bully around,
One day because of my parents' divorce,
Another one directed towards my appearance
Is there no one else around me?
No one to guide me through this dark time,
No shoulder to cry on when I need it the most
No one to lean on when I am weak
Maybe if I try harder?
Just look a little deeper in my mind
I hear hurtful things but I can't see them so I don't mind them,
Those voices are loud and pounding but I don't want to listen to them
People say those voices don't mean anything
But I know for a fact that they do mean something,
Those voices mean that they would rather waste all their time,
And spend it all obsessing over you just to make your life miserable
Some people look strong but are weak and helpless
Other people look weak but are very strong and brave
So, before you go out and judge someone, look what's on the inside
Those people may surprise you!

Caitlin Gakin, Grade 7

In the Morning

When I wake up in the morning
I hear the birds chirping outside my window
The sound of their voices sound like pens clicking

I see the morning sunshine coming through my window
I know it's time to wake up and get dressed up for school

I can smell the delicious pancakes that my mom is making
I then remove my soft cover away from me and get dressed and rush downstairs

When I start eating I can taste the sweetness of the syrup
The syrup was as sweet as having a thousand candies in my mouth

While I was walking to school I saw people walking their dogs
I see kids running to school with their huge backpacks

While I was walking to school I smelled the fresh air
The air was so fresh it was as fresh as the ocean

Then I finally got to school and I was so happy

Armando Roman, Grade 7

Miracles

Miracles are the summer sunsets where the sky can be any color.
Miracles are the views of long grassy hills.
Miracles are all the birds chirping to each other at the crack of dawn.
Miracles are the bright glimmering lakes, with all the pontoons on them.
Miracles are the bees on the job of the garden of a million flowers.
Miracles are the wet dew on the grass every morning.
Miracles are the little ice cream stands on a hot sunny day.
Miracles are the dogs on your door step.
Miracles are the millions of things that happen every day.

Isabella DiLise, Grade 7

Soccer

I play soccer
It's my passion
Seeing a beautiful soccer game
Is all I need
I join in the game
With my history soccer cleats
Which brings me memories
Running in the field
Crowd cheering for the team
I love soccer
It's everything I need
My mind cools down
From all the downs I've had in life
Just play, focus and learn

Jacelyn Islas, Grade 7

Over the Hill

Over the hill what did I see?
A bright sunrise smiling at me,
With hair of a million hues,
Everyone was rising from their snooze.

What did the sun happen to find?
A hedgehog trying to unwind,
A nest of birds with droopy eyes,
Just waiting to see the sun rise.

Over the hill what did I see?
A sun waking up a tall tree,
A sun just waiting to wake me,
Over the hill, over the hill.

Maeve Cavanaugh, Grade 8

My Favorite Season

Spring is near
My favorite season
I wish it was here
And here's my reason
I see the snow, the ice, it's cold
My nose is froze, so is my toe
This old man winter is getting old
Every year it seems so
Puffy clouds up in the sky
A warm and gentle breeze
Colorful birds, a butterfly
And pollen that makes me sneeze
Sun, warmth, new life we see
Like love, it's overwhelming me

Carrie Culek, Grade 8

Love

L aughing
O pportunity for feeling
V alentine's Day is when most love is shared
E motion

Alaina Portwood, Grade 7

Do You Know What I Am?

Do you know what I am?
Well for a hint, I have many sides
One day I may bring you the things you desire such as
    happiness, joy, and love
I may build your faith in a higher being,
    but just as I can build your faith,
    I can shake it until it is no more
I may bring another person to you to enjoy,
    that person that I brought to you may very well be toxic,
    but only I know
I may also bring you wealth when I see fit,
    but I can take all you have just as quick
I can also give me to a person who has not yet taken their first breath
The next day, I may bring a storm or a new struggle
As you may know by now, the opposite of me is death,
    and I could bring you that tomorrow
I give these things to everyone,
    some may have a larger dose of struggle or desire than others,
    but I don't care nobody said I was easy or fair
What am I?
I am Life

Mariea Coleman, Grade 8

Side by Side

Standing there tall with your arm around me tight.
Protecting me from wrong and encouraging right.
You are here for a laugh and make my day brighter.
In our home where our bond grew tighter.
I would run to you in the middle of the night,
When the darkness and monsters gave me a fright.
Through the same room we'd run and we'd play.
And watch our favorite show, SpongeBob, at the end of the day.
After school, I would ride home on the handlebars.
In a year or two you switched from a bike to a car.
We sang our favorite songs as loud as we go.
You would drive me to get ice cream even if there was snow.
Your days in high school were quickly descending.
After graduation less time we would be spending.
Sometimes I walk into your room if a conversation I needed to share.
I open up the door and realize there is no furniture there.
You are going to college two hours away.
Now I only see you on holidays.
Often, I think back to when we were young and want a remote to pause all the fun.
I shed a tear thinking of memories with my best friend.
Now I lift my head because it's almost baseball season.

Audrey Fisher, Grade 9

Nature's Luxury

Nature forever glowing; quiet, exciting, relaxing
Perfect visit is when the sun is blazing on nature
I respect nature and listen to the silence there is
Humans and animals stroll around nature admiring its beauty
I rest under a cherry tree
When summer wanders back again, nature and its climate is perfect
When everything is green and summer is at its best point, everything gets better.

Janeth Elena Perez-Medina, Grade 8

Times Have Changed

The Heart remembered
The happy days that were no longer
The memories that were worth while
She actually missed them
She wished she could do something
But it was too late
To save her best friends from back then

The group split apart
One moved away
The Second turned wicked and left for another group
Some managed to stick together
The Third lost all happiness
The Second threw out the heart
And fed it to the wolves
The Heart died

The Heart slowly came alive again
One returned from his long voyage
The broken Heart wanted to explain but couldn't
One had no idea what happened and didn't remember
The Second had won the wicked battle
While the Heart slowly lost all hope

Marie Miller, Grade 8

Red, White, and Blue

Red, white, and blue,
gold stars are there too.
Veteran's Day today,
we all know it'll be okay.

Heroes that walk upon the battlefield
make a promise that is forever sealed.
They said with their heads up high,

"We fight for freedom so please don't cry.
We keep you safe as you sleep through night.
We fight for freedom so do not fright."

Red, white, and blue,
gold stars are there too.

Kirsten Potts, Grade 7

March Madness

The regular season is done
The time has come
As we witness the 64 Elite
Trying not to get beat
If you lose your season's over
But if you win your legacy never dies
Brackets will be made by many fans
But upsets will happen and ruin those plans
In the end it will come down to the final two
Nobody knows who will win
And make it through

Colin Szczesny, Grade 7

Demons

They're everywhere
Most people think they're only in dreams.
But a lot of them come to life.
They're demons.

Some of them live at home,
Some of them go to your school.
Some have your blood in them
They're demons.

They haunt you for days,
You try to run, but they run faster.
You close your eyes wishing they disappear
But once you open them they're right there.
They're demons.

Escaping them is hard.
Not a day goes by when you don't see them.
Your only friends are your bed and the darkness.
You petrified of them judging you.
They're dreams.

Abigail Favela, Grade 8

Creature of the Grass

Slithering through the dry, damp leaves,
What do you wondering eyes see?
The scaled creature coming near,
This is my one and only fear.

This creature moves through the grass,
like a swimmer through water
jaws that bite just so
it's prey won't escape its trap of death.
Cruel, vicious, merciless, frightful.
The beast approaches nearer.

This creature can swallow its prey whole.
In one swift gulp
its food is gone, no longer here,
the beast is full, and coming nearer.

Slithering through the dry, damp leaves,
The disgusting creature draws nearer to me...
What is my one big fear?
It's the beast I have written about right here.

Karli Jerman, Grade 8

Beach Surrounding

Gladness seems coral,
Like a beautiful day spent at the beach with friends.
I see fish swimming on the coral reefs in the Indian Ocean.
I hear the coastal oceans washing up on the shore.
I smell the scent of tropical flowers against my nose.
I touch the tiny specks of sand surrounding my feet.
I taste a giant, icy glass of coconut milk under the burning sun.

Jenna Confer, Grade 9

Summer Is Blossoming

S ummer fun at the lake
W ading in the lake is my favorite
I nshore wind is coming
M any fish swimming around your feet
M ud between the toes
I ce cream breaks are always a grand time
N ewts running all over the place
G etting sunburned over and over again
Lauren Johnson, Grade 7

A Soldier's Song

Strength, dignity, and pride
All soldiers stand by our side
Dark nights filled with fright
Each soldier needs a light
To guide the way back home
Where they will never be alone
When they get home, they get to share
Great big hugs, everywhere
Abbie Dart, Grade 7

Summer

Summertime is finally here
There are summertime street fairs
People are filled with lots of cheer
Summertime is finally here
The fireflies are, oh, so near
We sit out in big, bright lawn chairs
Summertime is finally here
There are summertime street fairs
Grace Clift, Grade 8

The Relay Race

Life is like a relay race. Its starts
  out with excitement and joy.
It makes you feel so alive like never before,
But then, it gets tiring and you just
  want to give up.
It seems so dull now,
But it tells you to get back up and
  and finish what you started.
Kelsey Cappel, Grade 7

Softball

S pring and summer
O pen field
F un and exciting
T rying her best
B ase running
A lways playing fair
L aughing and competing
L oving the sport
Skyler Doss, Grade 8

The Long and the Short of Pegasus

Olympus has fallen.
Pillars of marble shattered like glass.
The only thing that can save them now and the rest of the world,
is a girl, the Daughter of Vest,
the holder of the flame, Emily.
Pegasus, the majestic winged stallion,
who, seems to glow in the black of the night.
Diana, a god on the mission with Pegasus
on the mission to find Emily.
Joel, Emily's friend and knows a lot about Olympus and the gods.
Palen, a thief who got them into the mess with the Central Research Unit.
Emily, a New York girl, but now determined to save her friends.
There's only two things standing in the way,
The Central Research Unit and the Nirads.
The Central Research Unit are cruel and nasty people.
The Nirads have no mercy,
brought Olympus crumbling down,
and four deadly arms.
The fate of the worlds are in their hands.
Will they win
or will they fall?
Dana Fry, Grade 7

Nebraska

Frigid winters and scorching hot summers
Mixed in with mild falls and springs
The 4 seasons are all unique
Each brings its own set of surprises
In Winter the blinding snow falls
The temperatures drop below zero
Freezing you inside your house while you sip hot cocoa
When snow begins to clear then spring is finally here
Warm showers follow and plants begin to bloom
The world is now a bright Kelley green
Soon after, the world changes again
The vivid greens, yellows, and reds have disappeared
You begin to sweat often
The sun directs its blistering heat straight upon you
This is a completely different beast named summer
Thankfully summer comes to a close in mid September
And a pleasant breeze blows in from the North
Fall is here and brings the harvest with it
Farmers work late into the night cutting down their well tended crops
A new kind of weather is here and turns everything a dirt brown
This is the first sign of the dreaded Winter, fast approaching
Brenden Andersen, Grade 8

The Collection of Musical Instruments

My family is a collection of musical instruments.
Mom is a flute skilled at nursing always soothing to others.
Dad is a tuba always loud.
Katelyn is a violin usually the spot light and sometimes annoying.
Ryan bass the largest and strongest in the group.
Alex is a viola the joke of the group.
And I am the cello usually in the back but I am needed to complete the group.
Carter Story, Grade 7

Goodbye Gracie

So Heaven has received another angel,
The night another star
Your life has become another lovely memory
I know you will never be far

I know you are watching over me
As my life goes on
I treasure the memories I have with you
I can't believe you're gone

You were a beautiful, caring person
You were there for me a lot
You will always have a place in my heart
A loving, treasured spot

You were really one in a million
A cut above the rest
Everyone that knew you would agree
You simply were the best

So Gracie I will say goodbye
I miss you with all my heart
As long as I have my memories,
We will never be apart

Erin Blaskey, Grade 7

Fireworks

darkness, black, no color at all
a shrieking noise and a blinding light shooting tall.
suddenly, the sky deploys
hundreds of star-like lights that depart
and fall to earth — it was just the start

one, two, three come firing!
it sounded like a war was starting
after looking up for awhile, my neck was tiring
and the noise, well, it soon became smarting.
but the beauty and the fun made it all worthwhile
the fireworks were filled with charm and guile.

after many explosions filled the sky
the war had ceased, the sights and sounds no more
I glanced up to see the last one fly
and felt sad, and felt poor.
without the fireworks, the night seemed bare
but I could still smell the fireworks in the smoky air.

while the crowds lingered and chatted for a bit
I found a box and fingered through it.
it was marked sparklers and
I had found a firework I can hold in my hand

Elaina Borg, Grade 8

Chalk and Graffiti

Children sitting on the sidewalk,
Drawing with some chalk,
Having a good time,
Not a mean or aggressive bone in their bodies.

They frolic around after school,
And do their homework, unlike a fool.
They are eager to learn,
And punish themselves if they fail.

You can look down the road, and see children playing,
Not a sad or troublesome person, day by day.
But if you go down the road,
It is a completely different city.

Here the children graffiti the brick walls,
And spray paint through the halls.
Toddlers crying due to hunger,
And vandals ransacking through the grocery store.

Even though it's the same road,
Each side has a different story to be told.
On one hand, good, the other, bad,
If only there was peace.

Adam Subora, Grade 8

Thoughts

A stream of thoughts constantly flows through my mind
They are both the pleasant and the evil kind
Battling against me the thoughts are
Each hurtful enough to leave a scar.

Pleasant thoughts are harder to choose
Fighting a battle surely to lose
For enjoyable thoughts quake in fright
Seeing sinister thoughts display their might.

Sinister thoughts will make one rigid with fright
Sure to keep someone awake through the long night
Surely to win the everlasting battle against the good
Although no one but the devil thinks they should.

The skeptical thoughts make me shiver
Always flowing constantly like a river
Asking vile questions just to see my reaction
The cheerful and bright thoughts need to take an action.

The sinister ones move to the battlefield
The pleasant thoughts try to put up a shield
For thoughts are monsters that live inside of me
And the ominous ones will not break free.

Jenika Smith, Grade 8

Dylan Limon

I am Dylan Limon
I am 12 years old
I have 2 dogs
I have 300 dollars
My dad is a cars salesman
My grandpa has been shot
I have 3 sisters
I have a wrestling mat in my basement
I have seen Michael Jordan in person
I am Dylan Limon
Dylan Limon, Grade 7

Team Fun

V iew the court
O ver play your opponent
L ove the game
L isten to your coach
E ncourage your teammates
Y ell when you are ahead
B e a leader
A lways stay strong
L ock the game in your heart
L eave as a winner
Jessica Confer, Grade 7

Veteran's Day

Veteran's Day is not just another day
It is all about supporting veterans
Veterans come in all sizes, big and small
Both men and women
They stand together to defend our country
And our freedom
They fight to save our lives
They are brave
Some die for us
We are happy for Veteran's Day
Alysen Burke, Grade 7

Fight for the King*

"All is not sweet, all is not sound,"
Rarely in life is joy found;
For life is a battle we all must fight,
Fight for the King who gave His life
And by His love relieves our strife.
He defeated our foe upon the cross
So our souls may not become a loss.
For when the battle is over and done,
He will come with the glory of the sun.
Marguerite Morgali, Grade 9
*Inspired by Ben Jonson.

Home Alone

Sleeping, house quiet
Finally, I eat alone
The big empty house
Jaise Heaton, Grade 7

The Tribal Sense*

My paint colors are symbols.
Turquoise for nature, healing, wisdom, endurance and confidence.
I know I am all.
I am confident in war, I believe in healing, myself and soul.
I am for the nature around me.

My black paint, for victory, success, power, aggression and strength.
I believe I am successful, I did not wear this paint for nothing.
I believe I am strong, and I have power.

White. White gives me purity and light.
White is for sharing and mourning.
I believe I have purity and light
I feel I can touch people's hearts with this gift inside me.

You may look at me and think I am just an Indian with paint,
But when you look closer, into detail, would you ever know what my paint represents?
Clare O'Neil, Grade 8
*Inspired by The Ritual Cache

A Miracle Shot

As I dribble down the court
I make my first shot; it goes down with a swish,
but for my second shot I could only wish.

I really want to make it,
Go ahead and save the game,
But instead I air-balled and felt really lame.
Coach called a time out and said I need the ball,
Steal it on the throw in and we'll win it all.

I dribble to the three point line, stopped, and popped a shot,
But out of nowhere our team grabs the ball and throws it back out to me.

I try to take the three again and this time it's a swish,
I never could have without our team's sweet dish,
My coach said I saved the game with my amazing Hail Mary Shot,
He jumped up and down and celebrated quite a lot!
Joey Gallardo, Grade 8

Invisible

Hello, did not see me there, did you?
That is all right, it's not as if I have always been there.
Ah, but if you only knew,
Everything you do to tear
Apart my broken heart bit by bit, 'till there is nothing left.
I am nothing but a minuscule ant on your extravagant sidewalk, waiting to be smushed
As I morosely lay there bereft.
I can never forget how you cleverly pushed
Me out of your life, like kicking a wimpy pebble down a dusty, dirt road.
I want you to know the real me.
Please try to ignore your awfully, harsh code,
I want you to see,
I wish not to make your life unlivable.
And remember darling, I am not invisible.
Rebecca Bora, Grade 9

Fair Life

Sitting on a wooden chair in the kitchen
Flies buzz by…buzz…
Drinking ice tea with grandma
Trying not to die from the heat
Life time-summer time

Summer is the best season
Going outside with my pigs
Talking to them about everything
Even though they don't talk back
But I know they are listening

Then fair time comes around
Pigs are ready but I'm not
Show days come and I get nervous
It lasts forever…all day
But is the best day ever

Now the worst day is sale day
You get money but lose the pigs
Got so close to them…
I cry all day because I lose them
Once my best friends and now gone forever…

Lyndsey Figgner, Grade 9

Family Forever

We work heavenly together and always forever
we could roam the earth for eternity
But when it rains
There will always be pain
It will always work out not like you want it to
but I'm sure it will make do
Like a baby visiting the zoo
Now spread the word
this is not under "confidentiality"
I know how it rolls "My mommy will be so proud of me"
but when you get home
she will yell loud to me
"I love you more than this world in reality"
And it would occur to me that we are now family
always and forever as we work heavenly together.

Marlonda Bell-Clark, Grade 8

Hope Cheney

H illbilly auctions are her life in the summer
O atmeal is her least favorite breakfast meal
P oetry is something she is not the best at
E very minute of her life, she is bored

C is for crazy
H ope, there will only be one like her
E asy to confuse
N ever nice to her brother
E very day thing is being a blonde
Y oung and energetic

Hope Cheney, Grade 7

Oh How I Love

Oh how I love my grandma
She was so nice
She was an amazing person too
If the family would fight
She would be the first there
She felt it was her job
To keep the family together and strong
She was so loving and caring too
You could be a stranger and she would show love to you
Oh how I love my grandma

Oh how I love my grandma
But one day my grandma got sick
We thought it was nothing
But we were wrong
It turned out to be worse than we thought
Grandma got worse, doctors started to say it was time
Every time I saw her I would say
Oh how I love you grandma
And one day I said my last goodbye
I wish I could see her one last time
Oh how I love my grandma

Ladislao Contreras, Grade 8

Grim

There I was, sitting on my chair
Waiting for him to whisk me away in the air
My death bed was sitting on horizon's ground
Listening for me until I come on round
Like a cat by a mouse hole
Waiting for him to come and be eaten like a roll
Until one day there was a rap on my door
But I was too weak to get up from the dying floor

After the coming of years passed and by
The door breaks open and just misses me by a fly
In comes a pool of darkness there
In there stood a man: tall, dark, and without care
"Come with me," he said in a hollow voice
I want to say no, but my brain says "You have no choice"
He picked me up with his old bony hand
And put his hand out proudly, like he owned the land.

"Who are you?" I meekly asked, "and do you wish for my reap?"
"I am only the reaper of grim?" he responded. "Now, go to sleep."
He waved his hand in front of my face.
And wiped me out from my own race.

Carter Sheehan, Grade 7

Out of this World

Our world is a beautiful place,
with skies of sorrow and wind whispering with many voices,
clouds of fury, like soldiers in the dark,
demonic waters of planets close and far,
and rocky shores that is home to different creatures.

Viktoria Adamyan, Grade 7

Warped Tour

There are many people,
In this tight space.
The screams come from my left,
And right,
I was screaming with them.
Everyone looking,
At the amazing people ahead.
I can't hear my own voice,
Over the noise,
And singing,
This is where I want to be.

Meagan Echevarria, Grade 8

The Beach

The beach is like
fresh air, blowing
through my hair,
which is refreshing
and clean, forgetting
about reality. Peaceful
sounds of the ocean waves
whipping and crashing.
Sand in my toes reminding
me of a child's dream coming
true on a summer day.

Dylan Beavers, Grade 7

Is She Really Fine?

She has a slight sweet smile,
Why isn't her smile bigger he wonders,
She seems so perfect and pretty,
She said she's fine but,
She's really not,
Behind her smile is sadness,
Behind her eyes are tears
That may fall if she doesn't stay strong,
She's just staying strong,
She might need someone by her side,
That someone might be you.

Megan Marquez, Grade 8

The Eagle

MJ is an eagle flying high
He can soar to the sky
He could fly down the court
He was the best at his sport
He could always handle the ball
He was graceful as he flew
Racing up points 2 by 2
He made the fans cheer
His screaming fans you could always hear
He was better than the rest
As you can see, he was the best.

Dante Daniels, Grade 7

Doughnuts

I can smell the wonderful aroma in the air.
The circle of despair; I know I'm on a diet, but it's just sitting there.
It's colorful sprinkles make me drool, Man! This doughnut is really cruel.
I finally decide to take a bite; I fall in love with this delight.
I'm definitely going to regret it tonight.
I can hear the crunch of the multicolored beads beneath my teeth, and
The silly dough beneath my fingertips. They taste fantastic!
I wake up from my slumber; blast it!
I was only napping.
I really want a doughnut.

Hailey Lanterman, Grade 7

I Am Matthew Majeski

I am an athlete
I dream that I will become a professional football player
I feel that football is the only thing that speaks to me
I hear the big hits that me and teammates make
I am an athlete
I pretend that I will throw the winning touchdown in the Super Bowl
I touch the leather football before every football game
I worry that I will get hurt in one game and will never play again
I cry when someone or something hurts me really bad

Matthew Majeski, Grade 8

I Am an Athlete!

I dream of playing at the University of Arizona.
I feel myself making the play to win the game.
I hear the crowd chanting my name.
I am an athlete.
I pretend that I meet Jackie Robinson.
I touch the baseball and my day gets 100x better.
I worry…worry? There aren't any worries in baseball.
I cry joy when I'm on Arizona's baseball team and we win the championship.
I am an athlete.

Ben MacIsaac, Grade 8

My Brother

You are a God to me,
You do everything for me,
You set good examples for me
You're always there for me when I have no one,
I am the only person you really care about
I don't think anyone one can say this like me,
But I love you like my mom, but even more.
We get into it but at the end of the day we'd always forgive each other.

Azark Cobbs, Grade 7

She Is —

She is an undiscovered wonder, a story untold.
She is a true beauty, the first flower to bloom after the cold.
You can tell her intelligence is strong, there is knowledge in her eyes.
Her kindness radiates like the sun and its light.
She is positively beaming, delicate like a bird.
But she is nothing if not humble and flawless in every form of the word.

Summer Thomas, Grade 8

Dog Tired

I'm tired.
I'm torn.
I'm trashed.
Not the muscles aching,
    From the 6 A.M. weights for football,
    8th period conditioning.
Not the sleepy all around tired,
    Because I was up all night doing homework,
    And studying for quizzes and tests, no.
Not tired like mom and dad from work,
    Taking the yelling from their bosses,
    Even when the bosses are wrong.
But the completely worn tired.
Tired of the expectations I should live up to.
Tired that the world can't help each other.
Tired that schools don't understand the work.
Tired that this team takes ten times the crap.
Tired that I need more money for college.
Tired that the country doesn't want to listen
Tired that I'm too tired to do much but stay tired.

Meher Tarun Pothanker, Grade 9

I Am

I am a dreamer.
I wonder what people dream about,
I hear people say I can't fulfill my dreams,
I see people give up before they even try,
I want everyone to reach their goals,
I am a dreamer.

I pretend that people will always dream,
I feel people will not try,
I touch the wish upon a star,
I worry that I might fail,
I cry about the forgotten dreams that will never reach the stars,
I am a dreamer.

I understand not everything will come true,
I say everything has a chance,
I dream of everything I want to be,
I try to make every dream come true,
I hope that people see the stars,
I am a dreamer.

Rose DeLateur, Grade 8

Summer Is

A warm feeling in the pit of your stomach,
The cool breeze through your hair,
The wet splash of sweat from your hard work and play,
The beautiful sunbeam upon your face when you awake.

It's a day with friends,
It's the trips,
It's the memories you make,
It's summer.

Ceyarra Hicks, Grade 8

A Great Book

A stupendous book is keeping my attention.
My friends keep trying to talk to me.
But until I'm finished with the book
They will just have to wait.
And I'm not going to be done anytime soon.
I feel bad for ignoring them,
But it's such an astounding story.
And it's too difficult to put down.
My friends are poking me,
Trying to get my attention.
But I just shoo them away,
And keep on reading.
They're saying the bell is about to ring.
But they must be lying.
Wait, was that the bell?
No, I don't want to go!
I want to keep reading!
I'm at a good part too!
This is so iniquitous!
I guess I'll sneak some pages between classes.

Katie Block, Grade 8

Family Vacation Time

Such a **F** un and adventurous time for all
In the b **A** ckseat of the car
Listening to **M** usic on my phone
    Wa **I** ting for the next time we stop
Talking and **L** aughing
    Sta **Y** ing in hotel rooms

    Tra **V** eling all over the country
Perceiving lots of pl **A** ces and cities
    Looking out the **C** ar window as sights pass by
    Trying to get to **A** ll 50 states
    A prodigious **T** ime with family
Even though fam **I** ly gets a little bothersome
    O n the way back to the airport
Not lo **N** g enough

    T ime sure does fly by
    I nvestigating places to go next year
Making **M** emories that will last a lifetime
Can't wait until the n **E** xt time!

Brianna Fry, Grade 8

Full of Family

C ompanionship of family and friends
H ope is what Jesus' birth gives to us
R eceive hugs and warm welcomes
I nside is full of celebration
S on of God is born as a human — incarnation
T rees lit everywhere
M ary becomes a mother
A ll of the candles are lit
S ongs are merrily sung

Claire Jacobs, Grade 8

Joys of a Guitar

It takes a simple strum
One pick of the string
Sticks to you like gum
Makes your heart sing.

The strings align so flawless
Each pertains it's own melody
They fill you with such calmness
Property tuning is the key

The body's shape oh so curvy
The polished wood has a glossy finish
Bending, curving all so swirly
All your stress seems to diminish
Guitars are works of art
Instruments made from the heart
Esmeralda Orozco, Grade 8

Cancer Free

Today was such a great day
When I found out about May.
The way to be
Is cancer free.
Five years ago on this very night
She fell to the floor at the terrible sight.
Through all this mess
There was a lot of stress.
To save her life
She went under the knife.
They had a lot of hope
But the doctor said nope.
The next day when she woke up
She felt like a pup.
It was the best day
The cancer went away.
Andrew Mulheran, Grade 7

Softball

Get to the field,
not many there.
Walking closer,
people stop and stare.
Two bags with me,
all full of gear.
Here I come,
showing no fear.
This isn't a game,
it's a passion.
All suited up,
no need for fashion.
Here comes the pitcher,
time to practice.
Out on the field,
this is my palace.
Gianna Trippiedi, Grade 8

Secrets

Everyone has their own secrets.
Some keep them locked up inside.
though everyone in their lifetime,
Can't let all their secrets hide.

If you look beyond the surface,
You'll see what lies beneath.
In the depths of one person's soul,
They'll let free what's underneath.

When you go inside someone's heart,
Be careful what you do.
You don't know the effects it will have.
You don't know what it'll brew.

Imagine you in this position,
Your secrets to conceal.
What feelings would you be having?
Feelings you won't reveal.

Some want to let their secrets out;
The burden's weight no more.
They feel freer than ever, now
Freer than ever before.
Olivia Mettille, Grade 7

The Battlefield

Arrows whiz by in the sky
The screaming sound as they fly
Shields bang against steel armor
Swords clash wounding each other

Loud bangs shake the red soaked field
The wounded cry for they yield
But it's too late their time comes
God takes them with the holy ones

Fire balls light up the gray skies
Exploding the ground nearby
The fire ignites some soldiers
Hits hurl colossal boulders

Less and less still stand
They wait for the war to end
Weak and being now breathless
Some soldiers are still restless

As the battle ends away
No one has a word to say
The victors raise their steel shields
Remember the battlefield
Blake Niewinski, Grade 8

I Will Stay Strong

People treat me, like I'm an animal
They think I'm strange, not normal
They think that I'm never there
And I don't care.

They call me stupid, they call me lame
They call me any other rude names
They will say anything to bring me down
But I will never keep a frown.

I have friends
Those will stay by my side 'til the end
And they will stand up for me
No matter what the odds may be.

I won't say anything in my defense
So people will assume I don't take offense
When I get a chance to hide
I won't take it, and I'll show my pride.

"I am not a girl to be bullied
I'm a person who won't stay too worried
I'm a girl who will stay strong
I am a person who won't say I'm wrong."
Jessi Ahrens, Grade 8

My White Dog

Remembers
The sound of barking
As I enter the room

Prints in the mud while she runs
Up and down the field
Like an athlete

The constant scraping
On the floor because
She's by herself

By my side when
I am alone. Comforting
Her when there's
A thunderstorm

Long belly rubs, lots
Of food, warm baths
Getting treated like
A princess. That's
Everything a good
Family can give a
Dog they LOVE.
Jaden Anderson, Grade 8

Veterans

With bravery and strength,
dignity and pride.
You served our country
with guns by your side.
The life you lived
was dangerous and rough,
but as you went on
things got tough.
You helped make me free,
to be the greatest
that I could be.
Paige Mendenhall, Grade 7

Love of Nature

We were all once green,
But we are never all forever,
Nature needs us to keep it safe,
We should cherish plants and animals,
Plants need sun and water,
Just like we do,
We need them for oxygen,
They need us for being taken care of,
We keep ourselves and them alive,
We shall all live life forever together
Bryanne Leiseth, Grade 8

Heartbreak

Tears stain the floor,
as I'm running out the door.
I don't turn back,
my heart can't take another crack.
I hear him shout my name,
but I am the one to blame.
I wasn't the one for him,
our love was only dim.
He grabbed my shoulder, "I still love you."
But with a sigh, I said "We are through."
Emily Jovanovich, Grade 8

Family

Fun to be around
Amazing and awesome people
My own
An inspiration to be like my family
Laughing, loving and caring
Yelling, laughing, screaming
Alexandra Farmer, Grade 8

Hero

Heroes are like green
They sound like a party
They taste like fresh dough
They smell like fresh air
They look like laughter
They make you feel graceful
Stuart Moser, Grade 8

Best Luck

I get the best luck in the world
It gets me far but I don't give a whirl
I get it all the time
It helps me where ever I go
But this is the luck that I want and I know
The luck is the best thing I ever got
I hope it stays with me whenever I'm not
The luck is my priceless possession
It's the best thing I have ever been given
Can't get this at Walmart
Can't get this at Kmart
Trust me you need it
I wouldn't be here without it
It's made my life better
It's also made my life a little weirder
It's made my life good
It's made my life bad
Sometimes it helps
Sometimes it doesn't
I guess that's the chance you take when you had the luck worth nothin'
Cody Westendorf, Grade 7

Dear Grandpa

I miss your welcoming face,
it was always there when I went over,
and there wasn't a time I hated seeing it.
The deep conversations we had, meant so much to me
because I knew you cared and was there to listen.

I miss the smile on your face when we would all be together.
And that's how I choose to remember, you with that smile on your face.

I miss the way I saw you before,
I knew you were sick.
It made me realize that I only had a limited time with you.
I couldn't believe it.
The man that watched me grow up wasn't going to be here anymore.
But most of all I couldn't believe that this was going to be the last time with him.
But the memories we made will live in my heart forever.
And I choose to think of you with that same smile on your face,
just like I remember.
I miss you grandpa.

Leea Rodriguez, Grade 8

Farm Boy Dragon Rider

Eragon was a poor farm boy, but little did he know,
One day a dragon would deploy.
He found something in the spine,
That is most certainly divine.
What he found is a dragon, that could easily fit in a wagon.
The dragon's scales sparkled like sparkling wine in a flagon
The dragon grew so fast,
That Eragon was aghast.
The dragon ate so much, that it could fit in a trunk.
But the worst thing about these meals is that they smelled like a skunk.
Isaac Wolfinsohn, Grade 7

Christmas

Candy canes coming down the Christmas tree.
Colorful lights commence to bright.
Everyone acting childish.
Room so crowded, yet connected like birds on a nest.

Cold, yet cozy weather makes everyone happy.
Classic Christmas carols flow out through my lips.
Confident Mr. Claus will come, we wait calmly.
Creatively we write our letters to him in cursive to seem classy.

Creamy coming out of the oven.
The crust is the crunchiest, yet delicious.
Carefully we place the caramel cookies under the tree.
Beside of them, some chocolate milk.

Lizbeth Montoya, Grade 9

My Life Is Like Being a Pirate

My life is like a pirate in so many ways,
I have to fight to be like a captain.
I must take charge to win every battle,
To reach my goal is like finding treasure.

Challenges will face me and I must surpass them,
Make a mistake and it's like losing your crew.
I have to choose my path as sailing a ship,
My crew are my friends they always support me.

The problems I have will make me stronger,
But I must know it's okay to cry.
It's like losing someone, but soon I must carry on,
But I must set sail to reach my goal.

Laura Flores, Grade 8

You

when others hurt you, forgive
when others praise you, forget
when you are given a challenge, do your best
when you are brought down, get up quickly
when others are brought down, lend a hand
when others are selfish, be selfless
when others show off, be humble
when others insult you, walk away
when others are insulted, step in
when others are cowardly, be brave
when others lie, be pure
and most of all
when others change the way they are, be you

Matt Misch, Grade 8

Shaffers Crossing

Clear sky,
Mountains all around an endless lake.
Empty wilderness surrounds the snowy patches,
Yellow, green and orange leaves hang upon thousands of trees.
Glorious sights above from peaks at Shaffers Crossing.

Jayden Ausland, Grade 7

Death on the Tongue: A Song About Bullies

Angry voices in my head
Dead bodies at my feet
Where will it end?
Wars erupt with words as weapons
Escalate and blood starts flowing
Where will it end?
Victims cower, but what was their crime?
Good grades? Their clothes?
Don't you know clothes don't matter?
Grades are just a ticket out of here.
What's wrong with you?
Or is it all about power?
Getting the best edge
Trampling feelings just to boost yours up
Where will it end?
Destroying your friends
Destroys yourself
When you are gone, will you be missed?
It's not too late to change.
Where will it end?

Tristan Poirier, Grade 8

The End

The line was moving all too fast,
We were sadly loaded last.

My friends told me that it would be lots of fun,
But all I wanted was to leave and run.

A lap bar and seatbelt was all they gave,
Still they insisted that it would be safe.

We were strapped into what I called fate
As my body reminded me of the food that I ate.

In front of us was a deadly looking drop,
"Oh, why can't this ride just stop!"

My stomach had started to flip and churn,
I screamed until my throat felt burnt.

The ride ended after a final bend
Never again, will I ride on the end.

Hanako Walrath, Grade 7

A Bad Choice

Dad stood angrily in the doorway and scowled.
I knew I had done something that wasn't allowed.
For Christmas I got an exploder gun.
I was told to use it only for fun.

The mistake that I made like no other
Was shooting the blue spears at my brother.
For this I now am sorry, you see,
Since I am grounded for more than a week.

Tristan Smith, Grade 7

The Last Round

Have you ever loved something
Where you stand out in the sun
Waiting for the green to clear
So you could have some fun?
Wishing you could go back
And have a mulligan
On the 15th tee?
What about a birdie
When you missed that putt
You practiced all summer for that
But now…what?
How that didn't sink makes me want to make a fuss
But there is always next season
For the greens to be clear
And everyone, everyone
Will give you a welcoming cheer.

Isaak Ramsey, Grade 8

Little Black Dress

I remember a little black dress
my mom gave me for my sixth birthday.
I would to go parties with my sister that
had a little black dress that looked like mine.
We were like twins when we would wear
that little black dress.
I would like when my sister would
wear the little black dress.

As I was walking down the street
I saw the little black dress in the window display
and reminded me of the old little
black dress I had when I was young.
I went home to see my little black dress
and started remember the memories with this
little black dress.

Ana Garcia, Grade 8

Wait For Me

If you ever want to know how I am feeling
Wait for me to slip on my headphones
Pay attention to the way I slump into my seat
and rest my head on my knees
Observe the way my toes move
and curl around the edge of the chair
Notice my shoulders relax
and the small smile that play on my lips
See my eyes as they slowly close
and my eyebrows rise in content
Look at my fingers fiddle
and play with each other
If you ever want to know how I am feeling
Do not ask me

Just wait for me to slip on my headphones

Julie Ly, Grade 8

Family

Together forever, through thick and thin
Jolly, sad, apprehensive, and mad
Fighting and forgiving until the end
Adding and celebrating
Losing and grieving
Together as one
Bringing joy and excitement
Making bonds and friendships
Creating stories and memories to share with all
Holidays and parties sprinkle the year bringing cheer
United as one whether together or apart
Above or on Earth
Miles or feet away
Blood and papers don't unite us together
But the memories we grow fond of year after year create us
Family is forever and ever

Molly Machala, Grade 8

My First Day of Skiing

When I got there I was freaking out
After we finished our class I wanted to go without a doubt
I started on the little hill
That was a big thrill
Next, to go on the biggest hill you need a lift
So we had to get to the ski lift
When we got to the top
My ears started to pop
Then when we skied to the main ground
We finally found
More of the bigger slopes
Than after we got the hang of the slopes
Run 1 run 2 run 3 run 4
All I wanted was more
This trip was a blast
I can tell this wouldn't be my last

Jason Klemm, Grade 7

Mouser

Mouser the cat is my best friend.
She is there for me always; when I'm sick she's there.
When I'm blue she's there to cheer me up.
Mouser is a very fat cat, but I love her so.
She is a funny cat; she bolts across the house.
She always wants to see you.
She is the best cat ever.
Mouser, the cat of everyone's dreams.
She is always beside you.
She misses you when you leave.
She's there when you come back.
Mouser, you are so old, but yet so young.
You already have grey hairs.
You're older than
Me.
Mouser

Jeremiah Hoekman, Grade 8

Spring

Spring is the time of a nice cool breeze.
I go outside and then I see
All the trees have suddenly turned green,
And everything seems so clean.

Spring is when we have Earth day,
And I must say, it makes for a good day.
I ran all the way to the recycle bin to throw away trash.
Boy, do I love Earth day.

I go outside and play basketball,
But I first must buy a new ball.
I have three hoops in my drive,
I love my hoops like bees love their hives.

During the spring, there are many storms,
Tornados break down the houses,
Hail cracks through a window,
And the water floods the basement.

School will soon be done,
Not having homework will sure be fun.
Sleeping in and staying up late,
These are the things that make spring great.

Grant Hatteberg, Grade 7

The Pains of the Morning

Cushy, cozy, and comfortable
All snugged up in my bed
I dream of things I can't imagine
Like sugar plum fairies dancing in my head

Then my heaven on earth is over
As I hear the birds chirp and sing
Then I hear the sun shout
"It's morning, get up you lazy thing!"

I hear my alarm clock screaming
And I try to ignore it
It's now morning time
Dream world may be gone, so I should just quit.

I will turn off the lights
Next, I will close the door
Shut the blinds
But for the shining sun, there is no cure.

I try my best
I try everything
But I will never beat
The pains of the morning

Eddie Haskell, Grade 8

The Berlin Wall

The Berlin Wall was a dreadful wall.
It trapped East Berliners and hurt them all.
Many different countries tried to help through this.
One of them was the U.S.

The wall built from 1961-1989.
People had to wait such a long time!
About 4,800 people escaped successfully.
200 people were not as lucky.

In 1961 JFK stated "Ich bin ein Berliner"
This meant he was on the people behind the walls side.
In 1987 Ronald Reagan said a well known quote.
It was "Mr. Gorbachev tear down this wall!"

In 1989 the wall came down.
People were happy all around!
Citizens walked and talked on the wall!
They were overjoyed it would fall!

Some of it is still up today!
But most of it has been put away.
I feel terrible for all that had to be behind the divide!
I wonder what it would feel like inside.

Nathaniel Blasen, Grade 7

The Meadow Dance I Never Had

Daisy petals dot the breeze
Silken violets dance around trees
Dainty orchids tremble and spin
By high command of the mighty wind

Beckoned by their joyous cries
From my parents, away I fly!
Thirteen rushing steps I skip
But over a jagged stone I trip

Dragged farther away from the friendly flower
What had seemed like seconds, was barely an hour
Countless years passed, yet even so I remember
This sun-speckled, wind-blessed day in September

Yet, as leaf subsides to leaf,
Eden and I have sank to grief.
So fiery dawn goes on to day.
Nothing gold can ever stay.

That verse is glued inside my head,
So honestly written, revised and read.
No other words can compare, to be true,
As lovely gold fades into despondent blue.

Sarah Kim, Grade 7

The End of the Game

Why was it me who had to strikeout
when there were two outs,
last inning, full count.
It was the middle of the tournament.
We had to survive or
drive home to Lawrence in shame.
I slammed my bat on the ground, felt horrible.
I had let my whole team down.
Why couldn't it have been somebody else?
Somebody else who could carry the team on their shoulders
and just hit a crummy single?
We knew we weren't going to win anyway,
but we still wanted to stay alive.
I wanted to stay alive.
I needed this one hit.
But no. It just had to be a strike out.
My mom and my coach said it was all right.
But it wasn't all right. We lost. I lost.
I ruined the game with
one
swing.

Wyatt Carson, Grade 7

Light

I'm almost to the light
It's so scary though
The dark is a better place
I'm used to it already
It'd be nicer
The light is horrible
Towards it gives me trouble
There's no way I can make it
There's way too much rubble
I'm going insane
It's ridiculous
Why did I bother to try?
The dark is where my home is, you live and you die
I've heard the light is paradise
But how can it be?
So much pain to get there
It's impossible you see!
Everyone around me in the light, laughing and smiling
And now I realize I was in the light all along
I'll join them now, singing my own silly song
Waiting for the rest in the dark, to join me in their own happiness

Kayla Kraft, Grade 8

Ode to My Grandma

My grandma is not like other grandmas
She takes long walks in the summer
And plants flowers of every color in the spring
Watches any new movies the library has to offer in the winter
Only lives down the street, there whenever I need her
Eyes a crystal clear blue and hair blonder than Barbie's
Always says I'm getting taller, but she is the one shrinking
Chocolate chip cookies are her specialty
Actually just baking in general
She is stronger than any woman I know with a heart of gold
Never asks for anything, but is always giving to others
As busy as she is with work, parties and vacations
She always has plenty of time to help whoever needs it
She holds so many memories
Florida has a special place in her heart
My grandpa's ashes are scattered on the beaches of Naples
Their favorite place on Earth
She helped raise me when my parents both worked
So generous and kind, her gifts mean the absolute world
I look up to her and cherish every moment with her
Time with my grandma, is never time wasted

Kristina Ferrari, Grade 9

Three Hinges That Support My Worst Fear

A wooden object that scares me at the night
hard to describe but will give one a fright
It keeps my clothes organized
But I can't stand it being open at night
I have bad dreams like on a boat being capsized

Its rectangle appearance gives me creeps
At night it looks like a black hole
Sometimes I wish I could sleep
By counting some sheep

In the morning when I rise
I can relax because I know it's all in my head
During the day I tend to forget,
But when it grows dark and it's time to go to bed
I think, "Oh no, here we go again"

This is my worst fear;
I hope someday I can cheer
When I have no problem with this fear
even though it may take a couple years

Michael Hart, Grade 8

The Way of Life

Like the wind,
We rush through crowds of people.
Like the trees,
We stand strong through the hard times,
And accomplish what others doubt is possible.
We follow our path through life,
And figure out we have to live our life to the fullest.

Concey Bader, Grade 7

Summer Fun

Excitement seems bright red
Like the color of a bonfire in midsummer
I see many people around the big fire
I hear the excitement in people's voices nearby
I smell the burgers cooking somewhere off in the distance
I touch the green grass underneath my feet
I taste the burgers fresh off the grill

Jake Hamilton, Grade 9

Life
You are perfect
You are loved
A perfect reflection of heaven above
The pain you feel inside
Is hidden by your smile
No one knows the real you
You try to hide from your demons
But, they keep on finding you
They whisper in your ear
"You are pathetic and worthless"
You scream back "No I'm not"
You want the pain to go away
You try not to believe them
But, soon enough you start believing it
You start wondering if you even belong here
Would anyone miss you if you were gone?
You think of taking your life
But, then you realize
You might be able to overcome your demons and live your life
Libni Funes, Grade 8

Those Who Deceive
I am cold and unforgiving
I wonder when the end will come
I hear the voices of what's right and wrong
I want the world to know how I see him
I am cold and unforgiving

I pretend to care and appreciate it all
I feel the hands of my anger and bitterness
I touch the calming waters of hopelessness
I worry his act of warmness will crawl into my heart
I cry for those who fall at his hands
I am cold and unforgiving

I understand not all are the same
I say, everyone gets what they deserve
I dream of a world where he has not transformed me
I try to erode the stone that is my heart
I hope the sacred flame will scare away the monster inside me
I am cold and unforgiving
Karen Romero, Grade 8

Untitled
Footsteps bouncing off the walls of my mind
Fake smiles fill the shoes
The urge to block them out
Is all my mind consumes

Weak broken beaten down
With nothing better to achieve
The fear and phony surrounds you
Now wishing you could just leave

What happened to sympathy?
Taken over by popularity
Nothing you do is ever right
Because you have sincerity

When you hit rock bottom
There is a way out
It may be hard to look up
But do so without a lick of doubt
Hannah Andrews, Grade 9

Honeybees
Honeybees fly on the days that are warm.
They hum as they work and greet every flower.
Then, if it gets hot, they begin to swarm.
But the pollen is what they like to devour.

Most people get scared when bees are around.
They will never hurt you unless you hurt them first.
They are fun to watch if you see them on the ground.
The nectar is the drink that they thirst.

Look up to the sky, there they buzz.
They like landing on bright colors.
You could watch them if they stop, just because.
They're out in the hot summer.

The best part about them is the honey they make.
It tastes so sweet, and it's good and healthy.
They do the job so carefully, with never one mistake.
Bees have a very big responsibility.
Ciera Bronnenberg, Grade 8

An Exciting Game
B allin' down the court
A s their eyes are watching me
S wiftly running by them like a slithering snake
K eeping the ball safe
E xciting game we are tied
T rying to score
B asket made, game almost over
A s we are ahead, I'm feeling great
L ongest second ever, we have to win
L ast game of the year was a success
Lindsey Johnson, Grade 7

Nick's Life
— Nick
Interesting, smart, funny, and generous,
Lover of winter, spring, and summer,
Brother of Alexis Kosiek,
Who needs steak, chicken, and snow,
Who gives kindness, support, and niceness,
Who would like to see the White House, space, and China,
Who fears spiders, height, and sharks,
Who lives in a big white house on Clifton way,
— Kosiek
Nicholas Kosiek, Grade 7

Crystal Clear

Now, it is crystal clear
What you said
Through all the fear
Now, it is crystal clear
The end of time is near
Eyes filled with dread
Now, it is crystal clear
What you said

Rebecca Neaterour, Grade 8

Sadness

Soft brown eyes,
Beautiful
Sadness in her voice
Had a family history of heart disease,
A sudden heart attack
Her father's death
Last look with sadness
Tears began to cry

Morgan Malcomb, Grade 7

Cat

A cat climbed up a tree
Then he got stuck
He wondered what he could be
A cat climbed up a tree
He couldn't really see
He fell in some muck
A cat climbed up a tree
Then he got stuck

Harli Handzo, Grade 8

My Little Brother

My brother acts like a dinosaur
He will scare you with his loud roar
He will make his feet go 'stomp'
Then he will go bite something; 'chomp'!
He will always show off his wings or tail
He will also run much faster than a snail
My brother is a dinosaur;
He will go to bed after his last roar

Claire Fink, Grade 7

Flying Angels

Soaring high in the sky light as a feather
Not giving a care about the weather
I chose to be free and fly with glee
with my wings spread apart
Flying here and there
Back to the nest
landing really light
here I am a baby bird ready to take flight

Asia Blossom, Grade 9

The Beauty of Winter

Snow shimmers brightly throughout the blue sky
The trees are filled with sparkle as high as they go
This world is like being inside a snow globe watching flurries pass by
A blanket of white falls apart above swirling into snow

Then the mountains and hills take their place in the wintery wonderland
Leaving the horizon to stretch as far out as the eye can see
Falling snow collects together to end up looking like a string of lace on the ground
Every little snowflake is unique and complete

Piles and piles of glistening snowfall being moved
Tiny fractions of the blizzard land on my gloved hands
Snow covered ground from fresh fallen snow
Trees weighed down from the mounds of snow crystals piled on their branches

Peeking out the window it looks like vanilla ice cream exploded all over
Walking through the multiple feet of snowfall
Gives the feeling of joy and adventure
Snow shines and glitters just like a shining star

Elena Stirn, Grade 7

Peace

If you really want to achieve,
you've got to believe,
Martin Luther King Jr., had a dream.
he did it by himself, he didn't need any team.

if you want to succeed,
instead of following,
you've got to lead.
Martin Luther King Jr., started small but grew like a seed.

When you are calm and kind,
you stand out and shine.
Martin Luther King Jr., marched in a line for what he thought was right,
but the white police took it wrong and made him pay time.

When you are going to lead,
you not only have to be neat, but teach.
Martin Luther King Jr., was a great hero,
who made lots of peace.

Mireya Rivera, Grade 7

Life

Life is like an undying friendship.
A companion,
With whom you spend your time with,
Someone to laugh with,
And someone to talk with.

Life is also like a black hole,
Filled with confusion and darkness.
A place where some people lose themselves.
A sometimes dark place where people are never found.
But sometimes, if you are careful, you can hold onto yourself and fight through it all.

Sarah Ingram, Grade 7

I Wish I Were Not so Irresistibly Attractive

I wish I were not so irresistibly attractive.
My intense hotness burns the floor I walk on.
Any pool I step into is instantly a hot tub.
I'm so beautiful I won America's Next Top Model
Six times with a broken nose and face cast.
I've been on cover after cover, commercial after commercial,
Without a single smear of makeup on.
I am the face that breaks necks when people turn to look at me.
If I were to die and be left to rot,
The soil I sink in would give off nutrients of cuteness.
The flower that grows will be stunning,
Not as stunning as me, of course.

Kailyn Bryk, Grade 9

The Best Kind of Dog

The best kind of dog is a Chusky
It's a mix between a Chihuahua and a Husky
He would be fun
And like to run
He wouldn't shed
And could never be put to bed
You'd have a best friend forever
But you would never
Know what he will do next
Sometimes he might even be a pest
Even though he's a troublemaker
You'll still love him the best

Molly Drogosz, Grade 7

Planting Time

I wake up at 5 and it's planting time, we spread the chemicals,
we till the field, we plant the seeds and wait for rain,
when it rains too much, it floods the fields,
so we re-till the flooded area, then plant more seeds,
and wait for rain, then let the crops grow,
then pick the crops, then next year,
we wake up early to plant the fields, we spread the chemicals,
we till the fields, we plant the seeds and wait for rain,
when it rains too much, it floods the fields,
so we re-till the flooded area, then plant more seeds,
and wait for rain, then let the crops grow,
then pick the crops, until next year we plant again.

Garrett Lamb, Grade 8

Golf Balls

Life is like a pack of golf balls.
First they are high and mighty on a shelf
packed for perfection.
Then they get bought by a new golfer.

It is thrown, and stomped.
Then he hits it close to the hole, this is great!
No one can miss this!
Then he gets a call. It's his boss he's fired
and it gets thrown into the duck pond.

Jonathan Leppert, Grade 7

Writing Your Days

As I write
my life away,
the cartridge begins to run low.

The antique profession of calligraphy awaits
my hovering hand of hope.
As my pen,
begins to shake,
from the thousands of words that complete me.

The smooth flow of ink,
the rough sound of the pen,
as it dances across my paper —
scribing the events of my life.

The scratchy feeling of its nib,
as the barrel embraces my hand.
The soft smooth touch of the gold and black utensil,
makes me feel I've shared joy with the world.

My bones begin to break,
my fingers growing sores.
I'm slowly disappearing,
but my writing has been spared.

Brooke Zielke, Grade 8

Summer Rainstorms

Smells of the air
Love when the roses are blooming
Tulips rising
Corn frying
BBQ on the grill for the night's supper
Cattle balling for their babies
As pigs are bucking wherever because they get to play in the mud
As the robin plays in the grass
Looking for the only worm for her chicks
The pounding on the tin of your shed
Summer rainstorms
Grass is green
Possibly a tornado
Soothes the soil when the rain comes down
Rainbows a rising for the person to get the gold at the end

Ty Groth, Grade 9

My Lovely Place

It is where I am alone and happy
I go there when I need to feel loved
I run through fields full of gorgeous flowers
I see bright, beautiful flowers and the most colorful butterflies
I hear the gentle wind swaying the trees side to side
And the wonderful sound of birds chirping
I choose to sit on the soft, comfy grass
And watch the magnificent animals roam by
I will go back when I am alone
I go back to my dreams always at night

Tressa LaBarge, Grade 8

The Shot

With the last second remaining I took the shot.
There was no way it was going in,
I was way too far from the 3 point line.
Everyone knew it wouldn't go through,
The defender was in my face,
I was off balance,
And I was having a bad game.
We needed that shot to hit,
So we could win the championship.
It was all up to me.

With the last second remaining I took the shot.
It went in!
I banked it off the glass from the 3 point line.
I knew I'd make the shot,
Even with the defender,
My off balance,
And the bad game.
I willed the shot to go,
And we won the championship.
All thanks to me.

Malik Jackson, Grade 8

Guardian Angel

I'm the wings that keep your sanity,
I'm your armor that treats you nicely,
I'm your sword that fights your fears away,
I'll be your jewelry that gives you grace and beauty,
I'll be in your heart until we part.

Like glue, I'll stay by your side,
If you are lost, I will always find you,
If you feel that I'm in the way,
I'll become your eyes,
Letting you see what you need,
You might find out we think alike,
What you hear, I hear.
What you see, I see.

We were meant to be.
Like the stars from above,
We will shine every night,
Like the ocean needs to
Exist to hold the sky in place.
From the moment we met.

Ariana Rico, Grade 9

The Sport for the Strong

Pride seems golden
Like the gold medals I can win from wrestling
I see championships and victories over my opponents
I hear the cheers of the crowd and my teammates
I smell the sweat from my hard work
I touch the new trophy and feel its value
I taste the blood from my accomplishments

Joel Hill, Grade 9

Divorced

Just because my parents are divorced
Doesn't mean my family is different from yours
Doesn't mean my family is not perfect
And doesn't mean I am different

Just because my parents are divorced
Doesn't mean I prefer one over the other
It doesn't mean I don't like my step-parents
Doesn't mean my siblings don't love me or I don't love them

Just because my parents are divorced
Doesn't mean I'm broken
Doesn't mean I wish they were still together
And it doesn't mean I need help

Just because my parents are divorced
Do you have to ask why they split?
How old I was?
Do you enjoy your step-parents and siblings?

I just don't understand why I am different from you.

Katarina Dodd, Grade 8

The Other Me Is RED

RED is a color
but,
it's also "her" name.
Even though there is a
resemblance,
we just aren't the same.
Childish, withered, arrogant,
is the hue of her vanity.
RED eyes, night hair, goth dress
—is her sanity.
Though playful, dense, and innocent as she
appears,
she counters my distance, shyness, an "incarnate" of my greatest
fears.
From laughter to envy, tears to criticism, disdain to scorn,
her emotion matched up
to her confided cat eyes, and cunning, curved smile
she had worn.
Transparent as a spirit, a "MONSTER" she was filed.
In truth,
she is me; a crying, lonely, "child."

Audrey K. Anonuevo, Grade 7

Respect for You

R emembering to mind my manners
E xpecting the truth and nothing, but the truth
S o I never lie to you because I know the punishment of what I do
P atience and silence keeps our visit calm
E xcited to hear what you say
C urrently attentive only to you
T rying to be the best company I can for you

Teagan Landenberger, Grade 7

Spring Serendipity

What is true serendipity?
the myriad of smiling blossoms
the liberation of bliss
the idyllic setting of peace
the evanescent memory
occurs only once a year
spring is the
only
true
serendipity.

Amy Zhou, Grade 7

Nature

The wind blows across
your garden.
The roses are skeletons
now.
As their petals fall they
die slowly.
What's left is their
leaves.
Those leaves are now
dead on the ground.

Gisselle Roman, Grade 7

Cities

The colors, so green
of trees and grass.
Objects so big such as,
buildings in the skies,
beige and white,
with mountains so far
with whitish/gray.
The feeling is frustrated
with a lot of buildings
and trees

Dalton Salazar, Grade 7

Poetry Is Like a Snowstorm

Poetry
Is like a snowstorm
Where no two snowflakes are alike
Free and unique
Dancing through the sky.
You can get lost in a blizzard of words
Blanketed with snow to keep their secrets,
And bring joy to the
People with a wondrous
Mind.

Kayleigh White, Grade 7

Ocean

Breeze, water, laid back,
Seagulls, flying, sand castles,
Blue, seas, deep, dolphins

Katana Donaldson, Grade 7

Mirror, Mirror on the Wall

Mirror, mirror on the wall.
Are you the one, who is judging all?
Is it true that you reflect what's there?
Is it really me who is standing here?

Through the mirror I see a girl
One with big dreams and goals
She is the only one with the power to make herself perspire

Sometimes the mirror holds lies, lies about myself
I look in and see a smile, but on the inside I see a frown

Mirrors only show the outside, you can only see the shell
Only you can see the soul that is underneath

Some of us want money, cars, or fame
While others only wish to be in a home again.
When I glance in the mirror, I see someone who is just laying around
Only worrying about themselves, and ignoring the problem around them

Who do you see when you look inside a mirror?
Do you only see what you want to see?
Or do you look in just a little bit deeper

Isabella Bucaro, Grade 8

Desert Horse

The sun breaks through the clouds, melodies flow through the air,
And a single pair of clip-clopping, can be heard above all.
Breath steaming in the crisp morning,
And an antsy leader, ready to let go.
Around he travels, 'til everyone's in tight formation,
Mares with foals, then a trumpet breaks the stillness,
Off they run, conquering the land, wild, untouched, and free.
Flowing like water over parched ground. Dust swirling in their wake.
Colors of all kinds blend together,
Hides gleaming in the afternoon.
Sun streaked spirits stretching towards the sky,
Dancing, twirling, playfully, poetry in motion, untouched by man.

A white form breaks the darkness, after hours guarding, and many more to come,
He is greeted by the mares, while foals stay wary.
He makes his rounds, only to take up his post once again.
Twinkling diamonds against black sky, light the way,
Dark shapes take up the sky, and quenching water falls to the ground.
The sun breaks through the clouds, melodies flow through the air,
And a single pair of clip-clopping, can be heard above all.
Breath steaming in the crisp morning,
And an antsy leader, ready to let go.

Sydney Wynn, Grade 9

A Person's Life

I soar as high as the sky, yet am grounded as a rock on the ground.
I express myself in an explosion of color, yet at times I feel so bland.
I can see a bright life in front of me, but am blind to the surroundings around me.
I feel sad about the day to come, but I am always happy about my life.

Cole Bowen, Grade 9

Here Comes Goodbye

It was hard as I stayed there watching you,
Holding on to your big, warm paw
Telling you repeatedly that I was here,
And I wasn't going anywhere.
I made sure that you were comfortable on your blanket,
And when I was ready I nodded my head,
As the euthanasia entered into your veins,
I went back and thought of all the things we did together,
And how I wouldn't know how to go on without you,
I was watching the syringe as the medicine was almost gone,
Then I looked back at you and you were starting to close your eyes,
I was telling you not to leave me,
And that I needed you,
And then you left me,
Sitting there with tears rushing down my face,
My head pounding,
My stomach feeling sick,
And my heart feeling empty.

Alex Ludwig, Grade 8

The Spring Time

The spring time is a season where things start to grow
grass awakens and starts to sprout.
Flowers start to bloom and smell pretty,
the start of a new spring time
for things to grow.

The spring time is when lots of rain falls,
and mother nature starts to water her own garden.
The spring time, when trees grow leaves,
and creatures awake from
their hibernated dreams.
The spring time the start of new things to grow.

The spring time is when the trees, grass, flowers, and
creatures have a new start.
The spring time is when you can smell spring and feel it.
The spring time rain provides life to every living thing.
The spring time is a start of a new beginning.

Michael Jimenez, Grade 8

Above the Sky

He stares up high gleaming at the moon
Wondering about the old tales and stories heard as a kid

I look close not sliding a single clink
I see the moon as it speaks to me

At the moment I know I am already a man on the moon
Seeing the dark craters in perfect ready position

I now know the meaning of the brightest in the sky
Not as far away, but a nice cruise

I am now on the moon

Trevor Lorek, Grade 8

Someone's Here

It's dark out, pitch black,
I'm lying awake in bed,
When I hear a "whack,"
I throw my covers over my head.

I know the sound came from downstairs,
My heart pounds in my chest,
I'm all alone, no one here but me,
But then I hear movements from downstairs.

I freeze like an ice cube,
I'm scared out of my mind,
I try to talk, but no words are spoken,
It's as if they had been stolen.

There's a creak from the stairs,
I get the feeling as if my whole life has flashed right before my eyes,
The doorknob to my room begins to turn as I fill with fear,
And all I can think is, "who's there!"

Makayla Houser, Grade 8

There Is No Place Like Home

Home is warm and inviting,
It is the place I like the best.
Home is where I feel the most comfortable,
I hate to leave the nest.

Home is the one place I can really let loose,
It is where I'm considered normal, not strange.
Home is where I can be myself without being judged,
I love that I will never have to change.

Home is where my heart lies,
It is a place I'm blessed to call my own.
Home is where I'm surrounded by love,
I never feel all alone.

Home is not just where I live,
It is so much more you see.
Home is wherever my family resides,
For they mean everything to me.

Maddi Swanson, Grade 9

Sadness

Tear drops dripping down my face like a waterfall.
Even though I said I would never fall.
We always get a second chance;
But I'm on my third.
Not always being happy isn't terrible.
Not everyone has a perfect life.
Even through thick and thin;
We try to stay strong.
No regrets,
No fear,
It's just this weird thing everyone calls Sadness.

Karina Sorensen, Grade 7

Bombing of Birmingham

September 15, 1963 is when it happened,
A nightmare that was unexpected.
The last time I would see my friends,
Because the explosion couldn't be deflected.

I remember the laughter of children,
Something that I enjoyed.
But then the explosion went off,
I wasn't overjoyed.

Addie asked "Does anyone need help?"
"Help with my belt" Denise said.
When she was done, Addie was tying her sash,
But when the explosion when off, everyone was dead.

I was blind because glass went in my eye,
I repeated "Addie, Addie where are you?"
My sister had to identify bodies,
But all she saw was Addie's shoe.

Ricardo Morales, Grade 8

Music

It can be the soundtrack to a summers day
What I would hear while sitting on the dock of the bay;
Music is number one on my top five
It just makes me feel alive

Whether I'm leavin' today
Or I'm going to play;
When I'm listening it sets me free
And when you see me let me be

When I'm down in the dumps
I just turn on "My Humps;"
It's also fun when I'm jumping around
Or I'm just homeward bound

Music is my passion
But doesn't change my fashion;
Music is the one thing I write
And keeps the light in my heart burning bright

Ryan Thiem, Grade 9

Dancing

I love to dance, and spin, and twirl.
If you have a chance, I'd give it a whirl.
Listen to your heart, and just let go,
Let your body gracefully flow.

It is a simple way,
To forget about your bad day.
If you feel down,
Do away with that frown.

Look in the mirror at who you are,
And realize your dreams are not too far.
Peace, happiness, and freedom are what you feel,
So try it because it's a big deal!

Step on that stage with those bright lights,
Make your first move realize it's not a big fright.
Breathe in, breathe out.
This is what dancing is all about.

Alexa Nelson, Grade 9

The Big Step

Stepping onto the court,
Rising to the challenge set up for you.
Playing in a game that brought courage,
Working hard to get into this position.
Getting the chance to prove yourself,
While playing with very talented girls.
Being the youngest of them all,
But working as hard as they would,
Or even harder to get to the level they are.
BAM! The attack of a large opponent,
Then the rush of exciting spirits.
The crazy feeling when you get the first dig,
On a court with the stands filled to the very top.
Believing in being better before you started.
Doubting you could fill those shoes
When really you should always think high of yourself,
As a young athlete and being able to play with our best players.
That chance and opportunity that was a first experience,
All starting with a single jersey and the courage to fulfill dreams.

Tessa Hedlund, Grade 9

The Unique 9-Year-Old

Nicholas Benedict one of the brightest of his age
Nobody could compare and were amazed
His sight so sharp could see anything
Could see so far and any being
Read books in an hour or less
Could read on people who were happy or depressed
Nicholas Benedict just like a dictionary
Easily memorize anything to store in memory
Little Benedict so kind and thoughtful
In the end, thinking all about other people

Octavio Gonzalez, Grade 7

Oceans

Oceans rage day and night
Oceans rock you to sleep
Fish swim calmly in its depths
Bright blue surrounds you from ocean to sky
Dolphins dive left and right
Sharks show up here and there
Oceans are mysterious
Oceans never cease to amaze
oceans are always stunning
Whales launch into air trying to escape the oceans rage

Henry Harrington, Grade 7

Procrastination Station

Whenever it's the weekend,
Although my homework isn't done,
Even though my chores are not complete,
As I lay on a couch,
I think of what I need to do without doing it.

Provided that I don't have homework due in a few hours,
Since there is a comfortable area to sleep,
Where there are no sounds,
While in the house,
I will sleep.

Rather than doing said homework,
Before an hour until it's due,
Because I'm tired,
While the facade of rest escapes,
I think of what I need to do.

Tommy Donelan, Grade 8

Papa Jim

Papa Jim was amazing,
He was funny and made us laugh hard,
Whenever we were with him we always learned something new.

I remember going to his boat every summer,
We used to swim and fish, or swim with fish
We used to play with his toy lighthouse,
Maddie and I's dolls used to live in that lighthouse.

I remember always eating doughnuts the next morning
After sleeping in his house boat,
After that he would drive us in his little boat to the beach
Over at the beach we would swim and watch parasailors.

Then we would go back to the boat and have more fun,
Memories of Papa Jim will roam my mind forever,
Wishing we could make more.

Grace Morganegg, Grade 7

Can You Feel My Heart?

"I have always liked you right from the start,
You were the funniest person I knew,
I always wanted to be there for you.
I like you from the bottom of my heart.
I would hate to see us both pried apart.
You are so lovable and gorgeous.
Our desire is harmonious.
For you I will do anything I can do
You have charming eyes of methylene blue.
You are like an angel sent from above,
When we meet and talk I can feel the love.
You are the one that I need just to succeed,
and our love exists, it just isn't guaranteed
Now I ask you this; Can you feel my heart?"

Raunaq Talwar, Grade 7

Butterflies

Did you ever see a butterfly?
Look at them as they fly by
You can watch them as they sip from flowers
Sit and stare at them for hours
Watch them when they soar through the sky
Notice how they fly so high
It seems as if they have powers
How do they fly so high above the towers?
As she spreads her colorful wings
You will think she can do most things
Even though her size is small
She is one of the most beautiful insects of them all
Even though they aren't the tallest creatures
Butterflies do have beautiful features
They get me in such a good mood
Watching butterflies gives me my great attitude

Emily Grice, Grade 7

A Dogs Love

When all humans fail
The dog is always there
Licking away your tears
Nuzzling away your sorrows with their muzzle
When all humans fail
The dog is always there
Waiting at the bottom of the stairs wagging its tail
Because you're the only one they want to see
When all humans fail
The dog is always there
Because a dog is loyal to the end
Unlike a lover or a friend
And though humans may last longer
How many can you say
Wait every day
Just to see your face

Gabrielle Brazzell, Grade 9

Zinkoff

Zinkoff was a very interesting boy
He loved to play with his giraffe toy
But one day when it got smashed
He smiled, walked away, and said that was that
He loved to learn and play each day
He didn't care what the other kids say
He always knew how to have fun
He ran down the street chasing cars in the sun
On a cold snowy day
He searched for a little girl thinking of where she would stay
They found the girl but not him
He was frost bitten from toe to chin
Zinkoff gave his trophy up
So he could make his big win up
Zinkoff was a care-free kid
And everyone should stride to be like him

Taylor Tomasiewicz, Grade 7

Springtime
Rain boots pulled up high
Children slosh through the puddles
Tears fall from the sky

Absent heat returns
Flowers thrive and grace dead fields
Lost beauty returns

Small fawns dash about
Running through the new found grass
The Earth is reborn
Megan Blaney, Grade 7

Track
The race set before you
The hair-raising sound of the gun
The courage to last 'til the end
The strength that He provides
The determination in you
The focus it takes
The resilience to bounce out of pain
The agility you need
The trust He builds in you
The confidence to finish
Who are you racing for?
Sydney Nystrom, Grade 9

Thunderstorm
Looking up at the blue sky
So big to the human eye

Complete with dark clouds
It rains on the crowds

Thunder pierces the sound
Bright yellow bolts surround

Small rivers form
In the huge storm
Joseph Angle, Grade 8

Family Is Forever
Family is about making someone smile,
even if it means going that extra mile.

You may have friends that push you away,
but family is here to stay.

Have faith and you will see,
family is key.

You may think you're pretty clever,
but remember — family is forever.
Hailee Presser, Grade 7

The Mime
He was always there *mocking me*, he would always wear the same thing as me.
Looking at me, *mocking me*, always looking like me.

Not any taller than 3ft just like me. Wearing the same shoes I get in the kid's section.
The same flashy lights as he walks. The lights calling out my name *mocking me*.

Taking my mom's attention from me, Why does he do this?
Dressed in my favorite blue dinosaur shirt. The same big T-Rex looking at me, *mocking me*.
Always looking like me.

Getting the same haircut, using the same gel and hairdo.
Same hair color and type, even the same eye color, his eyes *mocking me*.
Always looking like me.

His fingers look like mine, as long. The same skin color and texture.
He likes the same food as me, the same sport, wearing the same clothes as me.
Always looking at me.

One day I found him *mocking me*, every movement. I walked, he walked.
I raised my foot, he did too, I heard something behind me so I turned around.
It was my brother; I realized he always looked like me because he was my twin.
Emilio Reyes, Grade 8

The Void
Empty all day and night in a person living a lonely life
No one to speak or to be spoken to
An open abyss deep and dark
Acting as a roadblock from your mind to your soul
Life falls in and can't come out
Every second it grows large and wide
And less and less can get to the other side
Only one way to build a bridge
That will connect the road of life once again
Meeting someone new is the key to this
They will open your eyes to let the light shine in
On the road that is in blazing storm
A storm of crying rain and sobbing thunder
Will finally dry up from a caring sun
And never give up if you have searched far and thin
for the one that will fix the road that life travels on
The one whose soul will travel into your heart
Though many find the journey is hard
It may even be hurtful in the voyage of life but taking risks is the way to go
And all you have to do is follow your heart
For that is the way you will fill the void
Joshua Bonovich, Grade 7

Bully
If you are tired, go to sleep.
If you are hungry, get some food.
If you are energized, go run.
But how do you stop a bully from bullying?
Tell a teacher,
yah it will help for a little bit but the bully doesn't stop bullying.
If you really want to stop bullying stand up for yourself and others too.
Jazzmyn Adrian, Grade 7

Best Friends Are Forever
She's your best friend for a reason.
She tells you her drama and you tell her yours. You gossip about the latest news together.
You stay up all night blabbing on about your life. And she listens.

She's your best friend for a reason. She makes fun of you. She makes you jealous.
She lies. And she says sorry the next day.

She's your best friend for a reason. She sticks up for you. She defends you.
She picks you up when you fall. And you do the same for her.

She's your best friend for a reason. She makes you laugh until your stomach hurts.
She makes you cry because it hurts so badly. She keeps on making you laugh so you can't breathe.

She's your best friend for a reason. She sobs next to you over her most recent breakup.
She makes you stay all night so she isn't alone.
You sit there in silence watching a chic-flick while tears run down her face.
And you're her shoulder to cry on.

She's your best friend for a reason. You can act yourself around her.
You can look like a slob around her. You can have the best times with her.
And she says the same about you.

I don't know about you, but I have the bestest best friend in the world.

Olivia Morini, Grade 8

Ballad of the Battle of Red Cliffs
Background: The Battle of Red Cliffs was a decisive naval battle which took place between China's northern armies led by military genius Cao Cao, and the allied southern provinces led by Liu Bei and Sun Quan. China's most brilliant tacticians at the time decided to destroy the north's massive invading fleet of allegedly 800,000 with only 20,000 soldiers by crashing into them with unmanned flaming ships and setting them ablaze. Cao Cao's army was decimated and he escaped with a tiny fraction of his troops.

Note: This ballad is from the fictional perspective of a southern Chinese soldier.

The northern army's fleet is nearing,
We are as still as stones, we aren't fearing
Their tremendous troop of eight hundred thousand.

They think that our province is what they will earn,
But they do not know that we soon will burn
Their tremendous troop of eight hundred thousand.

Our unmanned ships are flaming dragons of death set free,
It will all be over when we can't see
Their tremendous troop of eight hundred thousand.

The brilliant tactics that we have employed
Have utterly doomed and destroyed
Their tremendous troop of eight hundred thousand.

Justin Ruan, Grade 9

California
California bright and sunny, palm trees waving and whipping in the tropical breeze.
The Hollywood sign big and bold, nice cars that make car buyers' blood go cold.
Nice beaches that supermodels and celebrities relax on, beach houses that only the rich can afford.
Nice clothes and glamour galore, it makes you think how much they actually paid for.

Kiara Thomas, Grade 8

What Summer Is to Me
Warm summer breezes
Blowing on the Atlantic
Hot under the sun

Relaxed lazy days
Wasting time watching Netflix
Reading great novels

Shopping in New York
Seeing brilliant Broadways
Nights in the city

Fun day at the beach
Swimming in the salty sea
Tanning on the sand

Cold melting ice cream
Juicy fresh watermelon
Mango water ice

Spending time outside
Needs to put sunglasses on
The sun is so bright

Days become shorter
Time for school to start again
Summer is over
Jeni McGlynn, Grade 8

When I Am Older
One day when I am older,
I would like to be a doctor.
To save the lives of others,
To ride in a chopper.

One day when I am older,
I want to go to Paris.
To see the Eiffel tower,
To be one of the fairest.

One day when I am older,
I would like to live on a farm.
To ride brown and black horses,
and to just have some fun.

One day when I am older,
I hope the sun will be brighter.
The sky will be lighter,
the world, a better place.

One day when I am older,
and that day will come,
I want to be with God in Heaven.
With his angels and his son.
One day when I am older.
Paige Brummel, Grade 8

Useless Things
Coffee without cream
Sleep without a dream
A pen without ink
An eye that doesn't blink,

A surfer without a board
A charger without a cord
A racquet without strings
A ball without bling,

Hair without bows
Feet without toes
Peanuts without shells
A ring without a bell,

An ocean without a wave
A bat without a cave
Love without hate
Marriage without a mate.
Lily Schoeck, Grade 7

This World's War
The world it spins
It goes around
Never again to touch the ground

No one hold it in their hands
No one controls the dirt and sand
No one will ever own all the land

The wars break lose
Some families lost
Yet no one really wins the battle

Many battles come to an end
Many good men lost
Many families are left to mourn

But this cruel world keeps going
It doesn't stop for anyone
Or all the people left mourning
Aryann Hoffer, Grade 7

Apology
I have pushed you down in the snow.
But you did a face plant,

And which was revenge
for taking my ten bucks.
Forgive me but it
felt good! (but cold to you)

You should know
I would do it again in
a heart beat.
Cole Maddox, Grade 7

Love Is
Love is what gets me up in the morning
And out of bed
It's what makes me go outside
Greeting this gorgeous day

It's what makes my heart beat.
It's what makes it stop when I see
That special someone to me

It's what makes me stay up all night
Or be in tears from a broken heart
It's there when I need a cast
When me and her are torn apart

It's there when I'm born
It's there when I die
And it's still there as my days pass by

Love is many things in this world
Love can be invisible
Or right in front of your eyes

Love can kill
Just like a knife
But love for me
Is just another part of life
Matt Rodriguez, Grade 9

State of a Spring Day
The sky growled
swallowing the sun
into a swirling storm of darkness,
and spring came that day

A sky clearer than glass
and the sun pouring out its rays
makes the flowers dance,
and it washes the darkness away

Animals feed on the dewy grass
mowing down each strand of green,
like loggers in the woods
and it starts to rain again

Noon awaits the day
fast like the traveling clouds
in a hurry to get to their place
in shapes of gray snowmen

The evening is cold
but the rain pours again
it is a cycle you see
no change or dismay
the typical state of a spring day
Nico Meyer, Grade 8

My First Goal

The soccer ball rolls down the field
I run down the side lines to receive it

Exhaustion from running
Fills each and every player

I struggle to control the ball
I panic under pressure
I notice rivals rushing toward me
I plant my feet

The ball is kicked
Gracefully flying over the defense's head
Disappointment strikes
The ball lands in the goalie's hands
I continue to wonder
If I will soon score my first goal
David Cooper, Grade 8

Music

I love music
It is my life
It is my escape
When I want to be alone
I turn to music
Music means something
Whether you know it or not
It teaches you many things
Music has different meanings
And each song is different
All music is different
Birds make music
Fast and slow
We sing many songs
Music is my escape
And I wouldn't trade music for anything
I love music
Olivia Hutchcraft, Grade 8

The Enemy

The world has changed
It's every kid for himself
All adults are zombies

No one knows what to do
Small children are scavenging like rats
Always fearful and hungry

London lies in ruin
Its buildings like destroyed Lego sets
And dead parents roam the streets

But if all kids team up
They will be able to conquer this new world
Where their parents are the enemy
Clayton Pfeifer, Grade 7

The Leopard Gecko

My gecko is lying in its home
it likes to be alone
his back is yellow
and anything but mellow.

The gecko is a demon
when he eats
he sees a cricket
Crunch!

When I hold him
he is a Ninja
he tries to sneak away
then he looks at me.

I can tell he wants
to go back to his house.
Michael Stark, Grade 7

My World

The skies are beautiful
The sun never stops shining
It looks like a painting
There is no fighting
We can do anything

I can do whatever I want
I can fly or jump incredibly high
I can run at the speed of light
I am famous and loved
This is my favorite place

I hear the sound of voices
I open my eyes and yawn
People tell me that none of that was real
It was very real for me though
I groan and get ready for school
Josh Oldre, Grade 8

A Day in Downtown

The beautiful sight
Of the downtown area
Made me feel like I was hysteria
BEEP! The sound of the cars
Speeding past me
In the evening the beach
Is the place to be
The cold water, bright sand
And hundreds of people
The building are tall as oak trees
But at night it looks better
The lights brighten up the city
Like stars gleaming in the moonlight
I have to say downtown
Is a wonderful city
Arbryanna Griffin, Grade 8

State Finals

With a slight click of a gun
The great race has begun.
Now the first turn was up yonder.
There's no time to ponder.
Just keep your eyes on the prize.

Passing my cross country friends.
My confidence extends.
My legs are turning deep red.
The uniform bleeds blue.
Maybe a gold medal too?

I'm tired and out of breath.
I'm refusing to rest,
Other racers were catching up.
My speed increased slowly
As the end got closer.
Bridget Landers, Grade 7

The Girl Who Twirled

My dreams are held as high as the clouds
Filled with grins, not frowns
All my fears filled with sorrows
Wherever I go they follow

People try to drag me down
No, I'm not going to drown
As people drive by
I hold my head up high

I know I can do anything, everything
Especially by expressing
My thoughts and doubts

I will be known all around the world
As the girl who twirled
Even when everything came crashing down
Nicole Carlson, Grade 8

Frosty Deer Hunt

Blaze orange in the tree,
Dogs flushing and the pheasants flee.
Sunset so pleasant to see.

Be still and listen.
Was that, not just the wind?
Snort, huff, and puff, not a grison.

Be still and listen.
Coyote or fox? My heart is rushed.
Snapped brush, his white tines glisten.

Be still and listen.
I pull my bow back, let the arrow fly.
Thwack, snap there the deer lies
Wyatt Fiene, Grade 8

Love

Love is when you have a friend there for you, even through the toughest times,
It's when you play a game with your family,
Love is when you share a joke and everyone laughs,
It's when you get sick and your mom and dad stay home to take care of you,
Love is when you wake up at 5:00 because your little brother is afraid of the thunderstorms outside,

It's when you accidentally feed your dog twice,
Love is when your friend calls you up at 10:00 at night,
Because they forgot the homework assignment, but you help them anyway
It's when you need help with something and your family or friends help you,
Love is when you get in a fight with your brother and then you make up,
It's when you do your chores,
Love is when you and your family and friends do nice things for each other.

Kyla McCabe, Grade 8

Fun Times

I remember buying for my first time a soccer ball with a shining emblem and rainbow colors that covered it
It was the first time I had one playing with it until it was dark
I remember when I used to take it to the park and have lots of fun,
whenever I couldn't find I would get worried.
I loved my rainbow coloring ball.

I remember when I went to the park.
I was kicking the wall until something went wrong.
The ball fell right to the sky and disappeared.
It was stuck on top of the school,
I loved the fun times we had.
I loved my rainbow ball and all those memories we had.

Jorge Serrano, Grade 8

Practice, Stay Committed, Eat Healthy

If you practice for any sport you will be ahead in the game
So ahead that you will win, win when the other team won't expect it
Because when they were slacking you were practicing and now you are ahead

If you stay committed for any sport you will be ahead
So ahead that you will win, win when the other team won't expect it
Because when they were slacking watching TV you were staying committed and now you are ahead

If you stay healthy for any sport you will ahead
So ahead that you will win, win when the other team won't expect it
Because when they were slacking eating unhealthy snacks
You were staying healthy and now you are ahead

Scott Tangney, Grade 8

A Delicate Delusion

My favorite place is inside a bubble. It's held together with a created sense of hope and optimism.
I don't get to choose when I go there, so it's always a surprise.
When I'm there, I'm building. I build huge walls around the inside to keep anything from getting in.
When I look around, I see people laughing and smiling.
When they stop smiling, my wall starts to crumble.
All I can hear is music and I want it to be louder.
When I'm there, I think I can do whatever I want, so I do.
When I'm in my bubble, I feel like the happiest person in the world.
But if I'm not careful, it pops and I'll fall out.

Devin Patton, Grade 8

A Perfect World

A perfect little world,
Not so perfect anymore.
Open the gates,
Enter the teenage years,
Experience a life you never imagined.

Carefree, drama free minds of youth gone;
Bright bubbly spirits faded to grey throughout the years.
Constantly torn down
By insecurities and voices of others invading the mind.
Nothing left but the feelings of confusion and anger;
Feeling afraid and betrayed.
Who is to blame?
Society.
The easiest place to put the burden,

You gain the freedom to be you once you seek the truth.
You must cross the bridge of realization;
You can't blame society because we are society.
Become tired of trying and striving for an image of perfection.
We only go forward on the avenue of life.

Erin Levesque, Grade 8

Paint Me a Zebra

Please don't paint me as I am.
Don't paint the pain, sorrow, or sickness.
Don't paint my arthritic body, and aging joints.
Paint me free, happy,
without pain,
arthritis,
and an ultra bendable body.
Paint me as a Zebra,
a warrior,
a survivor.
Paint me with my herd,
of other warriors fighting EDS.
Don't show our fear,
our shaking hands,
our numerous braces.
Paint us fighting,
battling through,
making it to the next day.
Most importantly,
paint us together,
paint us Free.

Taylor Nichols, Grade 8

Traveling the Distance

The day dances into the skyline as the moon drips to the ground
Slowly, but surely, melding into a landscape
A long and tedious trek it would be
But as time elapses and the future draws near
It does not seem to far
As it did
Yesterday

Natalie Pantaleo, Grade 9

Falling Skies

"Do you know where my keys are?"
"No. Did you check by the car?"
Before the skies fell down.

He drove away after kissing me
On my cheek, rosy with glee.
Before the skies fell down.

The reports started rolling in.
All the while, I did not grin.
Before the skies fell down.

I began to weep with extreme sorrow
As the roof fell down, with the building to follow.
As the skies fell down.

And as they searched, day and night,
I hoped and prayed with all my might.
After the skies fell down.

He now lives a happy life
With two daughters and me, his wife.
After the skies fell down.

Yet, we will never forget
The pain and suffering caused by that jet.
After the skies fell down.

Joey Carlisle, Grade 9

Dancing in the Rain

You are the hope
of refreshing drops of water on a
simmering hot desert day

You are the sudden
enthusiasm and jumping
up and down when the sky is sunny and a
single drop of rain falls
upon the window of the glass

You are the rush of
excitement when the
scent of sweet rain rushes
by and with the rare
conditions standing is not acceptable

You are the letting go of worries
and the flailing of your
arms while moving to your own beat
without any regrets

You are the few moments
that are remembered and reminisced because
there is no worry or with-
holdings and spontaneity is addicting and adored

Amy Leuszler, Grade 9

Don't Forget Me

Don't forget me,
Keep my pictures,
My memories,
Don't let them go away.

Don't forget me,
My voice,
My looks,
Don't let me wisp away.

Don't forget me,
My charm,
My attitude,
Don't let it disappear.

Don't forget me,
My work,
My care,
Don't let me flake away.

But most of all,
Don't let me forget myself,
Or you,
Before we go away.
Pablo Sanchez, Grade 8

Paradise

Ten days till I fly,
Ten days till I touch the sky,
Ten days till I soar like a bird,
Ten days till I land in paradise.

Palm trees sway,
Waves roll,
And the sun says hello.

Sand white as clouds,
Water blue as the sky.

People talking,
Birds walking.

Floppy hats with sunglasses,
Swimsuits and flip flops,
Sunscreen and beach towels.

I can't wait till I fly,
I can't wait till I touch the sky,
I can't wait till I soar like a bird,
I can't wait till I land in paradise.
Annie Wiacek, Grade 8

The Flower

After winter oh so long,
lonely flowers sing their song,
some are dull and some are bright,
bringing you joy upon the sight.

During spring they're sure to bloom,
sending scents into your room,
then you're outside again,
picking flowers, for the win!

Flowers, flowers,
red and blue,
their colors singing out to you,
saying pick me, pick me, pick me too!

When you're sick of winter's gloom,
take some flowers, fill the room!
Their colors bright, and so divine,
next you'll hope for more sunshine!

Then you look outside to see,
flowers, flowers, birds and bees!
Winter's over, and thus brings Spring!
Natalie Nanninga, Grade 7

The Forest of Books

My favorite thing I have to say
The thing I could do all day
Is sitting in the sun
Reading a book for fun.

The tales stories have to read
Is much like planting a seed
The stories grow in your mind
Leaving tall trees behind.

Soon you will have a forest
Were you can lay your doubts to rest
The stories tells of places
And a lot of different faces.
There's a lot of different people in books
Such as people who have scary hooks
There's books for all different things
Like how to be a human being.

The stories will unfold
As they are bought and sold
All pages do bend
When you come to it's end.
Tryniti Beiermann, Grade 9

Seas

The violent seas churn
Looking for ships to swallow
After the feast, still
Nick Kreinbrink, Grade 7

The Ride of a Lifetime

Beautifully groomed horse.
Gleaming tack.
Sleek, shiny black boots.
Professional black jacket.
The ride of a lifetime.

Announcer's booming voice.
Sweet aroma of horses, my adrenaline.
Distant whinnies.
Steady four beat walk.
The ride of a lifetime.

Sandy arena.
Announcer's booming voice.
Heels down.
Muscles straining to post.
The ride of a lifetime.

Announcer's booming voice.
The taste of dust in the warm air.
The smooth glide of the canter.
Silence.
The ride of a lifetime.
Breanna Penenger, Grade 8

Cold Floor

He calls my name
As I step out onto the cold floor.
The darkness is all I can see
Except the row of blinding lights above me.

All I can hear is cheering.
I fake a smile as I turn around
And strike my pose.
I wait for the beat to start.

It's so hot and hard to inhale,
I move my muscles across the cold floor.
If it wasn't for my melting makeup,
Everyone would see my true face; pale.

I'm feeling empty and all alone,
My mouth is dry and I tell myself
To keep holding on.

I stop and take a deep breath,
I raise my arm up and take a bow.
I'm finished, I sigh in relief.
I don't know why I love dancing.
Skylar Cunningham, Grade 8

Trees

Standing tall and proud
Giant beautiful and brave
Tall powerful trees
Niccolette Tindall, Grade 8

Fear

Fear is like gray.
It sounds like the nervous heartbeat pounding in your ear.
It tastes like the bitterness of a sour green apple.
It smells like the stuffy air on a hot humid day.
It looks like the deepest part of your eye.
It makes you feel uncomfortable and anxious.

Jenna Springer, Grade 8

A Stormy Life

Life is a harsh storm,
Suddenly wind blows rapidly;
It gets dark, rain and hail are pelting down;
Lightning strikes and thunder roars.
But then the clouds break away and the rain becomes a light trickle;
A rainbow appears in the clear sky and lights the rest of the day.

Haley Elmer, Grade 7

Self Portrait

My hair is as curly as a lion's mane.
My eyes are as dark as chocolate.
My fingers are like lightning when I start to write.
My mouth is like the wind singing in different speeds.
My heart beats like a drum when I'm nervous.
My skin is as tan as a desert.

Karla Rivera, Grade 7

Beauty

Beauty is not measured in make-up,
Or the clothes you wear.
Beauty is not measured in make-up,
Or how you do your hair.
Beauty is not measured in make-up,
Beauty is measured in personality and how much you care.

Julia McCoy, Grade 8

Summer Vacation

S and beneath my feet and between my toes
U nderneath the boiling hot heat
M ore places to explore like Hawaii and California
M elting chocolate ice cream dripping off my hand
E veryone's at the pool to get cool
R eady to go back to school and to learn

EmmaLee Archuleta, Grade 7

People

We are all people.
Every one of us has feelings.
Sometimes people decide to care for them.
After awhile they might gather them up and crush them.
Your true friend will come cheer you up.
Stay with you and make sure you're okay.

Mari Craighead, Grade 8

Life Is a Path

Life is a path with two directions the right and wrong one
We either pick the right choice or the wrong one
But sometimes we can't decide
Cause it might lead us to the wrong one
So then what do we do
From there that's your choice so it's time for you to find your path

Madeline Romero, Grade 7

You

You are my safety in every shape and form,
Like bright rays of sunshine you fill me with warmth.
You are a river so calming and clear,
You bring me happiness, smiles, and a world without fear.
When I think of you I am never alone,
When I'm with you my heart is always home.

Emily Leonard, Grade 7

This Is Me!

My hair is like Strawberries, Bright Red
My eyes are as light as a brown crayon
My fingers are like ice cubes, cold as if they are dead
My mouth is like night, silent as can be
My heart is like a drum at a steady beat
My skin is as soft as a kitten's fur

Reilly Beman, Grade 7

Self-Portrait

My hair is as long as a giraffe's neck.
My eyes are like a werewolf's, glowing, when they turn.
My fingers are tall like an elephant, on it's hind legs.
My mouth stays shut like a shell to a snail's back.
My heart beats as fast as a cheetah's speed, when on a roller coaster.
My skin is as smooth as koala's fur.

Mercedes Ensz, Grade 7

The Joy of Horses

H orses are the gateway to my happiness
O n a sad day they always lift my spirits and
R emind me of great times
S ummer is my favorite season so
E very day I can ride them
S orry if you're jealous, but they have my heart

Echoe Lennox, Grade 7

Together

F orever with me in times of need
R ight there when I need a shoulder to cry on
I ce-cream buddy for us in summer
E xcited to hang out with everyone
N ever running out of things to say
D etermined to always be there for him/her

Taylor Kinzer, Grade 7

The Windiest Night of the Year

Just standing there with nothing to hear but a mouse
Taking it all in and smelling the fresh smell of the air

You hear nothing but the whirling of the wind
Staring off into space like no one is there

Wind blowing everything off the benches
Jumping through the air without a care in the world

As cold as the snow in the winter
Wishing that it was over

The winter wind winding up in the trees
Whirling all around and never stopping

What would the world be like without the wind?
We may never know.

What matters most is what we know
Not what we don't know

Alyssa Faber, Grade 7

Darkness

Darkness is light to be
Just wait till the morning and you'll see
Morning light just waiting to be
Darkness is caving in
Light needing to come again
Bright light just waiting to be seen
No darkness no light just black
Drifting into deep sleep
Dreaming happy thoughts soaring above
Almost in a deep, deep adoring love
Soaring, soaring through the clouds
Suddenly hear something loud
Eyes awoken lying still
Light awake and I am too
Lying helpless in light
Happiness. Happiness is one of the many wonders
Working endless until it goes
Sunlight to be darkness
Life is just waiting, hanging by a thread
Circle of life just see, darkness here.

Callie Clinch, Grade 7

Nebraska

Nebraska, perfectly in the center of the nation
A state unlike any other
Corn fields going on for miles on end
If you don't like the weather wait a day, it will change
Snow and freezing cold one day
Searing heat and sun the next
A land filled with people of all kinds
Nebraska is a place where you are free to be yourself
Living here truly is the good life.

Eli Wibel, Grade 8

My Secret Life in Germany

I sit and wait in my dark escape.
Waiting for the day I can see the dawn break.
Death and life surround me in every place.

German planes take the air.
While bombs fall to the ground everywhere.
The sound of death's hounds fill everyone with despair.

Unlike the others I have found a safe place.
A friend's home with a secret space.
A place even forgotten by light.

Emptiness is all that I can see.
The only thing protecting me is a key.
For the key is what separates life and death.

Starvation takes over me.
Every scrap of food I see fills me with glee.
I wonder if there are other survivors out there.

So much has been lost, I have nothing more to lose.
Death has taken all and I'm the only one left that I can accuse.
Why am I still alive when the rest are dead?

I dream of the day that the U.S will come to my aid.
For that day is the day that I will be saved.

Bailey Bagnell, Grade 8

Germany

As I wake to the sound of tears.
I awake to my biggest fears.
Children crying and bleeding ears.

Life was always hard.
How have I gotten this far?
The hope I have is in the stars.

Living in this dreadful ruin.
I barely feel like I am human.
Why is this happening?
Is there even a point to be proven?

Bombs flying through the air.
I listen to the screaming of people driven to despair.
Wide awake and fully aware.
I start to wonder does anyone care?

Everything grows darker and darker.
Trying to survive starts to get harder.
I take cover before anything goes farther.

A bomb flies above my head.
Before you know it I am dead.
As I go I start to see the light.
I whisper to my distraught family that it will be all right.

Autumn Arnett, Grade 8

Useless Things

A plant without seeds
A bracelet without beads

Eyes without sight
lions that don't bite

Lucky without charms
Animals without barns

Nachos without cheese
Hives without bees

A head without a brain
An old man without a cane

Bread without wheat
A drum without a beat

Ice without its burr
A dog without its fur

Morgan Mander, Grade 7

My Name

A mazing times in Hayward.
L oving to other people.
E nergetic about running.
E X cited about the river.
I mpatient at the doctors.
S ociable to others.

G ood at school.
A ctive doing the mile.
B ashful meeting new people.
R esponsible with school work.
I nspirational with new things.
E ager to go on vacation.
L ong day at school.

B edazzle about my project.
I nane when someone tells a joke.
R espectful to others.
C omfortable for lazy days.
H onest about anything.

Alexis Gabriel Birch, Grade 8

My Escape

Music,
It's my passion.
It's my escape.
When life gets too hard,
When I'm on a borderline of giving up,
Music is there to give me faith.
Music is my savior.
Without music
There is no me...

Tonie Bright, Grade 8

My Adventurous Life

"Wow was that fun! Her life was like fireworks!
There were so many exciting things her life!"
She danced everywhere she went, never stopping for the world.
She was quite the burst of energy, leaving a loyal legacy behind.
Kayla helped everyone she could, and never gave up no matter what!
In her world there was never a dull moment, and every step she took,
was headed toward a new, astonishing goal she'd set.
Her family supported her in everything she did, and she loved them dearly.
She'd always appreciated how much her parents, and grandparents had done for her.
She'd donated blood, and went scuba diving,
"Which was so neat and colorful with all the fish swimming around."
Kayla had gone everywhere she'd dreamed of.
She was adventurous and kept herself busy.
She'd always wanted people to look up to her, and there are many that do.
She was a great role model, and she sure did leave a legacy behind.

Kayla Wheeler, Grade 8

Have a Great Day

This is an idea that gives you motivational thoughts
Sets the mood for a great day
This gets you excited for the day ahead of you
Gives you good and cheerful ideas to think about
This saying is a nice way to say so long to someone
Leaves them with a nice and thoughtful idea to ponder about
A saying that puts a smile on the face of the receiver
You can say this to cheer someone up
Or just to be nice and leave them thinking about great things
Sets the mood for a great day
Reminds you that the person cares about you
And how you feel
Have a great day is a saying that gets you cheerful about the day
It also sets the tone and mood for the way you act in the day ahead
So if you would like to put a smile on someone's face say "Have a Great Day"

Caden Jessen, Grade 8

When

When you're in an argument, hear what your friend has to say first
When life turns its back on you, think of what you will get out of the situation
When you feel distant from others, talk it out, someone will always be there
When someone needs help, give it, what goes around comes around
When everything seems wrong, think about how something will always come out of it

When you're going through obstacles, remember that life is just testing you
When you see someone upset, smile, it can be worth more than you think
When something brings you down, remember someone will always be there to talk to
When everything fails on you, there has to be someone that has your back

When handling situations between friends, listen but always stand for yourself
When you're frustrated about something, think positive about it
When you don't feel like something will work out, remember that it always will
When life give you difficulty, think on the bright side always

Claire Magnuson, Grade 8

My School
This school is the best,
Especially better than the rest,

We attend church as a class,
We pay attention in Mass,

We sing and pray together,
Every day in any weather,

We learn a lot from books and such,
I like St. Mary very much.

I love St. Mary's School.
Griffin Hartnett, Grade 7

Willow Tree
Willow Tree Willow Tree
where the guardian angels watch over me.
As I lay among the night,
I know that things will be all right.
when I have my ups and downs,
the guardian angels help me turn around.
When I lay beneath that tree,
The guardian angels lay with me.
We talk and talk every night,
talk about heaven's beautiful light.
Guardian angels guardian angels,
when you lay by me under that willow tree.
I know that heaven is right for me.
Gracie Scott, Grade 7

All Alone
All alone,
No one,
Is there,
No one,
To care,
No one,
Just there,
I need,
Someone to,
Help me,
Save me,
Comfort me,
Anyone?
Macy Grannes, Grade 9

Friendship
F riends can be nice
R uin your life or
I nspire you to be your best
E ventually, you will
N eed the strength of others
D epending on your needs
S tay strong or ask a friend
Kaylie Ewing, Grade 8

But It Is Just Nebraska...
Nebraska, just another state in another nation, wrong
It's the state of spirit and pride, of labor but some only see it as the corn or cattle state
It may not be bustling cities or stars walking down the street
But it is just Nebraska.

Located in the Midwest with probably the strangest weather in the nation
Brisk, frozen winters and searing, boiling summers to snowy springs and scorching autumns
But it is just Nebraska.

It oozes pride
We founded Arbor Day
Little Jack Hoffman scored a touch down in a Cornhuskers game
And every year millions come to the home of the College World Series
But it is just Nebraska.

We also made history when Edwin Perkins invented Kool-Aid
Harold Edgerton invented high-speed photography
Also when Joyce Hall invented Hallmark Cards
But it is just Nebraska.

It's not only Nebraska
It's the state of pride and love with welcoming smiles and hospitality like no other
But it is not only a state
But some say it is just Nebraska

Wrong, it's home.

Samantha Carter, Grade 8

Ode to the Internet
The greatest invention mankind has ever seen,
Wikipedia, Expedia and endless other medias,
I cannot thank you enough, you've saved me countless times.

Thank you for entertaining and teaching, connecting and preaching,
You are humanity's Holy Bible, the answer to all of our problems,
What's the Capital of Taiwan?
Internet
How do I build a computer?
Internet
How do I change a diaper?
Internet
What is life?
Internet

The world has been connected all thanks to you
Twitter, Facebook, Google and YouTube,
Thank you, internet, for providing us a place to escape to
For when reality has become too hard and we just want to start anew

You've provided a place for discussing, debating
Informing, complaining, you are the world's oracle,
Textbook, stadium, forum, journal, circus,
Home

Robert Filipiuk, Grade 9

That Day's Over

The sky used to be bright,
the wind gentle, the morning clear.
No rain, no fog, no hurricane,
could separate us,
but that was your fear.

The day grows on as we grow weary.
I was just too tired that day.
A word, a phrase, a look, an action;
what on Earth did I say?

You turn away, the darkness gathers.
You say what's done is done.
The night's not yet returned to that bright, clear morning.
God alone knows what I've done.

I'm sorry, I'm sorry, will you forgive
whatever I had against you?
I'm sorry, I'm sorry but I'm afraid the night
might have just about taken you too.

Annie Mattson, Grade 8

Rachel

My neighbor I've known forever,
Is beautiful and brave,
Who will live with regret never,
And cherish her young days.

Her sickness doesn't matter,
Because she is one of a kind,
As we climb through life like a ladder;
Rachel was an amazing person to find.

In hope of getting better,
And talking with her again;
I miss you Rachel,
Get better to have great experiences with new friends!

Wow! Your smile is spontaneous like the sun,
As warm and happy and fun!
In memory of the street and grass in summer time,
As the trees danced in a line;
Get better so we can have more adventures together!

Brianna Rush, Grade 7

The Rainbow

Red, orange, yellow, green, blue, and purple
The colors of the rainbow
Red is for something radiant inside of us
Orange is for the one and only
Yellow is for you to be you
Green is for the good inside us
Blue is for our beautiful selves
Purple is for the passionate part of ourselves
These are the colors

Elizabeth McAdams, Grade 7

She Will Only Get Stronger

You can push her to her limit,
She will always get up.

You can be mean to her,
She will brush it off.

You can take her friends away,
She will have her family.

You can hurt her,
She will only get up and walk away like the strong girl she is.

You can abuse her,
She will feel hurt and used but she will only GET STRONGER.

You can take her out of church,
But you can't take away what she knows is the truth.

You can plant her and water her every day,
She will grow up into the most beautiful young lady you have seen.

You can love her,
She will love you and will GROW STRONGER!

Jaiden Walker, Grade 8

Above the Ground

As I look down,
I start to sweat
"Just don't look down,"
says my best friend

The platform is yards from the ground —
many, many yards away.
I feel as scared as a fly caught in a spider's web,
like a mouse caught helplessly in a mouse trap.

I try not to look down,
but I look anyway.
I think I will faint,
so I take a step back.

I take a deep breath in;
I make my way to the railing.
I look over the metal rungs
to see an ocean of building stretching for miles
as far as the eye could see,
and I think to myself,
"Hey, this is not that bad."

Dylan Nguyen, Grade 8

Stars

Glowing and bright
You remind me of diamonds twinkling brightly in the dark
Shining in the dark night sky with wonder
I wish I could look down on the Earth with these beautiful orbs

Lizzy Schierling, Grade 7

Beautiful Mexico

Beautiful Mexico will someday want to be
To one day see again your beautiful sky
Filled with stars shining so bright at night
And to walk on your green grass that only you have

When I wake up I could feel that nice breeze in the morning
And hear the birds sing so beautifully
It gives me so much peace
To also smell the yummy food you have

I wish to see you again
Beautiful Mexico

Roxanne Ramirez, Grade 7

Dust

These particles flow free.
They could be on anything like a tree.
They fly so high.
But they cannot die.
Even if they seem pesky as bees.
You clean and clean and they're back again.
They are not our friends or enemies.
They are themselves.
They are not violent or hostile.
They keep to themselves.
It is everywhere at once.
Dust.

Jamie Mosley, Grade 7

Dogs

Dogs are great, dogs are fun,
Dogs love you more than anyone,
They shake their tails when you come home,
They try to get you to throw their bone.

They love to play, they love to fight,
They'll stay with you every single night,
Dogs don't hurt, dogs don't cry,
Even when they have to say goodbye.

But don't be sad, they go somewhere good,
You'll see them there just like you should.

Quincy Ellefson, Grade 8

I Am Lauren Theisen

I am a shoe lover.
I dream of my new shoes, dazzling on my feet.
I feel the new fur on the inside of my new Uggs.
I hear the click-clacking of my new heels.
I am a shoe lover.
I pretend all shoes came in my size, 6 1/2.
I touch the shiny surface of my new sky blue flats.
I worry the best shoes in the world won't fit.
I cry when I look at the price tag.
I am a shoe lover.

Lauren Theisen, Grade 8

Gossip

She won't walk her talk
And she's never learned what's true
She spreads faster than a wild fire
Yet, her fire's source is anonymous
Only time can put the fire out
But by then
All the trees and homes would be burnt to ashes
Words spill out of her mouth
That isn't even near the truth
She's like a viral virus with no vaccine
She's a pessimistic impact on our world today
It's practically impossible to get rid of her lies
She's someone who everyone constantly thinks about
She has the power to ruin anyone's reputation
In less than a day
She's not someone who you would want to be around
If anything, stay away from her as far as you can

Nancy Chung, Grade 8

Trapped

Life is truly a labyrinth;
Have you ever noticed;
That everyone wants to go to heaven;
But nobody wants to die;
Some go quick without a word;
Some leave us with something more;
A whisper, a sentence, maybe even a glimpse of the unknown;
Death is always hungry;
At the last moments of one's life;
The true realization of one's meaning, existence, and impact;
Comes into aspect;
And then and only then;
Do we truly realize how small we are;
And how exhausted life has made us;
We are finally allowed to close our eyes and rest;
Free from the maze;
Life is truly a labyrinth

Paige Peitzman, Grade 8

Knowing the Pain

Why? How? What?
Are the things I asked.
As my tears fell against the cold, clear glass.
I don't want to hear it! Make it go away.
They're lying mamma. This can't be true.
Why did this happen to me?
They say they have the cure, and they tell me they are sure.
How do I believe it I'm just a little boy?
They bring me through the door. Why so many chords?
Maybe they fixed me, maybe there is more?
I want them to be done, they have had their fun.
I open my eyes, it's my biggest surprise.
You mumble you love me, and I start to crumble.
As you push me through the door in the big chair with wheels,
I know how it feels, to remember something to terribly real.

Chance Tylar Hasty, Grade 8

Summertime

The summertime is nothing like the winter.
It is not cold out, and there is sunshine.
The weather is better and not bitter.
The sun stays out late enough for me to dine.

You can play outdoors and go swimming too.
Many people go running and walking.
They do not get cold, and the sky stays blue.
You can lie in the sun and go tanning.

The weather is great for ice cream sundaes.
Hot chocolate is not usually used.
Over the summer, I don't mind Mondays.
I enjoy each day and get quite enthused.

The summer is much better than winter.
It is so warm, and there are no blizzards.

Mary Kate Mooney, Grade 8

The Whistle Blows

The whistle blows everything stands still for a while
Down
Set
Hutt
The defenders rush

Receivers run out
And I dodge linemen
They call for the ball
I look left
        Then right
One person running down the sideline
The corner speeds up
It's all or nothing
I throw the ball
He catches it, touchdown
We win the game

Armoni Gause, Grade 8

The Inner City Struggle

I can see a light in the darkness of my life
Every day food is trying to come into our home
Luckily there might be a salad and a steak
I ask myself why we can't get help
In America, the ghetto children reach out together
The school has tattered books and metal detectors
Each day a student becomes a thug or educated
Our young children are given guns and drugs
I would give a child a basketball or a guitar
Tell them so and grow the youthful seed
To not cheat the growth of the life flower
Somewhere in the heart of our beloved country
Beyond the eyes of fortunate
Lost in reality's nightmare
Cries of help to the wealthy remained unheard

Max Schick, Grade 8

Pencils

You would think there's only one pencil
But I can't even find that.
They come in packages of 20's;
I take one out,
I have it one period,
it's gone the next
I borrow one from a neighbor and say I'll give it back later,
but then I lose it and they say, Noah, you're a traitor.
I bring one to school
but I keep losing my pencil,
drop it on floor, get a new one
in a week I find it under the couch.
I lost my pencil,
mom says look in your binder,
I say mom I can't even find her,
Look in your bag, my mom replies
It seems like all of my pencils vaporize.

Noah Cheatham, Grade 8

Fun in the Sun

The beach called my name
As the sun and the cool water invite me in
When I looked at the goldish sand on the beach
I could only see the baby blue sky and blue waters
When I walked along the beach the sand feels soft as silk
Between my toes the sand is hot and cool
From the pleasant and warm water
The air smells of salt water
It sounds like waves crashing and splashing
Against the rocks
I feel relaxed and loved by the warmth
As it warms you inside and out
The whooshing waves washed up
Along the quiet beach
No better place I'd rather be
Even though the beach is fun to go
I still want know how far it goes

Bryce Wyma, Grade 7

Idle Minutes Lost*

"Like as the waves make towards the pebbl'd shore
So do our minutes hasten to their end."
Those minutes are unredeemable
For time is non-refundable.
Procrastination diminishes time well spent,
Like wandering in a fog inescapable.
Listen to the footsteps in memory
On the road not taken,
The path to a door unopened.
Lost, forgotten, time's opportunity
Squandered and thrown away,
Until our minutes have ceased
And our pockets empty,
Nothing but judgment remains.

Elizabeth Payne, Grade 9
*Inspired by William Shakespeare.

Sports Legends

One can never play enough sports
Either in long pants or in shorts

With gear like nets and sticks
To score by throw or kick

With brands like Nike and Adidas
Wearing all these gears would be genius

A big honor is to be in the hall of fame
Because you showed your passion and love for the game

A legendary number in baseball is forty-two
Because Jackie took all the hatred and the boos

Chocolate thunder could throw down a dunk
Glass would come raining down in big chunks

The best time of year is the Madness in March
This time of year will bring smiles and break hearts

One famous name in Football is Lombardi
Won a super bowl and went to party

Baseball has the green monster
That homerun is a bomber

Baseball, football, basketball so many to choose
Play every season and no one will lose
Dylan Funk, Grade 8

I'm Sorry, Forgive Me?

I'm sorry, I'm not perfect.
But honestly, would it be worth it?

I'm sorry, I'm not the fastest sprinter.
But actually, I've trained all winter.

I'm sorry, I'm not the most graceful dancer.
But, I'm doing it for a friend who has cancer.

I'm sorry, I'm not the best at volleyball.
But, if it were a sport, I'd rather play dodgeball.

I'm sorry, I'm not the most flexible cheerleader.
But to be honest, I can do whatever, just let me take a breather.

I'm sorry, I'm not a straight A student.
But to tell you the truth, I'm really prudent.

I'm sorry, I make mistakes.
But lets be real, at least I'm not fake.

I'm sorry, I'm not perfect.
But honestly, would it be worth it?
Ariana Davenport, Grade 9

One Direction

My boys I remember when I first listened to them,
I instantly fell in love with their amazing voices,
and how I thought they were absolutely perfect.
After listening to the first song I remember,
wanting to learn every single small detail about them,
and watching practically every video they were ever in.
How my mother told me I was going through a phase,
and in the next two years I'd be hooked on something else.
Me telling her she was wrong because they were and
would always be my boys.

My boys I remember listening to their latest album two years later,
and still loving my boys as much as I had before.
How I know every single detail about them and
keep up to date on every video they are in.
My mother telling me sooner or later
I would get hooked onto another thing.
Me saying that she was wrong before and
is still wrong to this day because they were
my boys back then and would still be my boys
till the end no matter who else came around.
Destiny Gonzalez, Grade 8

Lessons from Literature

There are books that have changed me for good.
They inspired me to do things I never knew I could.
They taught me it is okay to shed some tears.
That being brave is facing your fears.
That you should fight for those you love.
That push should not always lead to shove
True friends will always be there for you
That you should hold on to your friends old and new
That family means no one gets left behind
That even villains can be kind
That even little people can do a lot
That you should never allow your brain to rot
True love is an amazing thing
That we should appreciate everything life brings
There is a hero in all of us
That we should fight for what is good and just
That childhood is precious
There's a fine, fine line between becoming too ambitious
Though people and books might be unlikely friends
They shall be the ones that will be with you until the end.
Cosette Laurice Marie Gutierrez, Grade 7

My Two Brothers

I have two brothers, lucky me.
They tease and annoy me, such pains they can be!
They'll joke and they'll prank and hide all my stuff,
sometimes I feel like I've just had enough!
But mostly they're fun and I love them, I do,
even if they smell worse than a dirty gym shoe!
I have two brothers, lucky me.
Without them how boring my life would be.
Hallie Miller, Grade 7

Dancing

Dancing, jumping, and leaping with joy
Listening to the music, and saying "oh boy!"
Laughing and singing to the beat
As we all tap our dancer feet.
Watching our shoes hit each other
While my friends clap hands with one another.
Our teacher says "girls lets dance."
We go to our spots as we prance.
Moving to the beat as the music starts
Feeling the thumping of our hearts.
With our smiles shining like stars
We all stand still like parked cars.
As the audience applauded loudly
My team and I walked off the stage proudly!

Emma Tuzicka, Grade 9

Ode to My Sled

Oh sled how you bring me joy,
You're better than playing with a toy.
When you go off the ramp and take flight,
I hold on really tight.
since you are so big and round,
When we land it makes a breaking sound.
I don't fall off because your handles are strong,
Even I didn't know I could hang on that long!
When people see you they say, "Wow,"
Also "I need that sled now!"
You may be old,
But you will never be sold.
It doesn't matter how old I get
I'm not done playing with you yet.

Riley Kraemer, Grade 8

Peace for the People

If wars were nonexistent
And all people were peaceful
The world would be perfect
No one would be hurt

All people would come together
And hate becomes invisible
To the people, they are impenetrable
To the horrors of today

Terrorists, bombings, corruption
Why is there evil in this world?
So the light will overcome and win
To make our people strong and know happiness

Nick Asuan, Grade 7

Moon

It shines down in a beam of light, to illuminate the foggy night.
A soft glow will show you the way, this object won't show in the day.
It glistens in the dark night sky, waiting for the stars nearby.
It shines down in a beam of light, to illuminate the foggy night.

Katie Beaudin, Grade 7

Snow Fox

A ginger fox
Her sleek fur speckled white from downy flakes
She trudges through heavy fallen snow
Carrying a goose carcass in her mouth,
Hurrying, she paces through slushy pools of melted snow
pausing only for a glance,
A cabin framed by emerald pine trees,
trimmed with silver lights
and hanging icicles, translucent and sharp
A scented bonfire crackles merrily in the stone fireplace,
the aroma tickling her sensitive nose
Soon back on the trail, she trudges,
leaving delicate paw prints behind
Silence veils the scene
The late evening moon rises,
while stars peak through the dark night curtain
She arrives at last,
her den entrance now framed with snow
Hurrying inside to her hungry cubs,
offering her feast of goose
Soon satiated, they curl together and drift into a deep, winters' sleep

Adrianna Pisarczyk, Grade 7

The Terror of Every Other Year

You may be asking, what is it you fear?
And I'll tell you, it's not something you're likely to hear.
My fear is simple
And yes, it may make you tingle.

The doctors say it prevents diseases,
But what if it just simply displeases?
I know they're good for my body,
But they are like sharp points prepared to pierce me.

Every other year I have to go back
Giving them their long awaited, tasty snack.
They are talking to me,
Saying, "We mean you no harm."
But I know they just want to puncture my arm.

The doctors say it won't hurt at all
But in reality, I'll be lucky if I don't bawl.
The tip goes in and it only hurts a little bit,
So I hang my head in shame thinking,
"Why did I throw such a big fit?"

Will Greder, Grade 8

Falling into Thanksgiving

Fall
Brisk, multi-colored
Jumping into leaves, drinking hot chocolate, eating pumpkin pie
Soft sweaters, wool scarves, Turkey, mashed potatoes
Eating a Thanksgiving meal, playing football, sleeping after dinner
Cinnamon smelling, family-filled
Thanksgiving

Keely Mahoney, Grade 7

Come with Me

Come with me and run like the wind.
Feel its gusts blowing through your face,
The constant "whoosh" in your ears.
Breathe in the cool spring breeze
As it seems to dance around you
And you feel alive and awake.

Come with me as we go to my special place
Where it seems all worries fade away
As our feet thunder on the ground,
Rushing to the door
Just as ancient memories seem to flow towards me
And I feel alive and awake once again.

Bridget Kos, Grade 7

Downtown Nebraska

Sun shines upon me nearside the Woodmen Tower
Down town Nebraska has certainly great power
At the Rose Theater people walk with crowns;
And adore the talented architecture.
On the Corner of the street,
I sight a marvelous store.
It's as big as an African elephant and more.
A very tall lady carries a baby
Toward the lake where children play
Cars Buzz by towering skyscrapers,
While the crowded Jazz on the Green begins.
The sun goes down but Omaha is still up.
Downtown Omaha, better than Council Bluffs

Da'Shza Powell, Grade 8

Nebraska Chills

I'm breathing in cold, chilling air
As I longingly wait for the appearance of summer
I think of all those "lucky-ducks"
In states with warm, spring weather
No one will truly understand our torture
Of waking up to snow in spring
Until you're Nebraska-livin'
Beautiful, spacious skies line the fields
Making the scene a painter's dream
The weather is a horrible, dangerous nightmare
Yet it leaves you wondering how life is truly
I wake-up some mornings to the Blue Jay's singing
But others, I awaken by the pit-pat of the storms

Kassidy Hart, Grade 8

Pursuit of Happiness

Happiness seems sky blue
Like the brightness family can bring to your eyes
I see the joy of others as they smile at me
I hear the sound of laughter through the light breeze
I smell fresh apple pie baked from a family's kitchen
I touch the grins that I bring to people
I taste the joy and freedom of many lives

Trinity Weers, Grade 9

It

There's a darkness that exists in every soul
To whom It has slight control
If you let It out It could conclude in your demise
But hopefully you and I can tame It likewise

For every man, woman, and child should build a wall
Fret for without that wall It will consume us all
And cause turmoil and war throughout the lands
For those who let It out will have blood on their hands

I'm explaining this once, not twice
Don't take this lightly; so listen and take my advice
For if you crack that wall, oozing out will be it
Every decision you make should involve all your wit

It shall always be there
And It will try to lead you to other's despair
I'll leave it to you to figure out what It is
For It dwells in darkness for It's own bliss

Kylee DeLuca, Grade 8

Gracie Goes for Gold

Ice skater Gracie Gold was her name,
Skating for gold was her game.
The Olympics was where she'd skate.
Winning gold, was up for debate.

Gracie's glides and spirals looked so nice,
While she was skating gracefully across the ice.
With jumps, spins, and footwork to show,
It is not easy to be perfect you know.

Gracie skated well in practice and was on a roll.
She worked so hard to reach her own goal.
Gracie competed with all of the best.
She focused on skating without any rest.

Out on the ice with beauty and grace,
Many people saw her cheerful smiling face.
Gliding, performing, competing her best.
Gracie outdid other skaters who were put to the test.

Alexis Storen, Grade 7

Sdrawkcab Yad

I got out of my clothes and dressed my bed.
I straightened my cereal and ate my head.

I put on my hair and brushed my shoes.
I watched the chair and sat on the news.

I pet the piano and played my dog,
Then I went out for my door and opened a jog.

What a frustrating day!
I don't know what else to say.

Nora White, Grade 7

In Life

In life you take in day by day barely making it through just one day,
forgetting the important things in life, like your little girl taking her first steps or your son finally getting his driving license,
your daughter losing her first tooth, those are the milestones in life that made life worth living for.
So make every day like it was your last and that it's something to be proud of and make it count.

Emma Morts, Grade 7

Friends

When you're having a rough and lonely day and nothing seems to be going your way,
you know that your friends are there to help you, if you have friends like mine, then you are the luckiest person around.
If you ever need a shoulder to cry on, or just someone to listen to you, you can go to your friends like a magnet to metal.

Shannon Haggerty, Grade 7

The White Phantom

Slowly, in the midst of night
The ground is peppered with flakes of white.

It starts in small innocent flurries—
You, in your bed, have no worries.

But soon, upon you is the ice cold ghost
Taking advantage of its wintery host.

The snow falls now with a purpose—
To cover the lively rock that earth is.

The Phantom now strikes with full force,
With a strong, unforgiving wind from the north.

The snow is free-falling and burying your land—
All your trees, grass, dirt, fencing, and sand.

The Phantom destroys all detail in the ground,
And covers it all in white without a sound.

You are in slumber and don't realize this,
Until you awaken with a house shrouded in mist.

The Phantom has struck you, and you didn't even know,
Until you woke up and peered out your window.

Oh, the shoveling you must undergo—
Because the Phantom has left you with a foot of snow!

Casey Lovejoy, Grade 7

Ten Little Pens

Ten little pens that were all mine,
One got lost and then there were nine.

Nine little pens were just being great,
One broke down and then there were eight.

Eight little pens were just like heaven,
One went the wrong way and then there were seven.

Seven little pens laid just like sticks,
One was fetched and then there were six.

Six little pens were loving the jive,
One got carried away and then there were five.

Five little pens were by the door,
One rolled away and then there were four.

Four little pens that were writing about me,
One went off topic and then there were three.

Three little pens that were brand new,
One got dirty and then there were two.

Two little pens were having so much fun,
One got bored and then there was one.

One little pen looked up to the sun,
He got a bad burn and then there were none.

Paige Nimrick, Grade 7

Life

life is like a roller coaster.
it starts off as an easy smooth ride.
you don't have to worry about being scared.
it gets a little bumpy. it gets rough and hard.
you start to see all the drops and all the heights.
you feel like you want to get off and give up,
but once you're on there's no going back.
It's a commitment. you don' want to grow up,
but it's something that we all have to do.
life is hard and short, but if you live it right, once is enough.

Mackenzie Creamer, Grade 7

Rain

Rain
it's a miracle
splish, splash
it drops
Rain, is medicine
it quenches the thirsty flowers and plants
day, and night
Walking through the clear, grey drops, trickles down your skin
cooling you, and gives you the urge to live
Rain, is what keeps us, and makes us feel alive

Franchesca Garcia, Grade 7

Theater

A member of the theater I am
With every production I am involved
To get one of the leads is what I plan
If not I'm sure that problems will evolve

In the spot light's where I'm always at
My mind is never full of scattered stuff
We block and block and block like one big fam
Rehearsal time can never be enough

Directors are exhaustive and insane
Things always have to be exactly right
I'm sure they think we are all lazy
They shout in to the great void of the night

Theater is what I love to do
It is my passion always through and through
Symon Knox, Grade 7

Skyscraper

Thanks for standing big and tall.
Standing broad, you tower over the city.
You look at the small little taxis rushing by.
They look like little blobs of yellow from where you are.
The world's problems seem to shrink as you stand up straight.
You are an inspiration to stand tall.
You are made of steel
And are as strong as people make you out to be.
At night, you light up the world.
It's a true sight to see.
Every day's a new day.
When it's nice and sunny
Your full beauty is accepted.
When it's grim and cloudy,
Your full self isn't showing.
It is hidden by the clouds in the sky.
You are an example to all.
Megan Lane, Grade 8

A Walk in the Park

The sun is shining high up in the sky
A river's flowing down the hill with speed
Some kids are flying kites up really high
The geese drink from the river with great greed

I feel the heat come through the summer sun
A breeze picks up and carries butterflies
A baby laughs because he's having fun
Most kids don't want to have to say goodbye

I see a small, blue Frisbee getting tossed
I hear a bird making a funny sound
Upon a big boulder I see green moss
Couples are having picnics on the ground

I hear a bark come from a running dog
Some runners pass me on their morning jogs
Shaya Haverkamp, Grade 7

Imagination

Your mind is a canvas for creativity
Anything you desire can easily come alive
Your brain is a conductor of wild illusions
That transforms your outlook
One idea is a new character designed
Everyone comes up with different spectrums
For your mind is a blank book to write on
Creativity is an open universe
For you to generate
Fantasies are always welcome
For they are accustomed
Inventions are little children
Begging for candy inside of your mind
Fabrications soon realize they are spells
Once you come to recognition
Your brain is a glass of water that recently emptied
For you awoke from your dream
Nina Bell, Grade 8

Regrets

When I was little, my family went to the carnival.
They asked if I wanted to ride the Ferris wheel and I sad,
"No, I'm scared."
I watched form the curb as my family rode the sky and I thought,
"Why didn't I do that?"

We went on a boat ride,
and stopped in the middle of the lake.
We had our life vests on and anchor down,
my dad asked if I wanted to jump in for a swim, I said,
"No, I'm scared."
We were leaving towards our home
and I realized how good the water looked
and I felt like going for a swim,
"Why didn't I do that?"

Jaqueline Ortiz, Grade 8

A Masterpiece Created

Poets are like artists,
painting words on paper.
Meaningful and dark or
silly and bright like the sun.
Mixing the letters together
to create the perfect image of the poem,
emotions dripping out of their soul.
Writers hiding the true color away from readers,
making it hard to find the stroke
of true meaning from under many different layers.
Fading the sentences together on the canvas.
The abstractness of every different page full of words,
each page being unique and different.
Each word and sentence splatter the designers paper.
To finish the masterpiece, they sign it as their own work of art.
Emily Floyd, Grade 7

Friends

Friends, friends forever.
Always together,
Always caring for one another,
Always trusting one another,
Always helping one another.

Friends, friends forever.
We would always do everything together,
We would always spend time together,
We would always go to parties together,
We would always laugh together.

Friends, friends forever.
We used to say,
We use to always be together now you ignore me,
You act as if I was not there,
You say you still care,
You say we are still friends,
But only when they are not around.
Friends! More like strangers…
Now you don't even say a word to me,
Now you look away…
Friends, friends forever…

Celeste Sanchez, Grade 8

Eminem

Every day I remember,
whenever I felt exhausted, excluded or nonexistent,
I would still listen to Eminem,

He'd help heal the huge wounds
on my hopeless, hurting heart.
and made me feel happier.

When I'm sad, I play his heavenly songs,
and fall soothingly asleep
I wake up to singing, surrounded by some of my siblings.

Slim Shady
The man who saved my life, helped me through my struggles,
who seized my never ending pain.

Happiness I have found, thanks to him
I have hope, I'm happy now,
Living my once lonely, hopeless life.

Thank you Marshall Mathers,
You were more supportive
Than my mother and most people.

Isabel Gabriel, Grade 8

Curtis Family Triplet

The Curtis brothers, I count three.
They love each other, but sometimes it's hard to see.
But no matter what they will always be family.

Jenna Gremmel, Grade 8

Look

You stand still here,
With the world spinning round and round,
Not blinking not absorbing,
Do you not notice the hurting you see?
This world you are staring blankly at is all you have.
How do you not care?
How do you just watch?
Your family, your friends are running away,
You are acting as if you are nothing, but a statue.
You are a part of this world.
Start believing what you see,
This is what our world is,
Not a blank canvas,
It is our life, it is our home.
Your eyes are open, but you're not seeing,
Look, look around you,
Is this what you want to see?
This world is full of strength,
Yet it still has hurting in it,
Understand this is how it is now.

Ryann Lewis, Grade 7

I Believe

He said, "Let there be light" and so it was,
And then he sent a man up from above.
The flood came and washed it away,
Except for one with his family aboard.
Many years later one woman was chosen,
She carried the son that was sent to save.
This special one was born on Christmas day,
No cry to come out of this newborn child.
Performing miracles as he grows older,
Many believed but many did not.
They sent him up to the mountain to die,
Hanging on the cross as it's hard to breath,
With nails in his wrist and feet.
He died for us,
Without asking for pay.
He rose again 3 days from death,
And went up to heaven with his father waiting to return.
You may not know about this beloved man and spirit,
But I call them Lord, my Savior, Emmanuel.
The 3 in one, Father, Spirit, Son.

Kati Moore, Grade 8

Grave

Dark clouds hanging over the horizon
transform the beautiful skies of Earth
Cold platoons of arrows fire at the wounded
creating a deeper gash.

To feel pain and agony
Of cold arrows piercing flesh
They fall when not knowing
the truth of the dark clouds and their beauty.

Tariq Portis, Grade 8

Crispy Kreme

I have eaten
the last doughnut
that was in the box
for my sister

and which
she was looking forward to
eating
for breakfast.

Forgive me
it was tasty,
sticky,
and so sweet.

Nick Davis, Grade 7

Truly Sorry

I have taken the
last strawberry
from the
fridge,

I know you
were probably
saving for
dessert…

I am truly
sorry but
they were very
fresh and chocolaty.

Rachel Evers, Grade 7

I'm Sorry

I have eaten
the rest of the candies
that were in
your bag

and which
you were probably
going to
eat after dinner

I'm sorry
they were
so sweet
and so sour.

Jimmy Stengel, Grade 7

God

God is a ray of sunshine,
He will be there through all the hard times.
Yet when it goes away, do not be afraid,
It will be back the very next day.

Eli Blankley, Grade 7

Creaking Swing

I passed that park, with that swing. That creaking swing.
It was worn out, and abused.
It was hanging there by a single chain, begging you with every silent creak to help it.
It was begging you.

Always creaking, but no one else seemed to notice.
Maybe they did, but chose to ignore it.
As long as it didn't finally break no one cared.
Ohh, that creaking swing, being pushed, over and over again.
Ohh, that creaking swing how it stayed strong to the very end, with its fake smile.

Just one more push, and that battered old creaking swing went down.
Down, down, down it went.
Then silence.
Now we noticed. That swing was never creaking to you.
Its smile was always real.
You didn't seem to notice it breaking, and withering.

Now when I pass, the silence is so loud.
The screams, the echoes of all those fallen pieces.
There they lay broken and scattered. Forgotten about, and deserted.
That creaking swing that just gave away. And down, down, down it went.
That swing, that creaking swing that was pushed one too many times. And "snap."
Then Silence.

Netasha Lopez, Grade 8

Ray of Hope

I look around at all the busy people and their bright strings of traffic lights.
Our changing minds hurt, betray, deceive, and smile evilly at us.
Our hearts cause us to love until it breaks, melts, or disappears
Everyone wears the baggage of their past,
But they know who they are and have hearts filled with happiness and strength.
I put on a show, a mask of happiness, for I must be the good girl,
But know that I am just a crumpled up piece of paper.

As I try and hide my face, some come to try and figure out what lies beneath it.
I have painted pretty pictures while someone smiled and scribbled over my canvas.
I have taken pictures of the blue sky, but others came by and turned it to rain.
And while I live with my own scars, I have learned to live with the pain.
I was not born with a silver spoon in my mouth and pearls around my neck,
But with flowers in my hair and a hand protecting me
So why do I feel like a forgotten leaf falling down?

As I walk slowly to string of burnt out artificial lights, a ray of sunlight stops me.
The sunlight smiles and holds out its hand, inviting me to join it.
As I place my hand inside of its sweet, strong hand, no longer feeling alone.
It leads me away from all of the traffic lights and the strings around it.
When I'm finally gone, I let go of its grasp and walk away,
The sunlight turns to moonlight, stars dancing on my shoulders and pulling me back.
For the sunlight has turned into something more than just moonlight, but a ray of hope.

Victoria Villanueva, Grade 8

Summer Fun
Beach balls bounce
Squirrels scramble up the trees
Bursts of fresh fruit fill my mouth
Crickets hum their nighttime tune

Twinkles of color fill the sky
The echoing sound of splashing water
Marshmallows fresh from the fire
Sizzling heat colors my body

The chlorine occupies my nose
Softballs fly across the starry sky
Worms dangle on fish hooks
The bright green of fresh mowed grass
Morgann Pospisil, Grade 9

Family Trip
It was awesome
We went to Disney World
My family and I
It smelled like a carnival
It was fun
We went on rides
We met Characters
There was a dog there that jumped
Like a human
We went to the three different
Disneyland parks
We went to a hotel
Then we ate some grilled crab
I hope we can go back soon
Avery Hyland, Grade 7

Boys
Boys make me upset, that I cry
To the point I want to die

I keep my tears tucked inside
Just to keep him by my side

He says he loves me, that's a lie
But it's time to say goodbye

He scared my heart I'm in pieces
He left me here speechless

You can say I'm done now
My soul is clear time to bow.
Mishelle Smith, Grade 8

Cloud
Dainty little cloud prancing in the breeze
Life is perfect and great
Until black and grey rolls in
And makes the sky full of hate
Brooklyn Stack, Grade 8

Pink-Haired Skeleton
She is a skeleton
All her muscles and ligaments and blood and heart and soul — gone.

She is nothing more than
Bleached bone, a tired shade of white
And pink hair, a wispier whisper of long-gone fuchsia.

She huddles in the corner,
Empty apertures to serve as eyes
And I look at her from a foreigner's distance
As she cries some unknown substance that drips down her lifeless frame.

After some time I walk over,
Finally sick of her sadness that stains the starless sky,
And sit down.

We sit there in a silence made up of inhales and exhales
As we fill our already smoke-filled lungs
And then empty pretty blue ice crystals
Into the air of those who don't care.

In and out
Up and down
And back again
We circle in our haunted carousel —

And wait for the ship to sink.

Sarah Zhou, Grade 7

It's Time to Say Goodbye…
There I am saying goodbye to you
For once and for all the day we all dreaded
Has finally come. Yet here I am,
The only reason being
There is no way I'm letting you leave without saying goodbye.

But the only words that come out of my mouth
Are don't you dare leave me, I need you.
Yet all I can think about is how much better
You'll be when you're gone and in heaven

Even though it kills me to say goodbye
I know that it is for the best.
But I know that God has saved a spot for you.
Up in heaven next to his side.
You deserve to be free of pain and free to fly away.

I know that once you're in heaven,
You will be watching upon me,
But not only as my brother but as my guardian angel.
You will never be completely gone,
Because you will always be in my heart.

I can still remember your amazing scrumptious meals,
But now that you're gone I will always carry you with me in my heart, goodbye.
Minerva Baca, Grade 7

My Two Sides

Sometimes I'm bright pink
I'm hyper and fun
I share with my family and friends
And I laugh all night long
Other times I'm dark gray
I'm easily irritated
If you make me angry
You will be sorry
But most of the time I'm pink

Kelsey Mulheran, Grade 7

A Box of Chocolates

Life is a box of chocolates,
  all sweet and tasty,
many different kinds to choose from,
  and waiting to be set on my tongue.

Then you set it in the sun, it
  melts and drips,
until there is no more and it
  is gone forever.

Haley Moustis, Grade 7

Draw Lines

I love to draw weird lines,
I'll draw lines all day.
Across papers and books and walls,
I won't erase them away.

Even when night comes,
I will continue to draw.
Never pausing, stopping, sleeping
I put everyone in awe.

Joey Ippolito, Grade 7

The Sport of Fall

F rowning because I was tackled
O pen for a deep pass
O ther team down by 30
T he opponents are furious
B reaking tackles every run
A t the 50 yard line and still running
L eft them planted in the grass
L eaving with a state championship trophy

Hunter Helton, Grade 7

Rainy Night

In the dark and shivering cold
Animals scurry to their nests
Even the ones attempting to rest
In the dark and shivering cold
Footprints flood the floor
Owners slam their doors
In the dark and shivering cold
Animals scurry to their nests

Jacob Posey, Grade 8

Overcoming Obstacles

There's always obstacles we must overcome in life,
It starts at the bottom, feeling lost and insecure.
People will drag you down and make you feel like you're just not sure.
Some will even try to end it by picking up a knife.

We've all struggled through more than enough,
With our heads down just wanting to give in.
We never thought we could win.
We all struggle through the rough.

But it's time to get our heads up and reach for the stars!
Because we all want to succeed,
And we're all capable of it indeed.
It's time to step out from behind the bars.

So now I hope it's very clear,
Stay confident and your dreams won't seem far.
Stay strong, keep negative thoughts locked in a jar.
'Cause we started from the bottom now we're here.

Janet Ortiz, Grade 8

Winter Blues

I've got the winter blues,
this sudden aching for the blossoming of spring and gorgeous colors
I've got cabin fever,
locking me up tight
Making me worn and torn,
split in half,
and tired of sweaters and cold weather.
I long for short tees and twirling skirts,
and to read a grand novel outside in my reading nook,
squinting as the sunshine blocks my view.
I yearn to gaze up at the stars,
and feel the humidity engulfing me up in one big swoop,
as I rid myself of coats and cloaks,
and replace them with skirts and shirts.
But winter is midway through,
and I'm earnestly trying to get a glimpse of this winter's hidden beauty,
but it's so hard not to take this snow for granted,
while daring to dream of catching a glimpse of a single blade of grass once more.

AutumnGrace Page, Grade 8

Rollercoaster We Call Life

Life is a roller coaster with its bumps and bends. It takes unexpected turns and
frightens you with its control.

Your curiosity got the best of you, though.
You jump on, waiting for the thrill and excitement of the ride to begin. There is no
turning back now.

The ride begins, but now you are having second thoughts. You wonder if the bars
secure you, or whether they will let you go.

This rollercoaster that we call life goes fast, however, so you can either scream
every time there is a drop, or you can throw your hands up and enjoy.

Suvidhi Shah, Grade 7

Unsafe

Statistics show that 1 in 4 women will be raped in their lifetime.
You might not be aware, but I am the 5th of 7 daughters. This is rape culture.

This poem is not fun. It is not about the sun, the rain, or the clouds.
But the tears on our cheeks. The alley ways that you speed walk past. This poem is unsafe.

In the city of Detroit, 11,000 untested rape kits were found in a back room of the police department, some dating back 25 years. In the first 10% tested after discovery, 46 serial rapist were discovered. Imagine if these were tested when they should have been and how many rapes could have been prevented. This is rape culture.

This poem is not fun. It is about a problem we face.
And the countless victims shamed for their existence. This poem is unsafe.

In today's society police ask what someone was wearing before they ask who had raped them.
They justify actions as teasing and leading a man on.
Women are told that they were asking for it, like men have no control once they are aroused. This is rape culture.

This poem is not fun. This poem is to show you that our society is corrupt. This poem is unsafe.

97% of rapist will never spend a day in jail. And Senators are still pushing for no abortion.
Leaving victims of sexual assault with unwanted children that remind them of their attack every day of the pregnancy.
This is rape culture.

This poem is not fun. It tells you to be careful. This poem is unsafe.

I'm not telling you to be afraid of men. I am warning you, that date rape drugs are cheap and undetectable once in a drink.
I am telling you, it was NOT your fault. This is rape culture.
And this poem, is unsafe.

Allisen Hallahan, Grade 9

A Brat

I remember being young, wanting everything
And if I didn't get what I want I would cry, but they told me
"Don't be a brat" so I stayed quiet

I remember wanting to go to a party with fireworks and cake
But my mother said no so in anger I yelled why, and she yelled back
"Don't be a brat" so I stayed quiet

I remember wanting to see my sister after being two months since we saw each other
But my mother wanted to go out with her friends, I wanted to cry but then I remember
"Don't be a brat" so I stayed quiet

I remember staying at my aunt's till midnight waiting for my mother after school
But she was celebrating and I wanted to yell why she could not celebrate when I'm home, but I didn't because I remember
"Don't be a brat" so I stayed quiet

I remember being at my uncle's, my cousins would be ashamed of me
Tell me why I wasn't normal like them and say other offensive things, but I did nothing because I remember
"Don't be a brat" so I stayed quiet

I remember wanting to speak, wanting to say what is really on my mind
Wanting to break from my shell, wanting someone to hear me out, but when I try remember
"Don't be a brat" so I stayed quiet

Desiree Muniz, Grade 8

Spring

The soothing breeze of the spring wind calms my soul to the touch.
Birds tweet to show their existence.
The acidic aroma of flowers and fresh fruit fill the warm and quiet spring day.
Trees sway side to side to match the beat of the careless wind.
The bees float to one flower to other flowers.
Squirrels go up and back down trees that have flower buds on them.
Some flowers are all ready to be picked for decorative accessories in big bright luxurious homes.
This is how I know spring is here.

Inice Johnson, Grade 7

The Place that has My Heart

My favorite place is Brazil.
I just got back from Brazil about three weeks ago.
I helped children and their families learn about God and built long lasting relationships with them.
I saw greenery and wildlife, but most of all I saw many beautiful smiling faces.
I heard babies crying, kids yelling, and lots of Portuguese being spoken.
I chose to help with school, play with kids, and I chose to spread God's love to these amazing people.
I am hoping to go back in two years.
I had the best time of my life spreading God's love with these amazing people and I know my heart is definitely in Brazil.

Matthisen Witzel, Grade 8

Raindrops

The raindrops beat upon my windowpane. Steadily they drum on my roof. I sit on my bed and watch it cleanse the earth. I watch it until I get restless. I rush outside to the front porch. Slowly I reach my hand out into the rain. I reach further and further until my arm is dripping wet. Carefully I put one barefoot on the top step. All at once I run into it, spinning round and round soaking up the skies tears, letting it wash away the frustrations of life. I fall to the ground and lay there with my eyes closed. My back soaks up the water beneath me and the raindrops give me feathery kisses as they fall on my face. In moments like this we understand why God made the rain. It's not there to depress us. It comes to make things grow and to cleanse the souls of many. Never cry with the sky. Remember the sky only has tears of joy

Adrielle Lodico, Grade 9

Winter's Hand

On a snowy winter day the wind blows and the snow blowers are out in the driveways roaring and snarling picking up and spitting out each individual flake.
And I can see the icicles hang from gutters and trees or anywhere else the cold will reach.
Yes, Winter's hand reaches out to many clouds squeezing them and forcing them to drop their glittering crystals among many towns.
Although the winter can be a time of freezing and cold, you must think of the wonderful things you love the most and realize that it won't last forever and take in the beauty of it all for there may never be another just like it.

Nicole Pruski, Grade 7

The Music

The music that was made long ago was only the beginning. Bang of drums, clash of symbols.
The sound of strings making a beautiful blend.
The music heard before is the one now long forgotten. But others don't know that the music of so long ago is still with us.
Living Breathing and singing with us.

Giovanni Reyes, Grade 7

That One Game

Fast ball, slider, curve ball it doesn't matter as long as I hit the ball is all that will matter to.
I don't care if I hit a homer or over the fence as long as I hit that little ball.
I don't want to walk or strike out all I want to do his hit that ball. hitting a ball can be easy or hard but I believe.
Then that ball come hurling at me I get ready to hit it out there pow there it goes flying into out field and then I run.

Matthew Krupowicz, Grade 7

My Passion

My fingers touch the keys
Making a note every time
The beautiful sound it creates makes me happy—

Competition is soon
I can't help it, but I still get uneasy
Nervousness, but then joy
You walk into the room,
Clean, but pure
The judge is ready—
I put my music on the stand
I block out the rest of the world,
Calm yourself, you will do great
As I start, I don't feel anything else but happiness—

When I finish,
I remember how much I love to play the flute

Samantha Warpecha, Grade 7

Spine

I glare at my reflection
Genetics have blessed me with a curse
I grasp the wooden bar
When will my spine be straight? When will the pain go away?
When do I get to stop wearing this brace?
"It's not even noticeable"
Lies lies lies
It's like a corset, but 1,000 times tighter and 5,000 times thicker
Why me?
It's kind of funny, there's an S in my spine
And it took over the other letters, leaving my spine as only an S
I see the clock in the back of the room, ticking, counting
10 more minutes until I can leave
I dread every second I have to be here
But deep down I know it's helping me
Lengthening my spine as straight as I can
Standing up straight is something we all take advantage of

Nina Connor, Grade 8

Big City Dreams

I could relate you to many things
I could relate you to the stars, the sea the sky
Your streets paint the land like strings
Your buildings reach hundreds high
You are a mountain range
Not varied, though, your mountains: rectangular
An outsider deems you as strange
Your range: everywhere
You are an attraction
You can be discovered, uncovered, your people want to be seen
Everyone sees you integrated into fractions
Your subways reek of big city dreams
We've got things to do and places to be
Try to figure who's in control: the city, or me

Derek Balogh, Grade 9

The Summer Nights

The sun starts to set,
Summer's warm day is coming to an end.
The wood is stacked by the pit,
Waiting and begging to be burned.
The fire makes a loud pop,
Flames reflect in our eyes.
The heat burns our shins,
Hot dogs roast over the fire.
Flames sizzle and spit sparks,
Ashes raise into the sky and become stars.
The moon lights the path to peace,
Trees sway in the cool breeze,
Fireflies light up the landscape.
The coals glow dimly in the bottom of the pit,
Telling us its time to rest.
The locust sings us a sweet lullaby,
And we drift off the sleep in the summer air.

Karley Zoucha, Grade 9

Broken

They speak and they laugh just because they can.
The words they speak, the lies they spread, they hurt.
They've pushed and they've shoved, and quickly they ran.
They buried a soul, they dug up the dirt.

The truth, the lies, lie down in deep disguise
The halls abuzz with murmurs and whispers.
They feel no remorse, it was no surprise.
They took, they stole, what has always been hers.

A faint crack appears on her glass heart.
She breaks, and she bruises, filled to the brim.
The pain they cause, piercing like a dart.
There's pain, no gain, flowing over the rim.

They scream, "Give up. A waste of space. Just die."
No one to save her, so she says, "Goodbye…"

Sahithi Muppalla, Grade 9

Pink Shirt

I remember wearing, for the first time ever,
a pink shirt with a tie and a light color, that color was purple.
They matched exactly to my sister's shoes.
We would to go the store,
wearing our pink shirt and her wearing shoes.
When we were together we wore that.

I remember the day that the shirt didn't fit me any more.
It was so small.
I couldn't believe it.
That pink shirt felt beautiful, it was soft.
I loved how they matched to my sister's shoes.
But most of all I didn't believe it didn't fit me any more.
That shirt would bring back a lot of memories.

Alexis Ortega, Grade 8

Value of Life

What will be something that is valuable in our life?
Or something that makes our life valuable?
We know it is not money
We know it is not authority
It might satisfy us and make us fulfilled
But it is temporary
What is valuable,
Is not temporary
It is family, who will be with us always
It is friends, who will carry us up when we are down
It is memories of our path we went through
Doesn't matter whether it's good or bad
Anything that is valuable will bring us
Warmth in our heart and
Smiles and laughter.
That will be something that is
Worth it in our life.

Alice Kim, Grade 8

Thank You For

To the veterans who have fought for our country
It feels so good to be free
And to those that have died
By sacrificing their lives
Thank you for serving your country

Only a few answer the calls or cries
To save soldiers' lives
And who takes care of the sick
Which is known as a medic
Thank you for keeping them alive

If only people who start wars could see
That everybody must live in peace
We wouldn't have to lose precious lives
And wouldn't have to hear hurtful cries
Veterans, thank you for keeping us free

Zane Belford, Grade 7

Document1

It's only a blank page
But soon words appear on it
Before you know it it's a forest
If you're not careful you'll get lost
This is one thing you can do with Document1
If you type just right
It can have a pretty shape
You can make it look like anything
It can remind you of things
Stuff you have seen
Before was almost a fish
Now it's a lamp with a shade
But if you open another it changes
It's no longer Document1
It has changed into Document2

Michael Wolfe, Grade 8

Snow Day

When I wake up
On This cold snowy winter day
As I go to grab my snow boots and coat
Scrambling everywhere before my mom is here
Hurrying to be at the slopes before the snow stops

Trying to be careful on the icy roads
Taking all of our sleds and gear out of the vehicle
Dragging our sleds all the way to the steep hill
Being pushed down the bumpy slope
Racing each other to see who will win

Soon we were all rushing to the car frozen
Going into the house
Making hot chocolate
Walking slowly by the fire to warm up
And laying on the couch watching a movie

Lucy Tjelmeland, Grade 8

Climbing

As I started to climb,
After I put on my gear
Before long I was at the top,
While my sister was on her way,
When all of the sudden my brother was already there

Although I had completed the climbing wall
After the fifth ascent,
If I said I was done we would have to leave
Since it was becoming late,
Before we left I went up another wall

As I looked at the mountain
As if it would become smaller,
So that it was easier to climb,
Although I was still going to climb it,
Before I become too old and wrinkly

Eli Ommen, Grade 8

The Beach

Taking the first step into the warm sand,
Your feet sinking in slowly.
Knowing that his is one of the best feelings to ever have.
Taking another step,
Feeling the sand hit the back of your legs.
You smile, remember how good it feels.
You smell the salty ocean water,
You haven't smelt in a while.
The sun shines onto your face,
You can't wait to soak up its rays.
You feel the breeze from the waves blow your hair back,
You forgot why you ever left this place.
You never want to leave now.
You love every bit of this moment,
And you never want it to end.

Grace Rieker, Grade 8

Crazy World*

Can we do what we say
What we do we have to live with every day
All we have is a lot of broken dreams and regrets
We just need to finally pay our debts

I can't watch the news and hear about the dead
I just look at the screen and keep shaking my head
Little baby boys and girls
Growing up in something I like to call a crazy world

Flash of the gun was bright in the night
The darkness of the theatre
One man was trying to make a fright
It wasn't a cult but he was the leader

I've said the same thing so many times
Everybody says the same punch line
Now they're on cloud nine
But their spirits won't die

Nicholas Grant, Grade 8
*Dedicated to the victims of the Aurora, CO shooting.

My Special Place

The sea creatures walk; The farm animals fly;
The birds swim; Welcome to my special place.

The fish walked by the pond; The horse flew in the sky;
The robin swam in the pond; This is my special place.

The shark walked by the pond; The cow flew in the sky;
The eagle swam in the pond; This is my special place.

The clam walked by the pond; The donkey flew in the sky;
The woodpecker swam in the pond; This is my special place.

The sea horse walked by the pond; The goat flew in the sky;
The parrot swam in the pond; This is my special place.

The blue whale walked by the pond; The pig flew in the sky;
The cardinal swam in the pond; This is my special place.

I walked by the pond; I flew in the sky;
I swam in the pond; This is my special place.

Alex Thompson, Grade 8

A Shining Beacon

Hope is a shining beacon
That pierces fearful darkness,
Which creeps upon this mortal earth.
The beacon is always steady, never moving,
Guiding lost ships to harbor.
Calm brightness, amidst the raging tempest,
"Sore must be the storm,"
That ever diminishes the gleaming light
That dances upon the tossing waves.

Elizabeth Mioni, Grade 9

You Can't Ask Me

What is it like to be in a crowd
Around people who smile
And are very loud
Who say, "Come stay awhile!"
I wouldn't know, you can't ask me,
For I am the loneliest lonely could be.

What is it like to laugh with friends
To giggle and talk with whomever
What is it like to tie up loose ends
To have life together
I wouldn't know, you can't ask me,
For I am the loneliest lonely could be.

What is it like to lose a loved one?
To struggle with pain of abuse
To cry blood and pain until you're all done
To always feel misuse
I wouldn't know, you can't ask me,
For I am the most blessed, the most blessed could be.

Kara Haglund, Grade 8

I'll Be Gone, But Not For Long

You are the friend everybody dreams for,
I couldn't ask for anything more,
You take in my pain,
and pour me some rain,
telling me to wake up,
though I can't seem to hear.
You tell me to be bold,
Yet my heart is too cold,
to listen or be controlled.
You flash me a smile,
and I stay there for a while,
to notice what has been wrong.
And that's when I realize, all along,
I did not have the courage to face my troubles, without you.

Though all of the years that we've been through,
all the bad times and good times too,
will never fade from my deep wide memory,
and I hope you will still be happy,
even without me.

Maggie Li, Grade 7

Deep in Thought

You want to know the place where I feel safe?
Where darkness is forbidden, time doesn't matter even if you're late.
I'm supposed to be here, I was brought here by fate.
Where I can get rid of my troubles, so hear the words I have to say.
Fighting with my feelings, this is the place I hide.
Deep in thought I write of what I feel inside.
Using music and rhythm, as my personal guide.
Where I can be myself
My place is in my mind.

Lee Holy, Grade 9

Ode to My Bed

It's comforting
When I'm tired
Or needing a break

The soft lavender color
Of sheets
And comforting fluff of my blanket

It helps me drift off
To sleep
With the comforting smell
Of lavender fabric softener

After long
Tiring days
It heals my wounds like a band-aid
With the soothing feeling
Of cozy sheets

Huddled beneath the blankets
Is safest
Hiding from things in the night
With a flashlight
And a yellow-tinted book
Caroline Shah, Grade 9

Rebirth

Rebirth happens in the spring
It starts to change everything
It makes me just want to sing
Of the rebirth of spring

Changes happen all around
Can you hear the beautiful sound
It rings throughout the town
Of the rebirth of spring

Birds hum out a beautiful song
The days grow so long
I can't help but sing along
To the rebirth of spring

We finally take the girl out
Everyone wants to shout
People start talking about
The rebirth of spring

Green grass grows super tall
As if it were an ivy wall
Everyone is called
By the rebirth of spring.
Jack Galloway, Grade 8

Baseball Dreams

Crack!
The ball goes over the fence
The crowd goes wild
Screaming
Jumping as I run around the diamond
I still feel
The ball hitting off the sweet spot
Of the bat

My foot bounces off third
I jog home in no hurry
I hear coach
Clapping
He is proud of me
My family screams
"Atta boy!"
I realize how much I love the game
We call
Baseball
Nicholas Dombroski, Grade 8

Broken

You look at her and think, "She's just shy"
But on the inside she's broken down
She's been tortured, taunted, and teased
Just trying to hide her frown

You look at him and think, "He's just quiet"
But at home he's abused
But he doesn't ever say a thing
He's alone and confused

They both feel so useless and scared
She's to the breaking point and so is he
They just want it to all end
They want to be free

The girl meets the boy
They know just how the other one feels
Now it's just them against the world
It's amazing how fast a broken heart heals
Abbi Martelli, Grade 8

Fall

The leaves change colors
Fall has fallen once again
The colors so bright

They fall to the ground
To make a bed of beauty
They fall with no sound

Their lives are complete
One more journey to their rest
Now wait for winter
Arianna Mercer, Grade 8

Child of Flowers

I saw her
The Sun on her hair of bronze
As small as a blade of grass
She wore a crown of flowers
She told me to look up

And I saw her
The Moon on her hair of silver
As big as the ocean wide
She wore a crown of flowers
She told me to look higher

And I saw her
The Planets on her hair of gold
As immense as the universe
She wore a crown of flowers
But she was just a child
A child of flowers
Anna Podborny, Grade 7

Approval

I walk into the room
A smile on my face

Wishing I could
Get a smile from her
I never tried this hard
To get approval

Day by day
I think of different ways
To get approval
No matter what I do
Or how I try
Nothing works

I walk into the room
A smile on my face
Waiting to get approval
Mia Hubbert, Grade 8

Bear

With the grass so green,
and the river so blue,
with gray rocks and
baby cubs all over.
Cheerful and excited
they are.
They can play in
the dirt and get
all dirty again.
With the baby cubs,
and mama bear excited
and cheerful
they all are.
Jordyn Deming, Grade 7

I Remember Good Times

I remember having good times with the
People I love. I remember the smiles,
The laughs, the cries, and the byes
I remember good times

I remember when visiting them, waking
Up to their beautiful faces smiling at me
I remember good times

I remember them all the time
When I think about them
I remember good times
JaUndra Bullock, Grade 7

De Fog

Shaking white clouds
Whistling in the night
Sneaking up through the trees
Getting bigger and bigger
Running through the night
Creeping up on houses
Breathing ever so quietly
Whispering in the wind
Ghostly chills down your spine
Until it gets lighter
Crawling away
Disappearing in the night
Brenna Dougan, Grade 7

Basketball

Basketball is my favorite sport!
I love dribbling down the court
Dribble, pass, shoot
It's a triple threat!
Basketball is my favorite sport!
The defense tries to make a fort
But they can't stop us
They can't even slow us down
Basketball is my favorite sport!
The other team wants to abort
Because when they see us,
They just turn and run
Nico Nasti, Grade 7

Nebraska

Busy city life fills the air.
Cars driving by, businesses booming,
but if you drive out west,
corn stalks reign supreme.
Towering vegetable giants stand tall.
Cows, pigs, chickens, sheep, horses,
farmers raise them until they die.
Nebraska is about cities and farms,
A little bit of both.
That is what makes Nebraska so great.
Adam Strasser, Grade 8

The Feeling of Success

Time after time,
Pouring heart and soul into the game.
Giving everything,
But it always ends the same.

Time after time,
Admiring the other team as they celebrate with cheer.
We shake their hands, glancing at their smiling faces;
But as they shake our hands, only sadness we appear

Time and time again,
Trudging away, noticing the team taking pictures in the background.
The trophies in their hands is a token of their victory.
As we proceed to the car without a single sound.

And time continues to go on,
Shaking off the loss and trying some more.
Motivated by victory, motivated by determination,
Triumph is what we look for.

And one day, there is that time;
The time we worked so hard to get;
And the feeling is like no other,
Because we know we've truly earned it.

Carly Manshum, Grade 8

Guardian of Scotland

On 1297, the 11th of September,
Was the Battle of Stirling Bridge, a day to remember.
The narrowness of the bridge gave the edge to Wallace,
Making his victory utterly flawless.

Britain's second invasion, the Battle of Falkirk,
By not showing up, Wallace made the British berserk.
When word came that Wallace was near Falkirk,
They thought of strategies thinking, "What will work?"

The event that took place that fateful night,
Had left the Scots with a heart full of fear and fright.
Wallace resigned as Guardian of Scotland in favor of Robert the Bruce,
Who would never give up or tie his own noose.

When William was captured, he knew he had met his fate,
While being dragged through the Tower of London's gates.
He was hanged, drawn, and quartered,
Then he was emasculated, eviscerated, and beheaded.

His head dipped in tar and placed on a pike,
And sitting on top was an old bird shrike.
With his head hanging on the old London Bridge,
His spirit still lingers on that well-known ridge.
Brendan Quinn, Grade 8

Sky

The sky is blue, white, or red,
Depending on the weather it ain't a dread
The sky is not the limits, but it shall spread
The sky is blue, white, or red

The sky is blue, white, or red
Just like my bears name fluffy Ted
As the wind blows on the riverbed
The sky is blue, white, or red

The sky is blue, white, or red
The sun came down and colored it, bled
It's time to say goodnight just like I said
The sky is blue, white, or red
Josiah Varghese, Grade 7

Youth

She's a beauty you see
She's fast and filled with
sudden fury
She can leave you heart-
broken for days maybe
even months,
She is capable of anything
as she feels.
She'll never let you finish
and she'll never let you
enjoy the moment.
because within seconds
she's gone, and it's all
just a blur.
Jasmina Gracanin, Grade 8

Facing Choices

It was just before the game,
Everybody was really aggressive.
Then they announced the names,
And the game started off very progressive.

After the first quarter,
The score was five to one.
Then Taylor was caught at the border,
And she decided to run.

She drove to the hoop,
Then she passed to Katie,
And she made a loop,
While Katie has made all her shots lately.
Nicole Casebeer, Grade 7

Clouds

Those fluffy, crisp, white
Pillows drift through the cold air
Rain, hail, ice, or snow
Hide inside
Jeffrey Austin Jr., Grade 8

Friends

Friends are the people who make us who we are.
They teach us the right and wrong all the time.
Friends are my number one support group.
When my family isn't around I know I can always count on them.
Friends are the reason I smile every day.
They always make me laugh at just about anything.
Friends are the best part of life.
Each moment you spend with them, is just another memory made.
Friends are different. Some are going to treat you right,
Others may treat you wrong, but that's how we all learn who is true and who isn't.
Friends are our guardian angels.
Even when they aren't around they will always be right next to you.
Friends are understanding, they always manage to help
And get what you're trying to say in every situation that you're in.
Friends are our coaches. When we are feeling low and insecure,
They are always there to boost our self confidence.
Dyani Cordero, Grade 8

Your Little Girl

We used to go everywhere to together but now we barely go outside
We used to tease each other but now we rarely see each other
We used to talk a lot now we never call each other
We have lots of memories but that was then
I was your little girl
I remember when I slept on your tummy and I could hear the rumbling
I remember when I always waited for you to come home
I remember when I never wanted you to leave
I remember when you spoiled me rotten when you could
I am your little girl
Now we became closer
Now we became happier
Now we have more memories
We are a family
I will always be your little girl
Love you, Dad!
Caley Bradley, Grade 8

Sea of Emotions

In a sea of emotions
Lost somewhere in between
Who can find an answer?
Or understand what I mean
In a sea of emotions
Who can find the light?
When fear and anger seem to stalk the night
In a sea of emotions
Few seem to find their way
To the happiness and warmth of the day
In a sea of emotions
Though scared and misunderstood
You will wake up to a friend who will find you, though deep under a hood
Through the sea of emotions
You will both find your way
And you will both learn to cherish the friendship that brightened your way
Joy L. Johnson, Grade 7

Night Is Coming

Sunsets
Cloudy swirls form
Illuminating orange
Making patterns in the night sky
Glowing

Ally Burhop, Grade 8

Rain

Dark clouds
Heavy, gloomy
Looming above my head
Until they can't hold more water
And cry

Cody Ainsley, Grade 8

Great Books

Great books catch your mind
Intriguing you to read more
Filled with great knowledge
Up to the very brim of
The pages, until the end

Steven Simpson, Grade 8

Rain

The rain
Soft and misty
Comes pouring down quite hard
No matter how it drops down, it's just
Water

Alan Albarran, Grade 8

Summer

Summer
The hot, dry days
Air conditioners on
Sun gets brighter, and life gets way
Better

Damien Crawford, Grade 8

Oceans

Currents of water
The big, heavy tides coming
Filling us with awe
Splashing, hitting, and forceful
When they come to the shore

Jennifer Moreno, Grade 8

American Soldier

All soldiers at war
Fight and live for their families
If you're "Army Strong"
Show pride and honor, right now
And fight for our freedom

Maxwell O'Brien, Grade 8

Writing

An idea strikes but quickly flees,
Lightning cracking, gone with a flash
Fantastic creatures and amazing dreams
Catch it then for it's precious ash.

For those remains can change many lives
With tragic plots, heartbreaks, and love,
Battles, dragons, tears, and knives:
All those options one can write of,

Yet each one differs, full meaning
The story it tells is created by me
With lots of help and careful preening,
Like a deadened bush trimmed down and free.

The finished project finally complete
Excitingly published and ready for show
The gnawing is over, the feeling so sweet
Like a statewide fashion it soon will grow

On my shelf, it stands there bold. I never forget the first one that's done;
With me it stands the story once untold. Now left for me my prize once won
The lives it touched forever affected, always in mind hearts forever connected.

Rylee Cannon, Grade 8

Grandpa

I am four years old
and a ballet dancer.
Death does not exist, but my Papi has cancer.
Mommy says it's a sickness.
Oh now I get it, like chicken pox.
Cancer cannot possibly hurt Papi.
He's as strong as an ox.

I am eight years old
and a ballet dancer.
Death is the passing of my friend's goldfish,
and my grandpa still has cancer.
Mom says cancer can be deadly.
My grandpa cannot possibly leave me.
He'll be here forever.
He's the best grandpa anyone could possibly be.

I am 15 years old
and a ballet dancer.
Death is the end of hope.
My grandfather had cancer.
Mother says he would want me to be happy, instead of living in the past.
But I've lost my grandfather forever.

Katie Gillette, Grade 9

Gray

If I could be a color I would be gray, because gray isn't a color gray is a shade.
I would be gray like the full moon unlike the hot sun which you can't gaze into.
But I would be gray mainly because gray has a different meaning for everyone.

Kassie Kunkel, Grade 7

Fall

Fall; oh what a beautiful season
The crispness in the air
The crunch of the leaves
The air whistling around the trees
Oh what a beautiful season

Apple orchards open
You can pick apples by hand
Or drink cool cider
But only in fall
Oh what a beautiful season

Leaves create a splash of color
Red, orange, yellow, and brown
Look at the beautiful colors
"Crunch" goes the leaves
Oh what a beautiful season
Amber Brooks, Grade 7

Connor

So innocent and small
Always up for another brawl

Tiny hands, tiny toes
Round cherry nose

Bright blue eyes, open smile
With such ease to beguile

You're unexpecting prey
Enough fun to last the day

Always slightly puzzled
Enough questions to need a muzzle

You drive me completely insane
I still love you all the same
Hannah Knaust, Grade 9

Spring

Spring time is a time
To take back all mistakes
Just plant them in the ground

The flowers will grow
From the chosen mistakes
Just rain and sun is needed

Spring time is time
To let go of the pent up feelings
It isn't worth keeping them

The flowers will blossom
From the words spoken in anger
Just let it all out
Julianna Borgia, Grade 7

An Ode to Imagination

Imagination
Everybody needs to think
Everybody needs to aspire

Imagination
Lets you see
what you want to perceive
Lets you change
what you want to change
It frees you
from your troubles
Lets you remedy anything
you want to fix

Imagination
Lets you do the impossible,
but nothing is impossible
You can do it
Every invention
Every creation
Every great idea anyone ever had
Started with
Imagination.
Neil Kelekar, Grade 9

Sports

Baseball is a sport, that many want to play,
youngsters throw baseballs,
made of yarn and clay,
and when the ball is hit,
the parents yell hooray.

Soccer is a sport, that many want to play,
youngsters kick kickballs,
and score goals all day,
and when a goal is scored,
the parents yell hooray.

Tennis is a sport, that many want to play,
players use racquets,
to hit the ball away,
and when the ball is missed,
the parents yell hooray.

Football is a sport, that many want to play,
youngsters advance the field,
and run many plays,
and when there is a touchdown,
the parents yell hooray.
Logan Edwards, Grade 7

Water

cold water rushing
misting me with a cool splash
leaving me freezing
Olivia Martello, Grade 7

Welcome to America

Welcome to America
Land of opportunity
Where men got independence
Welcome to America
Liberty and justice for all
Yet the government falls
In debt and they clash
And they bash
With other countries
Welcome to America
Where you can buy legislative power
From a governor in Illinois
Welcome to America
Where people like to live and
Will die for this country
Welcome to America
This is where I'll die and pass up
My life for a country I love
Welcome to America
This country will decide your fate
Ivan Arreola, Grade 7

Today

Today is just another day.
I can't see it another way.

Another push, another shove,
Another caught in war and love.

Another open yet closed gate,
Another fight between peace and hate.

Another obviously fake smile,
Another chance to walk the mile.

Another joyful happy face,
Another hope for human race.

Another step away from harm,
Another step towards righteous arms.

Today is just another day.
I can't see it another way.
Lily Spevak, Grade 8

I Like That Stuff

Slaves crave it,
Soldiers save it,
Freedom
I like that stuff.

Teens learn it,
Singles yearn it,
Love
I like that stuff.
Ava Reynolds, Grade 7

Softball
Softball
Running bases
Catching after the pitch
Watching the ball fly in the air
Pitching
Ashley Pruski, Grade 7

War
I lie
On this sad field,
Hearing the crying voices
Everywhere; hurt men are dying
Sadness!
Noah Mascal, Grade 8

Oblivion
My world replaced by
A soundless atmosphere that
Silences all noise
Darkness blinds my sight
From a hope of escaping
Brooke Melvin, Grade 8

Family
My life is complete,
With my family all around,
Filling me with joy.
I know I am always home,
As long as they're with me.
Kelsey Spears, Grade 8

Shame
S tupid pointless mistakes
H ang over my head
A imlessly walking with no where to go
M issing all of my friends
E very day I think of what I have done
Karly McDougald, Grade 7

Stars
S taying high above
T winkling in the dark night
A lways being there
R eady to come back soon
S hining down on us forever
Lucas Blankley, Grade 7

Sophisticated
books at hand
dressed bright like the sunshine
waiting for what comes next
ready for the future
Sophisticated
Olivia Warne, Grade 7

The Nameless Children
The children watch as the willow weeps
as judgmental peers do creep
they wonder why the willow weeps.

As the birds sing their sweet song they pray
that they could sing along
but society would see it wrong.

As judgmental peers do creep
they wonder why the willow weeps

Others brag of their conceit and their greed is a treat
as the children sit in a corner, silent and good
each time that they speak, misunderstood.

As judgmental peers do creep
they wonder why the willow weeps

Observers are they, watchers for God
to see when the time is right
and though it may be hard to watch

They cannot stand
they do not fight

We ask this question plain and clear for those of you who fear, cause fear
You may be judgmental peers who creep,
Would you know why the willow weeps?
Victoria Ault, Grade 7

Too Far Up
Whenever I have to think about fear,
There is a word I seldom like to hear,
But when my dad looks at the Sears Tower and wants to go to the top,
My thoughts and well being instantly pop.

The Sears Tower is a deathtrap way up high!
So close to the sun I will fry;
I'm so scared I think I will cry.
Please, God, I don't want to die!

For when I imagine myself there with all my fright,
I fall off and think that I can see the light;
Now thinking these thoughts, the floor feels really slick,
I'm so loose and wobbly; why won't my feet stick?

Why am I imagining these thoughts?
This is bringing back all the nausea I have fought —
The times I have fainted way up high:
Feeling unstable, oh my, oh my.

Calm down, Jack; it's okay.
You will make it off the deathtrap today,
No matter how much you can feel it sway.
Calm down, Jack; it's okay
Jack Harper, Grade 8

Can You Understand Me Now?

You never listen to what I have to say
Yet you scream at me every day
Can't you just stay away?
It's not like you're there for me anyway

Acting like you care
You're so unfair
Judging me by what I wear
How I truly feel I'll never share

I hide away all this hate
Like usual, you're always late
Can't your job and friends just wait?
Become a true mom before it's too late!

I want to shout!
Let all my feelings out
If you're not going to help then get out
That you'll understand me is what I doubt

But instead I stay quiet
Avoiding a riot
My true feelings you'll never buy it
All this anger, I'll just hide it
Nieves Camarillo, Grade 9

Addie Mae

I remember it like it was yesterday,
Sitting with Addie Mae.
"Help me with my belt?" Denise asked.
That was the end of Addie Mae.

The blast went off,
I really don't remember much.
"Addie. Addie." Was all I could say.
I just wanted to feel her touch.

It all went black,
the glass was in my eye.
It didn't hurt much.
I really just wanted to cry.

She's gone now,
My sweet sweet sister.
They took her away.
God, I really miss her.

I remember it like it was yesterday,
Sitting with Addie Mae.
"Help me with my belt?" Denise asked.
That was the end of Addie Mae.
Sadee Whitfield, Grade 8

Fallen Stars

When a star falls
An angel comes down
To take away
All the poor souls
Who have passed
Since the last fallen star

When a star falls
All souls are released
They are let go
Free to travel to heaven
Free from their ties
Free from pain and suffering

When a star falls
Remember
Those poor souls
For they are free
So do not fear
Do not feel mournful
A star will one day fall for you.
Tessa Kauffman, Grade 8

The Ghost of a Time

A swing hangs from a rusty bar,
Wind and idle songs play here.

Memories of scuffed shoes dig dusty
Trenches in long-since forgotten grounds.

A cracked yellow slide, the roof
Of a home in the sand, a castle.

A blackberry patch, overburdened
And conquered by blind growth.

A shared fence, once frequented
By friends is lonely and abandoned.

A house with closed shutters,
No one lives here now.

Silent laughter echoes at night,
A song was once sung here.
Caroline Meek, Grade 9

Veteran's Day

When our country is in trouble
you are always on the double.
With your weapons in hand
you march in like a band.
Things may start to get rough
but you guys are tough.
When you fight each day
we all say happy Veteran's Day!
Hayden Sechrest, Grade 7

Blossom

I know flowers blossom.
They blossom into beautiful colors,
flowers open up and change.
They grow,
get strong,
begin to glow
like a rainbow.
But then,
they weaken.
Shrivel up,
and later die.

I know humans blossom.
Humans,
when babies,
begin to crawl.
Then they stumble over their steps,
start to walk,
and grow into strong,
glowing human beings.
Until their time is done.
Tiffany Lozano, Grade 8

Chicken Pox!

Chicken pox! Chicken Pox!
Can you go away?
All over me,
Itching to scratch,
But not one bit,

Small,
And young,
I do not have a choice.
I have to cross my hands,
And do not dare,
Not even once.

Then they disappear,
Forever,
And ever…
And during the time,
I had them,
Not one,
Single,
Scratch.
Christopher Habrelewicz, Grade 8

Summer/Winter

Summer
Hot, sunny
Swimming, walking, running
Cookouts, bikes, snowman, snow
Sledding, playing, ice skating
White, wet
Winter
Mya Feeney, Grade 7

Military

Having someone in the military
You know it's not easy
They leave for a year
Maybe two
And maybe never come back

Some don't come back the same
Some lose their mind
Some lose limbs
It just isn't the same
And it never will be

I know no one wants family in the military
But who would protect our country
Who would protect you
And if you have someone in the military
Say thank you
Because they're saving you
TJ Sheehy, Grade 8

Stop

Stop
Stop
Stop
Stop
Please
I don't want to hurt anymore
I don't want to care anymore
I don't want to smile anymore
I don't want to love anymore
So please Stop…
But you can't
Because that's just who you are
Because that's all you ever do
Hurt me
Make me want to care
Then break me
So please
Stop I can't take it anymore
Haleigh Edwards, Grade 7

A True Dancer

Telling a story without a word,
expressing emotions for others to feel:
silent noises that well not be heard,
forgetting everything that seems real.
The leaps and turns put me in a trance,
and soon I become the dance.

Dancing can fill my free time;
it is a state of mind
Finding new mountains to climb,
dancing to music of every kind.
Working hard is the answer
To becoming a true dancer.
Tayler Cannon, Grade 8

Useless Things

Papers without creases
Parents without nieces
Doorbells without rings
Eagles without wings,

Sharks without gills
Kids without spills
Lacrosse without nets
People without bets,

Snakes without rattles
Horses without saddles
Boats without docks
Cement without rocks,

Bees without stingers
Phones without ringers
People without hunger
Heat without summer,

Parks without trees
People without knees
Lawns without grass
Cars without gas.
Isabella Milani, Grade 7

Useless

Trees without roots.
Feet without boots.
Maps without roads.
Trucks without loads.

Frames without pictures.
Batter without mixtures.
Clocks without hands.
Houses without lands.

The sea without waves.
Miners without caves.
Christmas without lights.
Performers without tights.

A country without a flag.
Clothes without a tag.
A house without a door.
A room without a floor.

A frog without a jump.
A tire without a pump.
Eyes without lashes.
Men without 'staches.
Olivia Manternach, Grade 7

You've Changed

"You changed."
Her voice is breaking up.
She can't see,
As the tear escapes my eye.

"You changed."
I try to speak,
But every sound,
I try to release,
Is mud.
Mud that has no form,
Or emotion.

"You change"
I'm starting to believe it,
But now all that's left
Are the memories.
Memories that will stay,
Because memories
Are the only thing
She can't take away
Izalina Santoyo, Grade 8

Fears

Sometimes I might be afraid
for one reason or another;
when I was a little girl
it seemed to happen more often.
In my years of childhood,
I was afraid of many things;
there were needles and sickness;
broken bones, even surgeries.
As the years kept passing by,
I learned to face all of these fears;
then I started to realize,
there were more as I got older.
The more I started to learn,
the fears would start to come and go,
they also started to change;
from spiders to family dying.
Then, I realized so much that
had been scary to me, really
had not been so bad for me.
Some of the fears made me stronger;
I learned to face my fears head on.
Ellie Brown, Grade 7

Mother

Mother
frightening, predictable
constant sense
a child's face as
she a happy little
girl to rejoin her
parents in a fantasy
Jacob Marsh, Grade 7

The Search

Look at the vines that grew over the gate,
Broken windows and a squeaky door,
Littered yards and ignored flowers of late,
Not to mention the overgrown moor.

The signs of Time is scattered everywhere,
Like little footprints littering the ground,
Time mindlessly destroyed things without a care,
Wearing everything down and all around.

Foolish Decisions assisted the destruction,
The greatest accomplice of Time,
The embodiment of a hidden demon,
It has made me commit the undeniable crime.

I have lost something special like so,
Where did my Life go?

Emily No, Grade 8

Everyday Things

I ate my hair and brush my pancakes,
I sat on my TV and watched my chair.

I cleaned my clothes and washed my room,
I washed in my clothes and put on my shower.

I visited my outside and play neighbor.
I get in the mall and shopped at the car.

I play my movies and watched computer.
I teach my cards and play brother.

I ate my book and read a pie,
I listened to sleep and fall a music.

All day it was a backward day,
I hope tomorrow is better, that all I have to say!

Say Meh, Grade 7

Dreams

Everything goes dark, he holds his guitar
He drifts till finally he sleeps

He awakens but in a dream, he holds a solid gold guitar
He is sitting on a stool, his fingers stroke the strings

A beautiful song comes from the guitar
He knows it's not real
When he wakes, this beautiful song will be gone

He still plays, not wasting one second
The notes mesmerize him
He closes his eyes, he begins to drift
Till finally he awakens
It's no dream, it's life

Priscilla Ocampo, Grade 8

Snow Under the Stars

Starry night sky sparkles overhead,
Lighting the way through the trees.
The full moon watches over everything,
Acting as a protector from all things bad,
Shedding light and giving hope.

The fresh snow glitters in the moonlight,
Looking so pure and white.
Afraid to make any movement,
You don't want to disturb such a beautiful sight.
Cold, crisp, clean air burns your lungs as you inhale,
Giving off warm steam as you exhale.

The wind screams through the trees,
Cringing as it burns your face.
You hear a snap,
It comes from an animal moving silently through the trees,
On a mission to get someplace warm.

Jaclyn Frey, Grade 9

My Gift

You are like,
The wind,
Always there by my side
even though I cannot see you.
The water,
Pure and beautiful
The center of my life.
The soil,
So rich and natural
Your soul is your beauty that shines as bright as the sun.
You are the greatest gift in my life
But now that gift is gone.
You are still in my heart and
in the trees
So calm
So peaceful
Even though you are not here I will love you
Forever and Always

Melissa Saettone, Grade 7

My Own New Road

I travel down that broken road
That everybody talks about, but doesn't know.
And with an already heavy load,
Everyone around me just says, "No."
"She can't do it; why does she try
When she already knows she can't actually fly?"

I start walking, trying to gain
What I've lost so long ago.
But with what I want comes pain;
I think it's worth it, though:
To stop following where everyone's life flowed,
And start paving my own new road.

Liza Nelson, Grade 8

Lifted Trucks

Big, lifted and black,
Diesel or gas,
Turbo or none,
I will have a way back,
In a lifted truck

Much smoke or none,
Extra long or short,
Stacked or straight piped,
There is much fun,
In a lifted truck

Chevrolet or Ford,
I like them both,
Radio or none,
It's hard to get bored,
In a lifted truck

Rain, sleet, or snow,
By the foot or inch,
Mud or gravel,
I'll get where I want to go,
In a lifted truck
Burton Hess, Grade 8

Just Me

I don't want to be
Another Brittney;
I don't want to be
Another Sam.
I just want to be
Me,
And that's just the way I am.

I don't want to be
Another Brittney;
I don't want to be
Another Sam.
I just want to be
The way God made me,
And that is just who I am.

I don't want to change myself
To be like somebody else
Because an original is worth
Way more than a copy.
God made me the way I am
Because I'm part of His master plan!
That's why I just want to be, Me!
Hannah Jenkins, Grade 7

Spring

Winter's icy clutch
Fades away to the sound of
Bird calls on the wind
Michael Stadler, Grade 8

The Place I Call Home

Pure joy is the feeling you get as you reach the path.
The trees reach for the sky while the grass waves "hello."
The tall pine wood trees protect you from the sun.
But there are places where they surprise you with amazing sights.
The little bright flowers beam with joy just to see you.
The birds sing happy songs to guide you along.
But I call it home because it's what I love.
My heart races as I come close to the top.
Finally I'm here right where the heavens reach the mountaintop.
The only spot that you can release your feelings.
I feel release, I'm calm yet I'm excited finally able to be at peace.
But the sun is starting to bed, and the moon is coming out to play.
Just as you're leaving that sweet musky earthy smell takes over your mind.
Open your eyes it's just as sweet as it smells.
Time to go now the sun has gone to bed and the moon is out playing.
Goodbye the trees wave, as does the grass.
For this is my home at last.
Christina Stopak, Grade 9

Snow

As the snow starts to fall,
While children come out to play,
When they start throwing snowballs,
Even though there are consequences to pay,
As the end of the day comes near, whenever they go inside, they'll have lots of cheer.

While snow falls to the ground,
Even though never making a single sound,
If the sun hits the snow just right,
So that it glimmers and shines like candle light,
As if a picture painted by hand, the snow is a winter wonderland.

Whenever the snowmen are everywhere,
While snowflakes fall into my hair,
Hills covered in snow which are so much fun,
Though sometimes I do miss the sun,
I love to go and sled, while others like to stay in bed.
Matt Reeves, Grade 8

Stadium Fun

My favorite place is peaceful, kind, and full of smiling faces.
It has purple and gray everywhere I go.
I go to this place so often to watch football, basketball, and sometimes baseball games.
I usually eat, cheer, and make new friends during these games.
I love watching the games, and having a grand time yelling
"GO CATS!"
I see Willie doing push ups and getting the crowd fired up.
I see the Wabash Cannonball.
I hear cheering and people singing the fight song.
I hear the crowd getting excited when Willie goes to the center of the stadium.
I choose to cheer, play, make new friends, and watch the,
Wildcats.
I will go back whenever there is a game to watch, and maybe attend college there.
Whenever I think about this place, it puts a smile on my face.
Bring on the cats!
Emileigh Dinkel, Grade 8

Freedom
When I look outside,
I look up at the sky.

It makes me feel free
to be what I can be

but then I'm brought back
and told what I lack…

The chance that I'll ever be free.

I am all alone.
My clothes need to be sewn.

I don't have a chance,
I've been struck by a lance.

I've been stabbed with what I lack,
and that phrase is now back…

I will never be free.
Emma Brown, Grade 7

Red, White, and Blue
Red, white, and blue
It's in for you
For the flag waves
Red, white, and blue
In the dead of the night
You risk your lives left and right
But still that flag waves
Red, white, and blue
Oh, red, white, and blue
Don't just stand there so pretty
Wave, wave your vibrant colors
Of red, white, and blue
You earned those thirteen stripes
So wave them hard and wave them pretty
Red, white, and blue
You survived World War I, World War II
So shout and cheer
For the veterans here
Who sacrificed their lives
For you
Red, white, and blue
Rosolynn Hegwood, Grade 7

Heaven to Hell
Heaven
peaceful, perfect
loving, caring, cherishing
God, throne, trident, devil
crying, paying, suffering
painful, regretful,
Hell
Kaelie Tomlin, Grade 7

The Awakening
The sun has risen.
Its color being orange and yellow.
Sitting next to the clouds,
Which are amazingly mellow.
Morning is near.

The sun dancing on the cold green grass.
Birds are singing,
and bunnies are springing.
Morning is here.

But something has changed.
I see wind blowing the branches and grass,
but I do not feel it.
The air brushing through my hair,
it is almost not fair, I want to feel.
Suddenly, I do feel.
The wind becomes stronger,
the day becomes darker,
and myself, terrified.
And then I wake up.
Abby Ignacio, Grade 7

Life, a Wonderful Thing
Sailing like a boat
Flying like a kite
Screaming through the journey
Laughing through the pain
Having nightmares
Living through dreams
Isn't life such a wonderful thing?
Traveling the world
Racing to you
Seeing the difference
Between the two
Craving many
Devouring all
The city is waiting
Just give me a call
We are free
Let's go out tonight
There's so much to
Explore
There's one thing to do
And that's to be me
Marisa King, Grade 8

Seasons
Winter
Freezing, Sledding
Cold, Long, Boring
Snowman, Blizzard, Ocean, Beach
Hot, Fun, Short
Swimming, Tanning
Summer
Emily Roach, Grade 8

Spring Has Sprung
Snow is starting to melt,
The sun is smiling in the sky,
Flowers are beginning to bloom,
While birds are flying by.

It's time to shop,
For things to wear,
Shorts and a bathing suit,
Because there is no need for another layer.

Later nights hanging out,
We have changed the clocks,
It's now lighter longer,
And that really rocks.

Vacations are prepared,
Either ocean or snow,
Seeing big snow piles,
Or feeling the warm wind blow.

School is almost over,
Summer is very near,
Spring will always be
A great time of year.
Amanda Krebs, Grade 8

Thank You
"The bus is here!"
I quickly take my place,
Tapping my fingers nervously,
A rather slow wait

The room becomes silent,
Slowly they process.
Guarding their sacks,
Uneasy and cautious.

Thank you sirs,
Teachers in disguise,
Humbling my heart,
Opening my eyes.

Showing me how to serve,
Allowing me a look.
Your faith and hope,
Open just like a book.

To you it's just a shelter:
A place for food and rest.
For me its service,
And for this I am blessed.
Mary Brinkman, Grade 8

Summer Nights

Moonlit trees along the street, casting silver glows
The ground is dusted with sparkly dew.
And the whole world is silent
Except for a dove's occasional coo.

The air is sweet like honeysuckle flowers
And the sky is speckled with pearls.
I tilt my head up towards the sky
To see the indigo swirls.

The squishy green beneath my toes
Is warm from the day's scorching heat.
It's moist and soft, and silky to the touch
Nights like these can't be beat.

The wind whirls through the night
Blowing all around me.
The flowers gaze and tree leaves whisper,
"Have you ever felt so free?"

Elyse Skolek, Grade 7

In the Jungle

When I walk upon the towering trees
I know its spring by the powerful breeze
Contours of timber lie along the ground
Like dark ink on paper and life all around

Up to my right, a spotted individual prowl
Its somber eyes glance until it lets out a growl
I notice her powerful jaws and broad head
She started toward me but suddenly fled

Creatures like these aren't seen every day
They appear unique in everyway
A great sight is when one lurks and creeps
But an amazing sight is when one remarkably leaps

And from that very moment
I visualize with great enjoyment
Of everything I recognize
And everything I specialize

Ryan Trost, Grade 7

An Eternal Gift*

"Sweet stream that winds through yonder glade,"
Its beauty resembles a virtuous maid.
The clear, cool drink that this brook brings,
Quenches the thirst of even kings.
A woman, by nature, nurtures the same,
Her grace and virtue reflect man's eternal aim.
Her soul is transparent with virtues from God,
Image of Mary, the angels laud.
We, too, may receive this same grace,
If we accept, as she did, our reward is His face.

Genevieve Zaharia, Grade 9
**Inspired by William Cowper.*

Just a Dream

The darkness pushes me under
I can't see
Can't hear
Can't breath.
I struggle to push up
Get out
My arms and legs flail
Finally,
I give up.
I'm trapped
I stop moving,
And sink down.
Down.
Down.
My eyes flutter open and I see the light coming through the window.
I'm in bed.
It was a dream.
Just a dream.

Dori Clausen, Grade 8

Fireworks of Joy*

The sky
Is filled with
Beautiful lights
We experience the
Lights rise
And explode

A time for
Joy and excitement
Has been introduced
This is a time
For celebration!

We must get excited
And fill our hearts
With a spark
Of light and hope

Ryan Theisen, Grade 8
**Based on the work of art "Fireworks" by M.E. Escher*

I, Verbena Ellen Colter

I am small and I'll never be tall
I'm white like a ghost
I'll never be able to boast about having a normal family
Because I'm adopted but not officially
I had a friend, her name was Annie
But she treated me like a fanny
And ditched me to be with Heather
Who she thought was much better
With Annie gone for the summer
My mom was worried my summer was a bummer
Then I met Pooch who thought I was a ghost
Of a girl who had drowned in the lake
I lied and said that he was right; he didn't realize I was a fake

Jillian Shorten, Grade 7

I Am and Always Will Be

I am a heartbeat,
beating with all,
My scarlet might,
Without holding a fight,
Because I am bright,
I am the sunlight,
Shining my strengths,
Willing to go at any Length.
I am the crack in the ceiling that's there,
nobody, to give me a thought.
I am a turtle,
Scared of fame,
Willing to go out there,
Even without a name,
If put down, then I settle for another,
So I can find another chance, but again face failure.
Because I am the youngest,
Because I am a writer,
I am and always will be important.
Since the very beginning.
I know I will and always will be.

Radha Patel, Grade 7

Melody

Words
There's millions of words
"Words have always swirled around me like snowflakes"
I'm 11
I've never spoken a word
Until this one day
I was able to talk.
The Medi-Talker
I touched the smooth,
Cold, Shiny
Keys with one thumb
Finally! I can talk
To someone else to show
I'm funny, maybe tell
Connor a joke
Show that I'm smart, friendly
Maybe tell Rose I like her outfit
I will always be
Puzzled about
Things like
Words.

Caitlin Pieroni, Grade 7

Fingerprints

Poems are like fingerprints.
They are alike yet different in many ways.
They help me get through the tough days.
Poems are like fingerprints.
They come in all shapes and sizes.
Sometimes they are happy and sometimes they are sad.
Poems always have cool surprises.

Zach Eighner, Grade 7

Arrogance

Arrogance brags about her money,
She hates unpopular people, Goodwill, and microwave meals.
Arrogance struts down the hall in high heels and,
A diamond encrusted dress,
Talking to all of the popular kids.

The bell rings,
And she doesn't flinch.
She takes her sweet time,
Getting to math,
Where she has a test.
She takes the paper and,
Circles random answers.

Arrogance doesn't care what grade she gets,
Because she is "too cool for school."
Arrogance goes home to her
Empty house.
She goes on Facebook and,
Updates her status about,
How much better she is than everyone else.

Kyle Macke, Grade 8

Human Paper

I am a piece of paper,
Waiting for my destiny to become reality;
Being written on.
It becomes true as I go on in life.

Many people can read me like a piece of paper;
Written all over to tell them who I am.
But sometimes I am not me.
I am someone else.

I do not like it when people think of
Me as being smart when they first meet me;
Stereotyping,
Just because I have glasses.
I am not just smart,
Nor kind.
I am many things.

I am a piece of paper;
Written all over to tell everyone,
Who I am.

Javier Reyes, Grade 8

Yummy

goodies
sweet, yummy
cooking, baking, biting, tasting
chocolate chip, snickerdoodle, pie, hot chocolate
chewing, drinking, making, eating
chewy, tasty
treats

Whitney Nightingale, Grade 7

The Dolphin

Jumping through the waves.
Splashing through the water way.
Deep in the ocean.

Splashing all the way.
Diving in the summer day.
Racing each other.
Aaron Kane, Grade 7

Flowers and Roses

The flowers are bright,
the flowers are colorful,
they gleam in sunlight.

The roses are cute,
roses are pretty and pink,
roses are red too.
Hannah Robben, Grade 7

Summer

A hot summers day
the sun high up in the sky
Children having fun

I love the summer
the weather so nice and warm
swimming at the pool
Abby Gatten, Grade 7

Tornado

Spinning all around
It's sucking up everything
Blowing down houses

Tornadoes are cool
The storm is finally gone
It is peaceful now
Alyssa Gatten, Grade 7

Waterfall

The rain washes down
On the waterfall it goes
Splashing high as day

The water is blue
Freezing the fish in the stream
The water is cold
Gerriel Greenwood, Grade 7

Creepers

Creepers.
Creepers watch me.
They explode when they're close.
They are green, mean blowing machines.
Minecraft!
Gabe Galindo, Grade 7

Quitting

Some people say I quit everything, which is somewhat true
It may be because sometimes I fall behind and don't know what to do
I get scared in some cases
Sometimes from the looks, words, or faces
But, I hide the emotions
I want them to see that I don't care about their notions
I mean sometimes these sports or clubs aren't even me
I'd rather do what I like and I like to be free
I've tried many different things, you know
But, they were never really me so I let them go
I have no real beat or hand-eye coordination
But, who knows, maybe I'll go on to be head of our nation
I'm okay with quitting, I've learned a lot
You'd be surprised as to what it has taught
I have many talents still
I know that I can use them to benefit me and I know that I will
So even if you're a quitter too
Remember, you're awesome and do what you love to do
Kaitlyn Schatteman, Grade 8

Amusement Park

You first walk in and you can already feel the goose bumps
on your skin but you don't really know why. It might be
because your walking straight to the roller coaster and remember
what you love about it, and think to yourself "The rush on a roller coaster"
It's the best feeling in the world when it zooms straight down
I feel the wind on my face I can't help but scream in joy when the ride hurls back up
in such a surprise. There is so many reasons why I love the ride,
but nothing beats the rush I get when I first get on the ride.
The speed it goes is incomparable to many things,
but maybe its as fast as a train or even a car.
But after the ride I know I have to move on
to other rides. I feel disappointed but then I see ice cream
and I can already feel my taste buds burst in flavor.
But I look away because I hear people screaming as if they were
about to plunge to their death screaming "AHHHHHH!!!"
But there is always that moment I have before I leave I feel as if
the fun was never coming back. Then I remembered all the smells
and fun I had there and say to the park I will come back again.
Enrique Duarte, Grade 7

A Day at the Zoo

I woke up this morning, and I got out of bed,
Thoughts of the zoo popped into my head.
The warm fresh air felt good on my face, I just couldn't wait to see that exciting place.

There were monkeys, and tigers, and elephants too,
I just couldn't believe I was at the zoo!
The birds were chirping, the butterflies flying,
The big tiger viciously growled so the kids started crying.

As we sat down for lunch at the Jungle Café,
We saw the baby monkeys getting ready to play.
As we walked up the tiresome hill away from the dome,
It has been a great day and I don't want to go home.
Hannah Baker, Grade 8

Baseball

Baseball
Challenging, Exciting
Throwing, catching, sliding
He is safe!
Fielding, sprinting, hitting
Tough, entertaining
America's pasttime
Weston Copperstone, Grade 8

Gifts

gifts
great, fun
tearing, opening, playing
in the box, out comes the gift
wrapping, cutting, taping
colorful, surprising
presents
Darius Rose, Grade 7

Snowflakes

snow
white, crisp
fighting, building, hiding
in the air, on my shoes
throwing, falling, icing
hard, heavy
flakes
Deveana Smith, Grade 7

Lights

lights
blinking, beautiful
changing, decorating, placing
green, red, blue, white
stringing, clinging, ringing
cute, cool
decorations
Blake Train, Grade 7

Indian Pride

I ndians are the best
N ever giving up on school work and sports
D ifferent than anybody around
I ntelligent, friendly, and polite students
A lways giving our all and getting the win
N o one stops us, we stop them
S t. Francis Indians are fantastic
Kouper McQuigg, Grade 7

Jasmine

My sweet dog, Jasmine
Her life is at journey's end
Too soon, though, it seems
She has a place in my heart
While she takes that final leap
Brandon Cate, Grade 8

Dreaming High

I can image myself
Becoming a well know famous person,
Wearing makeup and beautiful dresses,
Walking on a bright red carpet
With bright flashing lights
Taking pictures of me,
And meeting adoring fans.
I could give fans the chance to walk the red carpet,
While wearing beautiful outfits.
I could even sign autographs for free
Have a meet-and-greet,
And go on tour with a group.
I could even help make someone else's dream come true,
Share thoughts with my fans,
Donate money to a charity or the homeless and sick,
And make those who feel left out, feel welcomed.
All of these are soaring high to find a dream
That may possibly come true until you really put your mind, heart, and hard work to it.
Alisa Bitoy, Grade 7

Trees

Cherry Tree
Apple Tree
Peach Tree
To be blunt,
Trees are wonderful.
They have great uses.
Wisdom,
Strength,
And comfort.
When I run away,
I climb to the highest point of the biggest tree.
Stick my head out to the wind, take a few deep breaths, and close my eyes.
I feel safe.
Then I take time to think.
When I find clarity, I go home.
And I arrive with wisdom,
Strength,
And comfort.
Josey Tiemeyer, Grade 8

Train Ride Escape

I have never understood the hatred of trains
The constant bang of when you're passing things,
It's calming to some people you know.
Buses are cramped with people and it's hard to see the beauty of the outside world.
When you're just passing along on a train through a valley really look at it.
You can't see the beauty of the world if you don't even look.
Trains are meant for long distances when you have that time, take it.
There are very many stressors in this world: politics, education, and status.
Take the time to give the world a good look and more than a quick thought.
You may even discover what's truly inside you.
The most graceful and beauteous things in the world are easily passed,
Don't be someone who never gets that experience,
It's worth all the time in the world.
Elizabeth Memmini, Grade 8

Love Is Like a Rose

Love is like a rose
Petals fragile like glass, if there is a scarcity of care, it will perish

Love is like a rose
If you take care of it, it will live on

Love is like a rose
You can't pick it too early because it may not survive

Love is like a rose
Thorns will bite you like a break up
But it will draw you in with a beautiful smell, like heaven on earth

Love is like a rose
It flourishes at times, it can also shrivel and die

Love is like a rose
Will either prosper? Or wither up and die
Because we do not live in a perfect world

Love is like a rose
A beautiful delicate rose, take care of it
Tyler Harris, Grade 8

The Age of Information

The age of Information,
Or the age of Deviation,
From time which was once man's salvation,
For who can think when the TV blares?
and who can question when the ads ensnare?
And for many it is too much to bear,

Look at the math scores of our nation,
They really need no explanation,
For who needs geometry to watch TV?
And who needs the constitution?
As we participate in a new evolution,
From Philosopher to prisoner,
We enter into a new institution,
One without education,
but with instant gratification,
One without sorrow,
but with no tomorrow,
One without conversion,
And filled with diversion,
And this is the path we choose,
Every morning when we turn on the news.
Adrian Morrison, Grade 8

Spice, Ice, Nice!

There once was a boy named Timmy Carey,
Who loved anything that had contained dairy.
He liked milkshakes with ice
With peppermint spice,
Which really freaked-out his friend Barry.
Timothy Carey, Grade 7

Nebraska

Tall grass sways effortlessly in the wind,
Corn fields stretch over rolling hills,
Barns and stables settle in the nooks of the countryside,
We are labeled as idiotic hillbillies,
Who don't know anything of "the city life,"
Our buildings stand tall and proud,
Metallic material glaring back at us,
We have as much as the city life as New York,
But with an easy going pace,
Cement roads are cracked and dry,
Trees innumerable and lush,
Animals scampering, free of fear,
Our weather "changes every five minutes,"
From dry humid summers with no rain,
To wet heavy winters where you can't see the ground,
This is my home, the one that I love,
Nebraska, equality before the law, strong and true.
Molly Ptacek, Grade 8

I'd Rather Write a Song!

Whenever I see an assignment of poetry,
Before I can start, I complain and groan,
Rather than working effectively.
If only poetry was like a song:
Oh wait… It is!

When I write a song,
Although it may be tricky,
As I'm searching into my heart and soul,
Since the words can be hard to find,
I'll see what I can come up with.

As long as I don't compose any music,
After I am finished writing,
Even though I was technically writing a song,
Until I have another poetry assignment,
I won't have this much fun again.
Carrie O'Dell, Grade 8

Friends

Friends are some of the most brilliant things in life.
A lot of friends just come along and then just go away,
Like a leaf in windy storm.
But some of them stay with you forever;
They stay with you and help you through very hard times.
And when the time comes you can also help them,
They are there for you whenever you need them.
You can go to them and tell them whatever you want,
And they don't give away your secrets.
You can always hang out and talk with them.
And it won't be awkward.
They are always open for questions,
And they will be open to answer.
There is always that one friend for someone;
Friends are some of the most brilliant things in life.
Carson Childs, Grade 8

Notebook

A notebook filled with emptiness…
A notebook filled with memories…
A notebook filled with creativity

Creativity is not always
what you want it to be…
A notebook is not always perfect…

A notebook's pages could all be different
A notebook's pages can only handle so much…
A notebook's pages only has a limited amount of space…
A notebook's pages could be ripped…

In the pages…
There's something hidden…
A message or a story, no one knows…

A notebook can hold secrets
A notebook can hold ideas
A notebook can hold marks

A notebook can be easily damaged…
A notebook can be easily lost…
A notebook can be easily forgotten…

That notebook is ME…

Jocelyn J Gonzalez, Grade 8

Unknown Deception

Holding onto memories as long as I can
Fears, fatalities, frankly I don't understand
Not as easy as one can comprehend
Creeping and attending the doomsday of a family
Takes the breath out of you, like the loss of a friend

Lurking in the darkness, waiting to attach
Can never convince fate when to hold back
Dreading the day when everything will end
One loss, and no one can pretend

Hoping is all we can do
Never ending paranoia is all that presumes
Holding on to smells like scents of perfume

Wishing, regretting, praying, denial
It all seems so permanent
Like the loss of a child
Fate is supposed to bring you closer to yourself
All it does to me is rip me apart

Taking family, friends and foes
ending them, making my sensitivity show
thinking of it, I cry myself to sleep
Please, please, just let me be

Jaden Moore, Grade 8

Sunrise

As I come over the horizon
You wake up and do your chores
After that when I am half over the horizon
You and your family eat your breakfast.
When I'm almost at my highest point
You are playing with the kittens and horses.
At noon I watch you eat a sandwich
Under the tree with your sister.
When I start to fall behind the horizon
You do your final work and eat supper.
And then when I'm fully gone
You are in bed until I come back to play again.

Edna Galey, Grade 8

Nebraska Football

Fans cheering in the stands,
Fun and excitement in the crowd.
Bo lifts the cat to the sky,
Young players stepping up to fill the new spots.
Drills and strategy displayed.

A good start to the year,
Past players were there to interview.
New players were showing how well they were prepared.
Defense will be strong for the fall.
Returning to Memorial Stadium for the show of the year,
the maturity of the team was clear.

Matt Eilers, Grade 8

Sorry Daddy

Three years ago. February 27th
I woke up and I heard bickering downstairs.
I listened carefully as you yelled forcefully at your wife.
I crept down to get a better of view of the situation.
I watched as the tears slowly fell from my mother's face.
I rushed to my mom and he threatened us again.
To hurt us. To kill us. To burn the house down.
I knew this needed to stop. Today.
I slowly slipped my phone out and called those three numbers
9-1-1. I'm sorry daddy. I'm really sorry. You need help.

Jackie Koepp, Grade 8

Cup Noodles

Noodles hard when raw.
Noodles soft when cooked.
Noodles tasty, soft and yummy.
Noodles, when ready they smell delicious and delightful.
Noodles wet, squishy and slippery.
Noodles are easy to make.
You hear slurping when eating.
The smell of broth.
The salty taste.
Noodles the one thing everyone likes.

Jazzmn Correa, Grade 7

The Most Important Leaf in the Universe
The most important leaf in the universe
grows only in one spot.
That spot is lying on a tree
next to the hoary worn road.

That leaf must grow in the same old tree
until it is old,
old enough to be—
the most important leaf in the universe.

That leaf must fall at the exact time—
the time that is passing by—
timely enough to be
the most important leaf in the universe.

That man must walk, that leaf must fall—
fall to the face of that man.
That car must drive, the woman must run,
run to save the man.

The leaf must grow, the leaf must fall,
to be the most important leaf in the universe.
Brie Nielsen, Grade 8

Cherish Childhood
You are running through the park dashing not to be tagged
Behind a dog on a leash who was practically dragged
Screaming with laughter as the wind passed our ears
Being tagged by the other was your new greatest fear

You are dressing up in an abundance of dresses
Poised as a princess who makes no mistakes or messes
Thrashing through your closet deciding who to be
Shall I be a princess?
Or shall I just be me?

You are little and plastic oh what a joy!
You look like a person, but act like a toy
We move your arms and legs
Pretending that you're me
With all the special treatment
The Barbie's made me feel free

We're holding our babies pretending we're mothers
In our house full of girls we weren't bothered by brothers
We mimicked our mom as we cradled our dolls
You could hear our playful voices through the paper thin walls
Abbey Heller, Grade 9

Poems Are Like Puzzles…
Poems are like puzzles
With twist and turns and every piece
Has its own space
They block all thoughts to anything and everything
All complicated to make everything fit
Kendra Miles, Grade 7

My Daddy
My Daddy always curled my hair and took me to church
He went jet skiing with Mommy
But one day he got hurt
I visited him
The hospital smelled like death
But my Daddy was alive
I could hear his heart beating
But in three short months
Jesus called my Daddy home
And he was dead
No more hair curling
No more church with him
Just me and Mommy
Jamie Whitworth, Grade 7

My First Wave
I'm in the water,
The wind is blowing hard,
It's the perfect day to learn something new.
In my wet suit and the surfboard in my hand,
Off to the distance I see the waves crashing against boats,
Then…all of a sudden,
It's coming!
Now or never! This huge wave is coming my way,
Ready as I'll ever be I jump in and I'm off,
Deep in the ocean,
I take a deep breath and I dive in,
I did it, I'm riding the wave,
It was the best feeling: that I could do anything I put my mind to.
Ciarra Todd, Grade 8

Need a Friend
After a fault,
Maybe your own, maybe not,
Life can be scary or not worth it if someone gets hurt,
After mistakes, you can't look back,
Pain will seep into the cracks in your heart,
And you won't let go,
Looking forward can be a challenge as well,
More pain like the pain in the past can be caused,
And tears will fill your experienced eyes,
But you can look beside you and a true friend will be there,
And they will have a shoulder to cry on,
And they will be with you through every challenge to come.
Adrianna Rupert, Grade 7

Love
Love is a feeling for every human being
It moves the world along with me
Loving someone is more than just seeing
Love is a feeling for every human being
This feeling is full of comprehension and hearing
Experiencing this feeling fills one with glee
Love is a feeling for every human being
It moves the world along with me
Maria Villalobos, Grade 8

The End of the Road

Walking down this road of truth and lies
I realize the sadness in my eyes.
This road is dark, scary, and deprived
I hope this walk won't lead me to my demise.
I feel the sharp pain like a rose bush
Under my feet. I see this dirty lake
A pool of lost dreams barely see my reflection
Staring back at me.
"Crash" the sound of thunder
Screaming at me not feeling glee
I'm going to run I'm going to flee.
I feel a stinging burn like salt water
In a cut. Like a bird with no wings
I can't fly but, I see the end of the road
Shinny and clean. Take a deep breath
And run to the gleam.

Caden Baumgarten, Grade 8

Shy

She thought of herself as a tide,
When others resembled an ocean.
She thought of their lives as a prize,
While hers was stuck in slow motion.
It felt like life was repeating itself,
It was begging to jeopardize her health.
She wanted to make a difference,
But she couldn't find the courage.
She let her fears get in the way.
The words that she needed to say,
Will forever remain unsaid,
Imbedded into the back of her head.
The pain causes her memories,
To replay in her mind.
She thinks of how she could've redone them,
But it is far too late for her mind to be kind.

Cami Teasdale, Grade 8

The People with Nothing to Say

Everyone goes to the theater, excited for the play.
Little do they know, the best are the people with nothing to say.
They stand behind the stage, dressed in all black,
Moving the set to the front and back.
They sneak onto the stage, and move the trees,
Then move to the back like a bunch of busy bees.
No one to appreciate or understand,
They don't come out and bow, hand in hand.
They have no big part in the show,
Their names most people don't know.
But they are still people, even though not known.
Without them, the play could not be shown.
So what we must learn as people, is no matter what our job,
Everyone is important, even those that are a slob.
Do me a favor, see what they say
When you next go to see a play.

Lauren Dalton, Grade 8

Rainbows Are Like Life

Rainbows are like life.
When it rains for a while a rainbow appears
Why
I was told to brighten people's days
Just like in life

Everyone goes through tough times
Trust me I've had my own times,
But in the end everything turns out
To be good or even better than what
You even imagined

Basically the rain represents sadness in life
While after the rain stops a rainbow appears.
Which the rainbow represents happiness
Therefore rainbows are like life

Mya Delatorre, Grade 8

In the End

In the end when it's all said and done.
Blood has been spilt, the battle was won.
The sting of sacrifice leaves tragic scars
But turn around, and look at this, you've made it so far.

Through flame and fire, when your goals were dire
fueled by determinations, you outlasted all the liars
Climbing a mountain, standing tall through a storm,
The confidence of success was born.

The shadows swarmed like moths to a flame,
Fear and uncertainty, rabid emotions you tamed.
Fighting valiantly, never surrendering.
Growing stronger and always remembering.
This is not the last battle, you held the enemy at bay.
But never forget all that you've learned today.

Cooper Dammrich, Grade 9

An Icy Mission

Suited up; ready to go,
I go on out and meet my foe,
He bites and pains my open skin,
And stings me like a sharpened pin.

My face is cold; warmth I'm yearning,
Wear a scarf (I was now learning),
Next I reached my destination,
And then on back before frost-ation.

And now I'm in a full-blown sprint,
Before my skin's a bluish tint,
Open the door and into heat,
Now I'll rest and admit I'm beat.

Jack Frost just didn't want me to get the mail today.

Ethan Van Sickle, Grade 9

Words

Words are essential.
Part of everyday life.
Part of everyday communication.
Long words.
Short words.
Easy and hard to pronounce words.
Good words.
Bad words.
Make-my-day words.
OR Break-my-day words.
Words are quite powerful.
I like words.

LaShawn DeNoyer, Grade 9

Sleep

It's time to sleep.
A time for imagination,
A time where I can be whoever I choose.
Let's see, Let's see,
tonight, who shall I be?
I can be a hero of the land,
Or a king whose rule is just.
I can be the leader of a band,
Or simply a man whom everyone trusts.
Sleep.
A time to be me,
A time to be free.

Daniel Alcaraz, Grade 8

To My Valentine…

You are:
The goal to my field,
The spikes to my cleats,
The number on my jersey,
The Nike sign on my shoe.

You are:
The chocolate to my strawberry,
The cheese to my mac,
The milk to my cereal,
The sugar to my cake,
You are all I need from the world.

Rachel Weber, Grade 7

Child's Realization

A child's imagination
Imagination, the key
Key to happiness
Happiness we've lost
Lost with our age
Age bound our minds
Minds being controlled
Controlled by society
Society, the death
A child's imagination

Ian Doering, Grade 8

Life's Story

Life is like a book.
You never know what will happen next.
You are forever unknowing.
You are forever oblivious.
But are you really?

Everyone's story is different.
Everyone's knowledge may be limited, but not to a complete extent.

But in all of our journeys,
We all know one thing,
We know that even when you think it's over,
and you're all alone,
That this, my friend, is the moment when an even grander chapter begins.

Lauren Nyder, Grade 7

Jose

Jose
Quiet, calm, mellow, unpredictable
My siblings of 5
My love for the family
Who cares deeply for my family and my newborn sister and friends
Who feels that most things are just natural to happen and happen randomly In life
who needs people in his life to care for and help
Who gives kindness and respect to people
Who fears the death of people I know and my family and myself
Who would like to see the world in places with nature and different cities And my future
Resident of Omaha Street South
For feeling of happiness and care for different people I know but silent
Maravila

Jose Maravilla, Grade 7

Nebraska

Nebraska
Bright golden cornfields and thick green grass
The scenery strikes a glimpse in your eye
With mysterious weather like fresh snow in March
Large open land filled with wooden homes, stone building and friendly people
Whisper roar through the winds
Birds soaring across the clear blue sky past the gleaming yellow sun
Dandelions flutter in the wind
Particles gently land in the garden
Many dreams waiting
For a better future
Than today

Tony Le, Grade 8

Beautiful Rainbow Forest

My favorite place is the Rainbow Forest
I'm going there to see the butterflies, unicorns, zebras, and much more
I'll hear animals running and butterflies flying right by me
I might just lie down on the quiet, peaceful ground
I will go back to my Rainbow Forest when I'm feeling down or upset to visit my dream world
I like being there because it is peaceful and quiet which makes me feel better

Jesica Pacheco, Grade 8

War

Bang, bang
Shots from both sides
Men falling everywhere
Soldiers scream battle cries and run
Sadness

Madison Wachowski, Grade 8

Mustache

Mustache
So warm and fun
They are very comfortable
They are very fun to have too
Get one

Haylee Ruiz, Grade 7

Daytime

Sunshine
It keeps us warm
Shining during the day
Gleaming brightly its rays of light
The sun

Shannon Brennan, Grade 8

Bullying

Bullying starts with
Little pushes in hallways
And grows every day
Children become unhappy
And start to wither away

Ashley McCurdy, Grade 8

Thunderstorms

Rain falls from the sky
Thunder rumbles around me
Lightning cracks the ground
Vibrating inside of me
Storms have stopped; the sun now shines

Emlyn Krasnican, Grade 8

Reflection

Mirage
In the water
Like nature's own mirror
Showing the vast landscape around
Reflect

Lydia Andina, Grade 8

Strong Survivor

In the barren sand
There is a green survivor
His name is cactus
He has grown sharp and rough
His pricks are as hard as steel

Jeremy Banzon, Grade 7

Dance Competition

After countless hours of packing all the costumes,
So that nothing can be left behind,
Before the long drive,
Until we finally arrive at the competition,
Where I'll be surrounded by people who share the same passion as I do.

Unless you're super human,
Although you've spent months preparing, you're going to be nervous,
Because who wouldn't be,
When performing in front of loads of people,
For at least 2 minutes.

Whenever everyone is finished performing,
Since there has to be one winner,
If the judges liked you,
While you were performing,
There is a pretty good chance you could win.

(And there is nothing better than knowing all your hard work has paid off)

Chandler Dixon, Grade 8

My Stage

The blue curtain opens to another production.
The birds and the trees offer their applause;
My stage is set.

The lush green carpet encompasses the stage like a blanket.
The gentle sound of birds singing and leaves swaying plays in the background,
A huge, single spotlight illuminates the entire theater.

The stage, however, changes every performance.
Every scene brings new challenges and problems,
But it is up to me to contribute my own lines.

I have eighteen scenes to show my skills.
I have one theater to give my performance.
I have one performance to prove myself.

I am a golfer and the stage is my course.
I am a golfer and my props are my clubs.
I am golfer and I call my own shots.

Charlotte Roberts, Grade 8

Peace

Peace is where the heart is.
The heart is where love is.
Love is where kindness is.
Kindness is where mercy is.
Mercy is where others are.
Where others are?
You don't need to look far.
Looking too far is way too hard.
Just stick to the family and friends that love you with all their hearts.
Peace comes in many ways and forms.
You'll know it's peace when your heart is warmed.

Selena Castaneda, Grade 7

Spring
Spring is here,
Summer is near,
School is almost out,
And I cannot wait to scream and shout,
And it would be cool,
To go to the pool,
And to see my nephew and nieces,
If they don't show up,
I will fall to pieces,
I cannot wait till summer,
To go down to Nebraska,
So I can go to Saturday in the park,
To enjoy my summer vacation,
And then I have to come back to school,
To come to see my friends,
And come back to do more Homework,
But I don't know why,
I'm leaving Middle School,
And it is going to be cool,
To be in High School,
Here I come high school.

McKenzi Soulek, Grade 8

Beauty
She has long hair.
She has blue eyes.
He thinks she is beautiful.
She looks in the mirror,
She sees horror.
He sees beauty.
She wakes up,
uses makeup.
He couldn't care less.
She heads out the door,
hoping to look acceptable.
To him she is clearly perceptible.
With her every step
He sees perfection.
If loving her was a drug,
He had an addiction
How could one love someone so much,
If they don't love themselves?
She needs to look in the mirror and see,
If beauty is in the eye of the beholder,
Why can't that beholder be me?

Linnea Nelson-Sandall, Grade 7

Mirror
Mirror, mirror
on the wall
tell me something
tell me whose the loneliest
of all
Just tell me
oh, please, something
who's the loneliest of all?
Mirror what's inside me?
Tell me how
can a heart be turned
to stone?
Mirror, mirror
Save me from the things I see
I can keep it away
from the world
Why won't you let me
hide from me?
Mirror, mirror, tell me something…
who's the loneliest of all…
I'm the loneliest of all…

Sari Anna Ballard, Grade 7

Ode to Books
Books with their
Musty smell
And smooth pages.
It's textured words
And colored pictures.
They call out to me to be read,
So I flip the page
And it whispers
Of stories to be told
And legends to be shared.
Like doorways to worlds
Filled with magical creatures.
Or portals to places
Just across the ocean.
All the knowledge of the world
Encased in a paper cage.
Its magical properties all bound
In a single place.
Waiting.
Calling.
Begging to be read.

Eileen Huang, Grade 8

Country Life
At Dusk
I am
alone
outside
singing
softly.
Breathing
the cool
air. I
look at
the land
around
me with
rolling
hills and
dense woods.
I smile.
Life's good
away
from the
city

Anna Swoboda, Grade 8

Just Because I'm Quiet
Just because I'm quiet
Doesn't mean I'm shy
Doesn't mean I can't talk right
And doesn't mean I cry

Just because I'm quiet
Doesn't mean I can't yell
Doesn't mean I hate talkers
Doesn't mean I'm in my shell

Just because I'm quiet
Doesn't mean my life is rough
Doesn't mean I need your help
Doesn't mean I need someone tough

Just because I'm quiet
Does volume really matter at all?
Or does the content of what you say do?
If I talked more would our boundaries fall?

I guess we'll find out if I do

Teresa Gottwald, Grade 8

Basketball and Baseball
Basketball
Shooting, Dribbling
Hard, Skilled, Intense
Fouls, Shots, Runs, Steals
Sweaty, Dangerous, Active
Catching, Batting
Baseball

Fernando Rodriguez, Grade 8

Family
Family is forever
You will always be together
Sometimes we may fight
But we are all together at night
You can always rely
They'll always be by your side
Family is forever

Adelyn Sldes, Grade 7

Winter/Summer
Winter
Snowballs, cold
Snowing, playing, gatherings
Christmas, family, flowers, growing
Swimming, tanning, relaxing
Sunscreen, tropical
Summer

Jenna Wulf, Grade 8

Me, Myself, and I

Me, myself, and I
Are all that are here
Feeling motionless
Daydreaming
About something that will never be
They laugh and tease
But why?
I dream of a life that will never be
Me, myself, and I
Forever lonely
Katie Workman, Grade 8

Together

All that I am,
started with you.
All that I was,
left with her.
All we can be,
is everything.
all we can do,
limitless.
together,
we love.
Spencer Navara, Grade 9

Poems Are Like Friends

Poems are like friends,
Which are sweet,
Connected by the heart,
Talented, joyful,
Word by word—tender,
Sentence by sentence,
Loved and adored,
Paragraph by paragraph,
And never leaving the story
Of life without each other.
Grace Schmidt, Grade 7

Ear

I hear all your secrets
meant only for your best friend
I hear the sounds
of the birds high in the sky
I hear the silence
of the night as the crickets sleep
I hear your thoughts
even though they aren't spoken into words
I hear all things
even those not meant to be heard
JashwaAlan Cummings, Grade 8

Bugatti

I drive in a car
The fastest in the world
Bugatti Veyron
Albino Rosales, Grade 7

Ode to My Mother's Hair

My mother's hair black and frizzy and poofy and messy. A dark forest.
Where no one would dare to dwell
The hair which we tamed together, the hair which I inherited
I loathed her hair along with mine, its chaos I couldn't untangle
It wasn't as straight as the lines on the expressway
And it wasn't curly like the hair they showed in the commercials.
It was a burly bush amidst a meadow of sunflowers
My hands hurting from dragging a brush through the knots
Which was as hard as tying two glued shoelaces or walking on a thread
Her hair was an ocean, a pool of a unknown darkness that was stiff down her back
But then one day my mother came home she sat me down and gently said, "Listen"
She told me about her best friend, the one whose hair had disappeared
By medication which became her only option. Whose hair was stolen
from the drugs that floated through her blood and pulsed through her dark blue veins.
And I now look at my mother's hair as a blessing
A black and frizzy and poofy and messy blessing.
And the black curls that cascades down her back
And in the mirror I admire my own hair the way a lion admires his mane
Gently bringing a brush to smooth out the curls
Every thin strand I treat like thin gold chains, the beautiful mess I inherited.
Because it reminds me that I'm like my mother with a frizzy dark forest upon my head.
Nabeela Syed, Grade 9

I Am a Soccer Player

I am a soccer player
I wonder what it's like to be the best
I hear the ball getting kicked like someone's head hitting the ground
I see me at the top 3 like a lion, the king of the jungle
I want to be the best
I am a soccer player

I pretend I've made it to the top
I feel the rush of playing at camp now
I touch the ball as I make the winning goal
I worry I'll never make it
I cry that I'll make it and get an injury that will end my career
I am a soccer player

I understand it's not easy to make it
I say it's all about team
I dream to be the best
I try to make it pro
I hope I'll make it there
I am a soccer player
Brandon Ruiz, Grade 8

Springtime Days

As I was walking through the garden in springtime.
I felt the beautiful air on my skin.
I could hear the humming birds singing,
As I am strolling in the park, I hear kids laughing and playing.
Buzz, buzz, bees are taking the pollen from the pretty flowers.
The great big trees are growing their leaves on their branches.
People are coming out of their house to go to the park and lay down on the smooth grass.
Some people come out just to lay down and look up at the clear clean wonderful blue sky.
Aimee Kyle, Grade 7

Sisters

Someone to look up to
Giving me hope,
Giving me courage,
Giving me support,
Giving me a helping-hand,
Giving me a whole-hearted smile,
Giving me warmth inside,
Shaping who I am,
Sometimes fighting, but always there.
She's sun on a rainy day,
She's a blooming flower in winter,
She's water in a drought,
She's the courage in all fear,
She's everything I could ask for,
And much, much more!

McKenzie Friedman, Grade 8

Principles of Success

Plan your vision;
Preparation is key.
People aren't always driven;
Passion is found within thee.
Progress will take time —
Patience is definitely needed;
Pleasing all can be an uphill climb
Possibly impeded.
Pain will be endured;
Problems are sure to arise.
Perseverance assured,
Pleasure will surprise.
Pushing through the stress:
Principles of success.

Maggie Pollard, Grade 8

Useless Things

An orange without a peel
Michael Jordan without a steal
A bride without a groom
A mop without a broom

A Dalmatian with out spots
Polka without dots
Baseball without umps
A model without pumps

A princess without a crown
Up without down
A cow without a moo
Me without you

Sydney Elliott, Grade 7

Ducks

Ducks in the hot sun
Splashing in the cool water
Ducks love the summer

Cali Wright, Grade 8

My Favorite Place in Europe

My favorite place is Germany.
I am going there this summer.
When I go there, I am visiting my relatives.
When I'm there, I will go on walks in the wilderness or to amusement parks.
Everywhere I hear German being spoken.
I choose to play games with my younger cousins.
I might revisit Germany in two years after coming back with my family.
I think Germany is a great place to visit because of its natural beauty.

Nick Paulsen, Grade 8

Christmas Joys

Snowflakes tumble so gently down the sky
Each are different my oh my!
Lights light up each house on the block.
The cold chill brushes past in a flash
The Christmas carols rolling off the tip of the tongue
As the melodies dance in your head
Family surrounded around the Christmas tree on Christmas morning
At last, Christmas has arrived.

Miranda Pospisil, Grade 9

A Wonderful Place in the Mountains

My favorite place is Montana at my uncle's secret fishing spot
I am going to Montana this summer
When I get there, I'm going to fly fish in the magic river
I see the beautiful lines on the fish, and the amazing waterfall
I hear the loud roar of the waterfall dumping water into the river
I choose to fish all day and then sit around the campfire at night
I will go back to that amazing place whenever I can
This place will always be one of my favorite places to go during the summer

Tate Busse, Grade 8

Escaping the World

My favorite place isn't too far away from the ordinary world
When life is too stressful, this is where I find myself
Playing with all my childhood toys is what I do here
I see slides, and all sorts of children's toys
Laughter filling the air, along with no care in the world
I choose to be carefree and just play
Going back to my favorite place is in the near future
In my head is where I can escape the world and become a child again

Hanna Bracelin, Grade 8

When All Else Fails

When all else fails in your life don't cry,
Don't be depressed don't say my life is over,
But pick your head up roll your shoulders back,
And say my life is worth living so why should I mourn.
When you are down remember all the good things like they were yesterday,
Then also remember the bad things and think to improve then forget them.
Always remember you are worth it and so is life.
When all else fails don't cry but make life better.

Harrison Jensen, Grade 8

A Pair of Sight
Some people call them windows,
However no one actually knows.
Everyone has them and they can see all,
But how is it possible if they are so small.

Each as different as a person's fingerprint.
Brown, blue, and green.
Everybody's is different with his or her own tint.
Remembering anything seen.

Surrounded by white,
And can look at both dark and bright.
Covered by lashes and lids,
Can be passed down onto people's kids.

A camera controlled by the brain.
Changing direction and the ability to shift.
Each pair is complex and nothing close to plain.
That's why they are God's gift.
Colin McKay, Grade 8

Mirror
I look in the mirror.
I hate what I see.
A repulsive beast is staring back at me.
Her hair is too dark; her skin is too pale.
She's as ugly as sin and as fat as a whale.
Her eyebrows are too bushy.
There are lines under her eyes.
She'll never be perfect no matter how hard she tries.

I look back in the mirror.
I re-examine what I see.
This girl's not as bad as I thought her to be.
Her smile is the sun.
Her eyes shine like stars.
Her dimples are flawless.
She's so perfect it's bizarre.

So re-examine the person you are.
Find the good in yourself and you will go far.
Julie Dunlap, Grade 7

Wrong Way day
I dribble my food and eat my ball.
I watch my couch and sit on the TV.

I ride the school and go to the bus.
I cut my rock wall and climb my hair.

I hangout with my book and read my friends
I walk my football and throw my dog.

My day was weird but that's okay.
I hope tomorrow will be a better day.
Logan Amdahl, Grade 7

Life with Friends
Why does life have to be so hard?
Sometimes it is like a deck of cards.
Say you lose the card Five,
it doesn't matter, you're fine.
Maybe in one game it doesn't matter,
but some games you'll get bored and start to chatter.
Why do you have to try so hard for others?
Some boys are just like your brothers.
Sisters are sisters, sometimes you fight and can't stop,
Some friends are too clingy you just want to drop.
Why do you worry so much about friends?
Sometimes maybe your friendship will end.
Some friends aren't there forever, they're like vapor.
Some friends are like sandpaper,
they will rub on you and make you beautiful.
they will be useless after a while, you will become beautiful as usual.
Most regular friends are for never,
but Best friends are Forever.
Natasha Adrian, Grade 7

Merely But a Dream
In my head I live a perfect life.
In my head, there's no pain—no strife,
In my head I can always dream,
I can be anything I want to be,
But when I open my eyes I can clearly see,
This world is just too cruel—too mean.
The people's heads hang low with sighs,
Whose countenance say we're ready to die,
The skies aren't blue nor the breeze crisp,
Where even the smartest are confused,
And everyone mutters what should I do?
So I just keep my eyes closed and dream a big longer,
Praying soon one day I will be stronger,
I'll pick up the world and shine the light's beam,
Hoping that things are not as they seem—
But like I said,
It's all in my head,
Nothing merely but a dream.
Hanna Dunn, Grade 8

Mentally or Physically?
So many people told me I'll never be it.
They say they'll never believe it until they see it.
Well, you see me now…right?
Ready for take off and soon be in flight.
I'm going to be something in life believe it or not,
and trust me, when I start, I'll never stop.
There is no limit to success.
It's not about your appearance or how you dress.
Success comes from the mental state.
It's not that you're smarter than anyone else;
It's the amount of confidence you have in yourself.
So many people told me I couldn't be it.
They say they'll never believe it until they've VISUALLY seen it.
Brittney Maxwell, Grade 9

Aviation

That greatest feeling ever —
Being fast and free —
I know I'm hooked forever,
That aviation is the thing for me:
The power of having control
And able to do a barrel roll.

Adrenaline pumping in every vein
Like I'm weightless, nearly in orbit
I must be going insane!
I've reached the point: I am a pilot.
Better look out below —
Flying daring, fast, and low.

Seth Breyfogle, Grade 8

Basketball

Basketball is a great sport
Dribbling up and down the court
Shooting the ball
Hoping it will fall
Splash! The ball went in
Right through the rim

I want to play like LeBron James
When I play the Holy Ghost Flames
I want to win fair
With my Jordan air
It is always my dream
To beat the other team

Joey Mosny, Grade 7

Silent Love

The love I have for you is like the love a
mother has for it's baby.
But I can't show you, I'm afraid like a boy
is afraid to lose his best friend.
Your eyes sparkle like the blue ocean
you're beautiful like the glimpse of the sun
early in the morning.
You make me feel like I can fly
high sky in the air with the birds.
But I can never show you the love I
have for you it's silent like the wind
with no sound.
But I will always love you.

Alejandro Martinez, Grade 8

My Dream

Basketball is sleeping
Going to state is my dream
The buzzer is my alarm clock
My jerseys are pajamas
Shoot for the moon
Steal some z's
Jump into bed

Bailey Reigle, Grade 9

My Family Is Crazier Than Yours

My family is busier than Santa and the elves on Christmas Eve
after a UFO exploded all the toys
half the elves got struck by lightning
and Mrs. Claus got malaria

My family is funnier than 500 clowns
hyped up on sugar
and breathing laughing gas

My family is grosser than New York sewers
after the bathrooms have been broken down for weeks
and everyone got food poisoning

My family is sportier than a room
with Michael Jordan, George Forman, Babe Ruth, and Shaquille O'Neal
all having a show down

My family is so competitive that when one of us loses
we have to go to counseling for years,
and that doesn't always help

My family eats so much we ask elephants,
"Are you gonna finish that?"
and then,
"Are you sure?"

My family has to be crazier than yours!

Allanah Rolph, Grade 7

Night

Wings of night, wrapping around the east in one last instance of brilliant western color.
Stars and galaxies pirouette on the performing night stage.
Twinkling lights that waver and wander
Through the wisps and waves of space, of night, of dark

Black of the night that procures blindness
Pierced by shining raven's eyes
The Heavens never appeared so dark
To a single wandering glance

The young raven that flies — carries
Comets and fireballs, dashing through the vast openness
Illuminating its path
Alerting other ravens of its presence

Squawk! The wings of night retreat from
The east curtains rise, revealing a flash of blinding light
The sphere of brilliance and illumination just a ball in the sky
The unseen — see

The
Night
Just
A
Wink

Robert Mills, Grade 9

Save Me...
I am drowning,
Not in water
But in my own thoughts.
A wave of emotion is about to hit.
Save me.

The current of feelings are getting stronger
I don't think I can hold on any longer.
My sanity is getting washed away.
Save me.

Help is on the way I always hear,
But is it ever really here?
I'm slipping away and now people care,
But now I'm left to gasp for air.
Save me.

Help was always on the way.
All I had to do was obey.
But I was always to scared to stay.
But now that I'm here I am okay.

And now...
I'm saving myself.
Katie Durkin, Grade 8

Useless Things
A Man without a friend
A book without an end
Dinosaurs without roars
Fire trucks without horns,

Pens without its ink
Girls without their pink
An elephant without its nose
A garden without a water hose,

Glue without its stick
A hay barrel without ticks
School without its students
Workers without apartments,

A book without its words
The sky without its birds
Lockers without locks
Boats without docks,

Fishing line without a rod
Me without The Lord God
A husband without a wife
Useless things without life.
Aaron Mickelson, Grade 7

Wishes
I wish I were an Indian.
I could hear the wind talk;
See the animals walk.
The Earth can be like my mother —
The Black Squirrel, my brother.

If I were to awake under the sky,
I would see the birds as they fly.
I would smell the soil beneath my back.
I would feel the Earth; I wouldn't lack
A sense of love for Mother Earth.

The rapid river runs by
The tall trees of my tribe.
The Indians are fast jaguars of the land.
A totem pole outside stands
Only if I were an Indian.
Laura Durkin, Grade 7

My Little White Sheep
My little white sheep
I got from my mom
As a gift before I left.
On a trip to Mexico with my dad,
I took it along to remind me of home.
I had it everywhere I went
At my grandparents or my aunts
and then back home.

My little white sheep
When I left I forgot it.
I cried and I cried
but it was never found.
I drove my parents crazy
until they gave me a replacement.
I was happy until I figured out,
My little white sheep is still alone and lost.
Aimee Lopez, Grade 8

Your Beat Makes Me Dance
You are the beat to my music.
You are the words to my song.
You are the moves to my steps.
You are the headphones to my ears.
You are the pictures to my phone.

You make me want to dance!

You are the controller to my xbox.
You are the light to my tv.
You are the victory to my game.
You are the steps to my path.
You are the poster to my black light.

You won my heart like my game!
Madison Rosinski, Grade 7

The World Keeps Turning
The boy will fall
And then get right back up
And the boy will then go on

The dog will be yelled at
By the next day he will forgive
And the dog will then go on

The rabbit will be chased
And get away
And the rabbit will go on

The world will be at war
But then all will be silent
And the world will keep turning

The girl will be bullied
And then find more to life
And the girl will go on

The deer will be hunted
And be scared
But the deer goes on

The lion will be mad
But then learn to forgive
And the world will keep turning
Carl Nielson, Grade 7

Her
All these days,
All these nights,
You have been in my heart.
I have to be smart,
To tell you what it's like.

That one day
Was August 24th
Since then I hear her name,
Replay in my head every day.

The First time I heard that name,
I knew it wasn't going to be the same.
The first time I heard her voice,
There was no other choice but to rejoice.

The first time I saw her smile,
It was caused by a friend of mine.
The first time I saw those eyes,
They made the world spin a million times.

Woah! Was the only thing I could think,
I had some water to drink.
I tried to be clever,
Which changed the future forever.
Dieter Villegas, Grade 8

Softball

Dirt surrounding bases
The players running around
Umpires yelling
And you're out

Izabella Vietti, Grade 8

Puddles

The leftover rain
Kids splashing in the water
Getting their feet wet
Muddy mess

Carsyn Bacha, Grade 8

Rain

Slowly it falls to
The dry ground that is begging
For it, and the earth
Soaks it in

Nick Yanello, Grade 8

Dogs

You remind me of my brothers
Kind and loyal
Jumping in to always help me
I wish you would never die

Maddy Redeker, Grade 7

Stars

Stars in the night sky
Shooting across the moon so high
To wish upon a star
Starry night

Madison Osborn, Grade 8

Friendship

Friendship is a blessing
That you should never take
For granted, for a friend can change
One's life

Megan Scarber, Grade 8

Horizon

Setting is the sun
With hues of orange and red
And the warm light is
Fading fast

Gabe Molina, Grade 8

Sky Diving

High up in the sky up on a tiny plane
Got my jump suit on and I'm ready to play
Jumpin' falling, free as a bee
Nobody can ever touch me

Samantha Bohling, Grade 8

A Deep Dark Killer

A creature oh so sweet,
But one who creeps underneath,
Many think of it as a peaceful thing,
But can change oh so fast,

A creature who lives in the darkest of water,
A creature who I will never bother,
"King of the sea" many have called it,
But it is the scariest thing I have ever seen,

Its skin is black and white,
Making it invisible on the darkest night,
It has a thousand tiny sharp teeth,
making it the fiercest creature of them all,

It has been said,
that they are the smartest creatures of the ocean,
But I wonder if any other animal has challenged it in such freezing water,
This is why I fear the deep dark killer of the freezing ocean.

Ben Perrin, Grade 8

Joyful Joe

Joe
Brother of Kate
Cheerful, well spirited, and creative
Lover of my family, friends, cats
Who feels happy, and free spirited
Who needs food, friends, and family
Who fears losing a family member, losing a friend, and death
Who gives ideas, friendship, and happiness
Who would like to see Zombies, future technology, and my birth mother
Resident of Riverside
Lemon

Joseph Lemon, Grade 7

Inside

These emotions inside of me
Threatening to spill out
To reveal all my secrets
That no one knows about

These emotions inside of me
They're clawing at my soul
Spinning in my head
I'm slowly losing control

These emotions inside of me
They're making me crazy
Everything I see
Is becoming hazy

These emotions inside of me
I cannot speak of
Because they show the real me
That I can't seem to love

Alaina McBride, Grade 8

Night

The sun may rest its tempered light
To bring about the sacred night
That doth, with the raven's gentle crow
Does mark the start of fair moon's glow

As Nyx's black cloak shimmers nigh
To cover all the shining sky
That gives all men a way to see
The Heavens and all eternity

Its gift to those with wandering eye
To see the star speckled, dim-lit sky
And truly what a sight to see
Our whole existence presented to thee

So we thank the power that does bestow
Its dim, humble light to crowds below
And after awe at such a sight
We simply turn to say good night

Peter Kishler, Grade 9

boxes

boxes
the bane of our existence

they say you are this or you are that
the jocks, the nerds, the artists
the depressed outcasts, the performers

they put us into boxes stuffed so tight that we can't breathe, can't move, can't escape
if you do escape you feel like you belong nowhere, box-less and alone

it is a crippling emotion but it can also bring freedom

why can't I be friends with kids who are one thing
and kids who are not at the same time?

why aren't the boxes open?
why can't the labels be removed?
why have I been stripped of my individuality?

why do they tell me to 'be myself' if they don't really mean it?

I feel as if I've been manufactured
boxed, stacked, and labeled

the smallest defects or the slightest flaws are cause enough for me to be thrown into the box labeled "undesirable"
my box should not be taped shut and the only label that should ever be on it is "free"

I don't want to be one thing, I don't want to be constrained to one box
my box is open
is yours?

Fiona O'Brien, Grade 8

Listen, Look and Learn

I always did these things mindlessly, I really don't know why.
I wish I could volunteer to do these things.
Mostly because it's not as cool to be smart anymore,
Just like brand names are important in order to be cool, but not necessary to be a person.
How often we are judged by other's simple thoughts is amazing.
If you knew it was happening.
You didn't think about, what the people thought, or if they thought something good or bad.
If they stereotyped you by the clothes you wear, the shape you're in, or the color of your skin.
There are people who do think about this.
They constantly worry that they aren't cool enough, or thin enough, or that they just don't belong.
You probably judged one of those people today.
You probably didn't think about what that person thinks about themselves.
You probably NEVER thought that the person was hanging on by a thread.
You probably thought they were just average.
That they didn't think about the eyes watching them.
That they thought they were as far from normal as possible.
That's where you're wrong.
Listen, Look, Learn, DON'T JUDGE.
Things we never think about doing.
Until we read the thoughts of the people...like them.

Ebony Belt, Grade 8

Football Field
My favorite place is in a great location I call the football field
I am going there for the next four years of my life
I play the great game of football
I see players using all they have to win the game
I hear a roaring crowd cheering us on to win the game
I choose to give the best of my ability to help our team win all the competition thrown our way
I will go back there every time a game is in session,
Or whenever my team needs help to win the game
The football field is a place where my mind can be cleared,
And where my mind can be set on competition

Luke Lampe, Grade 8

Looking at the Footsteps That Have Been Made on the Beach Before They Are Washed Away by the Ocean's Tide
I stare at footsteps
Swallowing the beach
Like whales swallow fish.
Only allowing
Small patches of sand
To be kept untouched
And feel the sun's warmth

But they do not last.
As the tide comes in,
The footsteps vanish.
But the memories
That were made there stay.
All of the fun times,
That these people had
Making the footprints
Cannot be erased.

When these ones have left,
There are new ones made.
When these wash away,
It all starts anew.

Grace Kinsey, Grade 8

City at Night
A rainbow of lights,
Sparkling and luminous,
Looking exquisite.

Casey Duong, Grade 8

Winter
The white scenery
With pretty, shimmery snow
The early sunset.

Triya Mahapatra, Grade 7

The Temptation
We face temptation
We face drugs and alcohol —
Always say, "No way!"

Sierra Travis, Grade 9

The Forest
The sea of trees all fit in nature
It seemed like they were speaking to me
As soothing as the sound of rain
Chirp chirp chirp the sound the birds always made

All of the leaves fell in a swish
Autumn has now began
The animals fit in perfect
Buzz buzz buzz the sound a bee makes

Trees are mother natures skyscrapers
The sweet smell of the honey fills the air
Natures like calmness and tranquility
Squeak squeak squeak the squirrels go

What are the sounds of nature
It can be loud, soft, calm and even disruptive
But natures unpredictable no one knows what comes next
Swish swish swish the leaves are falling off the trees

Matthew Logan, Grade 7

Family
There is nothing like family

They always stand by your side
give you courage
give you pride

Wherever they are is home
give you hope
they will never leave you alone

They accept you for who you are
give you love
heal your scars

They will make you feel strong
give you confidence
you will always belong

There is nothing like family

Serena Gilliam, Grade 7

Lost in Wonderland

Flowers biting, creatures hiding
Smiles in the dark;
Alice wandering, soldiers pondering
And the Queen of Hearts.

Silent whispers, quiet tricksters
Many have gone mad;
Hats are flying, time expiring
Here in Wonderland.

Plants are singing, animals clinging
Things are upside down;
Paths are clearing, things are fearing
Nothing like her hometown.

Heads a-rolling, mushrooms growing
Taking her final stand;
Locks directing, Walrus inspecting
Here in Wonderland.

Brianna Parkhill, Grade 7

A Walk in the Timber

The dusty trail leads the way.
The tree branches hang so low.
There is no toll you have to pay,
So you can take it slow.

The bird's melody is oh so sweet.
You can hear the squirrel's chitter-chatter
The mulberry trees hold a tasty treat.
Listen for a deer's quiet pitter-patter.

The sun shines through the green leaves,
Lighting every stick and log.
Everything that God sees,
Will be covered in fog.

Now, on that stump you should sit,
And close your tired eyes.
As you suck on a cherry pit,
In nature there are no lies.

JT Klein, Grade 8

Seasons

With changing seasons
tiny buds wake up and yawn
spring is in the air

The leaves of autumn
lovely gold and brown colors
painting the landscape

The cold keeps coming
as the days heat fades away
bringing winter near

Jake Kritz, Grade 7

The Summer Fun

Summer is so fun
Jump into pools of water
Can't wait to begin!

Aayush Chanda, Grade 7

Winter

Winter is quite cold
It is right after Autumn
Snow is ev'rywhere!

Amrith Balachander, Grade 7

Star Light

White star light
Beautiful, full, bright
Make a wish!

Mackenzie Randall, Grade 8

Burning Fossil Fuel

Global warming stinks!
Icecaps are slowly melting.
Polar bears are sad.

Jack Vomacka, Grade 8

Useless Things

Books without words
The sky without birds
A guitar without strings
a bell without rings.

The store without food
A mood ring without moods
A politician without bias
The Bible without Matthias.

A house without lights
A boxing ring without fights
The mall without clothes
A fight without foes.

A printer without paper
Communion without wafers
People without legs
Pirates without pegs.

Shoes without strings
Wives without rings
A chimney without smoke
A comedian without jokes.

Grant Florence, Grade 7

Please Forgive Me

I have borrowed
my sisters shoes
without asking...

That she was
going to wear
to school;

I apologize,
but they looked
perfect with my outfit!

Kate Ross, Grade 7

Index by Author

Index by School

Author Autograph Page

Author Autograph Page

Author Autograph Page

Author Autograph Page